SO THIS IS WAR

A 3rd U.S. Cavalry Intelligence Officer's
Memoirs of the Triumphs, Sorrows, Laughter,
and Tears During a Year in Iraq

CAPTAIN CRAIG T. OLSON

Bloomington, IN 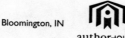 Milton Keynes, UK

AuthorHouse™
1663 Liberty Drive, Suite 200
Bloomington, IN 47403
www.authorhouse.com
Phone: 1-800-839-8640

AuthorHouse™ UK Ltd.
500 Avebury Boulevard
Central Milton Keynes, MK9 2BE
www.authorhouse.co.uk
Phone: 08001974150

Disclaimer: "So This is War" has been reviewed and authorized for public release by the 3rd Armored Cavalry Regiment and the Department of Defense Office of Security Review. Names of military members have been deleted or changed in compliance with DOD Directive 50.8 dated September 11, 2001.

First published by AuthorHouse 3/29/2007

ISBN: 978-1-4343-0449-0 (e)
ISBN: 978-1-4343-0451-3 (sc)
ISBN: 978-1-4343-0450-6 (hc)
Library of Congress Control Number: 2007902150
Printed in the United States of America
Bloomington, Indiana

This book is printed on acid-free paper.

Cover Page (top to bottom, left to right):

1. *Tiger Base Operations Center in Sinjar, Iraq.*
2. *Catching some shuteye during an operation in the "Triangle of Death".*
3. *A soldier burning the crap at the Rabiah base camp, overlooking the Syrian point of entry.*
4. *The sign on the plywood crapper at Tiger Base in Sinjar: "Do not Urinate in the Shit Box, Wet Shit Will Not Burn".*
5. *An Iraqi policeman on patrol in the "Wild West" town of Biaj, Iraq.*
6. *Making a pit stop while on patrol north of the Sinjar Mountains.*
7. *The author with a group of kids outside of the predominantly Kurdish town of Sununi, Iraq.*
8. *A mounted patrol on the streets of Biaj, Iraq.*
9. *The Christmas Day soccer game pitting the soldiers of Tiger Squadron against the 3rd Iraqi Army Battalion, 3rd Iraqi Army Brigade at Tiger Base. The Iraqis won 2-1 in overtime.*
10. *The author posing with the Squadron Commander, Command Sergeant Major, and their favorite Yezidi tribe, who we called the "Lavender Tribe".*
11. *Soldiers fixing a blown track on the M-88 on Market Street in Biaj, Iraq.*
12. *Children in South Baghdad awaiting the weekly food distribution.*
13. *The 4th of July Luncheon at Tiger Base in Sinjar.*
14. *An Iraqi Border Patrol soldier watching over the Syrian border.*
15. *2nd Iraqi Army Battalion soldiers proudly surrounding their Division Commander in Biaj, Iraq.*

Dedication:

To Jennifer, Cade, and McKenna for their unconditional love and
being my life.

To the hundreds of family and friends who prayed for my safe return and enjoyed reading my stories and spreading the word of the good we are doing overseas.

To the men and women of our Armed Forces, all of our first responders, and
our 3-letter agencies and their families who are in this fight every day.

CONTENTS

A Soldier is Born

"Regard your soldiers as your children, and they will follow you into the deepest valleys; look on them as your own beloved sons, and they will stand by you even unto death."
Sun Tzu

Like a lot of young boys, I grew up wondering what it would be like to be a soldier fighting in a war for your country, the kind of adrenaline-filled action and exhilarating combat that Hollywood glamorized. I pondered which service to join during my junior year in high school in Phoenix, taking the free lunches from all the recruiters, and narrowed my choices to either the Army or Marines by Thanksgiving of my senior year. Despite high grades and my choice of college cross country and track scholarships, I wanted to take some time off from academics, do something exciting, and see someplace exciting and new. There was no better time for that, as it was 1985, President Ronald Reagan was in office, and the Cold War was still alive and kicking. I selected a two-year Army contract that locked me into a place (Germany) and a job (a Forward Observer which, as I later found out, was projected to have a 30-second lifespan in the event of a Soviet onslaught through the Fulda Gap) that looked adventurous. Both would surely satiate my curiosity to serving in the military and possibly experiencing the thrills of combat before I moved on to other things in life.

It turns out that I took a liking to the regimented military lifestyle after a year each in Nurnberg and Stuttgart, Germany, but I also found that I had a surprisingly strong desire to return to school. One day at work, while scrubbing the floor in the unit's command center, I asked one of the officers about a

1

picture of an old castle that was hanging over his desk, a picture that turned out to be West Point (his alma mater). He told me all about the unique qualities of the school (enough not to scare me off), its valued place in American history, and the mental and physical challenges. I rarely heard about West Point while growing up in Arizona and I always thought that the Army-Navy football game consisted of a bunch of soldiers and sailors lining up against each other. The Major introduced me to the West Point Preparatory School in Fort Monmouth, New Jersey, which was the perfect place for a guy like me to improve my SAT score and running times at the school known as West Point's athletic feeder program. I sent in my application, was accepted, and the course of my life over the next 20 years changed dramatically.

I actually enjoyed my four years at West Point. Sure, the entire first year of hazing and belittlement (the unofficial motto is "high school hero, West Point zero") was full of stress and discomfort, the exact conditions that lead to amazing memories, but I fulfilled my dream of competing in cross country and track at the Division I level and loved the tight bonds that adversity and challenging environments form best. I missed out on Desert Storm during my junior year when that war only lasted a few days and the speedy conclusion quickly dispensed the rumors circulating around post that centered on early graduation for the Cows (aka juniors), an event that last occurred during World War II. Four remarkably short years later, I was a newly commissioned Second Lieutenant in the Military Intelligence Corps bound for Fort Lewis, Washington and the 7th Infantry Division (Light).

The Army rarely lets you go long without a challenge, so I quickly found myself competing for a slot to Ranger School and lost 30 pounds over the ensuing 90-day course that consisted of four phases in Fort Benning, Georgia (Jungle Phase), Fort Bliss, Texas (Desert Phase), Dahlonega, Georgia (Mountain Phase), and Eglin AFB, Florida (Swamp Phase). My reward for finishing was slapping on the Infantry cross-rifle insignia and leading a light infantry platoon of thirty-five soldiers, each of who could hump a 90-pound rucksack for days without a complaint. My Infantry Company soon shipped off to Saudi Arabia for six months after one of Sadaam's feints back to the Kuwait border and, after that, we trained to replace the 10th Mountain Division in Mogadishu, Somalia before the U.S. pulled out of there following the deaths of our Rangers in 1994. So I was close to combat a couple of times, anxiously in search of the ultimate adventure and ready to take my years of training to the big game, but the tyrants of the world went quiet and our Air Force and Navy fighter jets and bombers took care of our foreign policy and vengeance for several years afterwards.

The Army reassigned me to Fort Huachuca, Arizona in 1995 so I could be near my Dad as his fight to ward off the cancer accelerated. He started going to nearby Tucson for chemotherapy treatments and was recovering on and off, but the doctors gave him less than two years to live at that point. I made the decision to leave the Army in 1997 and return home to Phoenix to attend graduate school at Arizona State University and be close to my family. It was the place I needed to be at the time. My Dad ended up passing away less than a month after I left the Army. His last words to me, scrawled awkwardly on a hospital notepad because he couldn't talk, stated, "I've always been very proud of you".

Over the ensuing six years I finished up a couple of Masters degrees at ASU, worked in Scottsdale as a financial engineer where I enjoyed the stark contrast to the military as I wore shorts to work in an office overlooking a gorgeous golf course, and took a job as a Director of Finance for a start-up semiconductor company in Tempe where we raised over $32 million from Silicon Valley venture capitalists in another story that could write itself. I made a lot of money, worked a lot of long hours, met my wife Jennifer while on a layover at the airport (she later moved to Mesa, Arizona from Portland, Oregon for a teaching job), bought a home in Scottsdale, and became fat (literally) and content. As nice as my life was, it was missing something important to me—something that only my past lifestyle could provide.

I applied for the Voluntary Return to Active Duty program in June of 2002, when the memories of 9-11 still weighed heavily on a lot of us and just before President Bush and Secretary of State Colin Powell made what is now considered to be a far-fetched case for going to war with Iraq. Life went on and I almost forgot about the application until a call came in a year later saying I was accepted (it was actually a difficult process to return to active duty at this point—a couple of years later, as young officers left the service due to the increased overseas demands, the Army readily and quickly admitted ex-officers). We weren't pregnant at the time and my wife and I both thought it would be an exciting chapter together. Selfishly, I had several other reasons to return. I left active duty in June of 1997 in part to be with my Dad during his fight with cancer and in part because I had a desire to see how the other half lived and to see if I was really missing out on the coveted civilian lifestyle. I quickly found that I sorely missed the camaraderie that is fast to form in the military, the bonds with the other soldiers that quickly appeared in Germany, West Point, and in the Infantry but never in the civilian world, where Happy Hour at TGIF's was the closest thing that brought everyone together. I realized that money wasn't a big motivator in my life and doing something I could feel good about was. Plus, the Army life wasn't nearly as stressful as the daily fear of being laid off or laying someone off that civilian life after the market crash in 2000 provided. I also had only 11 more years to go before retiring, something that couldn't be said for the civilian sector and a point that was driven home when the kids came along and I envisioned coaching their teams, attending their plays, taking long family vacations, and fathering kids who I could someday be very proud of.

I left the Army during a time of relative peace and I knew that it would be a drastically different Army during the Global War on Terror. In the old Army we had well-defined training calendars and if you did get deployed it was for a maximum of six months, unless you were stuck with the dreaded one-year assignment to Korea. I knew it would be different and dangerous, but I had no idea what was really in store on the advent of "The Long War".

My reporting date back to active duty was September 1, 2003. At that point, we were six months pregnant with twins, sold our home, and moved three hours down south back to Fort Huachuca, the home of the Army's Military Intelligence Center located in the beautiful Chiricahua Mountains. My first assignment was to complete my advanced military schooling prior to rejoining the real Army. It was while waiting for the class to start that we had our first jolt of our new life: Jen and I were in the town's mall on the day before I was due to fly to Kansas for a six-week class and her water broke—it was October 29th and the babies weren't due for another two and a half months. She was airlifted 80 miles west to Tucson and the Army released me from the class and allowed me to join her. Cade and McKenna, our son and daughter, joined us in this world on the very next day, weighing in at 2 pounds-10 ounces and 2 pounds-2 ounces, respectively. Our lives over the next two months basically consisted of living next to the kids' cribs at the University of Arizona Medical Center's Neo-natal Intensive Care Unit. I never fully realized how close we were to losing our little miracles as they fought their own war to stave off infection and blindness and breathe on their own through the night. The doctors graciously agreed to let us bring the kids home two days before Christmas, even though they were both well under the required 4-pound weight and had to sleep with probes stuck to their tiny chests to warn us whenever they stopped breathing.

Six months later, at the conclusion of the career course, my first assignment back into the "real Army" was being assigned as the S-2 (Tactical Intelligence Officer) for one of the three combat Squadrons (consisting of about 1,000 soldiers each) in the historic 3rd Armored Cavalry Regiment (3rd ACR), a unit with a remarkable wartime lineage since it was first formed in the Indian Wars in 1846. I arrived in Colorado Springs in the summer of 2004, when the soldiers in my new unit were coming off of their vacation after a year in the rough Al Anbar Province in Western Iraq. Morale was high, for one because they just had a couple of months off and, secondly, nobody knew at this time that they would be returning to Iraq in less than 10 months. I arrived just in time for the intensive train-up that every deploying unit endures in the six months before marching off to war and 70 percent of the recent Veterans of Al Anbar were scheduled to make that march with me. I wasn't initially excited about joining the 3rd ACR because I knew we were tossed around on a short rope to return to Iraq at any time, but six months later I realized the benefits of going to war with more firepower, to include our own internal Apaches and scout helicopters, than most combat units three times our size.

Before I deployed to Iraq, on the day after Jen and the kids flew to her parent's home in Portland and the day before my unit departed Fort Carson, I sat on the couch in our cramped on-base house with a small tape recorder and made three tapes. I never told Jen this and didn't expect to—in the worst-case scenario if I never came home she would have found the tapes sealed in three separate envelopes in my sock drawer. On each of Jen, Cade, and McKenna's tapes I told them that I loved them more than the world itself and that they completed my life, but I died doing something that I felt was very important and serving in the military—going to work in the uniform every day with hundreds of amazing people next to me—was something that made me feel good about myself and about our future, the kids' future, and our country's future. I told Cade and McKenna that I would be very proud of them if they ever decided to make the same decision. I prayed to God that I would return in one piece and we'd be together again. It was the first time in my life that I felt a tear fall down my face.

I finally had my chance to experience war, that dreaded concept that is all too common in the world where man sinks to a new low in a violent attempt to create peace, and at that point I would have given anything to get out of it. Over the next 355 days I was going to experience a collage of emotions and events, both in Iraq and at home, as we made our way from Kuwait to the "Triangle of Death" in South Baghdad and then up north near the city of Tal Afar after President Bush prioritized the defeat of foreign Jihadists entering across the porous Syrian border. After participating on 18 combat missions in areas covering a third of Iraq, building and settling into our own base camp, burning our own shit for a year, and sharing more piping-hot goat fat and sweet Chai tea with the Kurdish, Sunni, and Shia people than I ever thought possible, my year was over as if it was just a dream. One long, bad, ugly, frustrating, and at times refreshingly beautiful, dream where I found out that war is much more than the pure mayhem and destruction I once imagined.

This is my story of a year at war.

MARCH 6, 2005: AND WE'RE OFF

"Never, never, never believe any war will be smooth and easy, or that anyone who embarks on the strange voyage can measure the tides and hurricanes he will encounter. The statesman who yields to war fever must realize that once the signal is given, he is no longer the master of policy but the slave of unforeseeable and uncontrollable events."

Sir Winston Churchill

After a long start to what will surely be a long year, I'm finally in Kuwait and settled into a large canvas tent with dozens of others. Our first night in the desert was frigid, but it sure is nicer than the wind and blizzards that I left behind in Colorado Springs. We'll see how I feel a month from now when the temperatures spike. I'm thinking that the summer will be similar to that in my hometown of Phoenix, with the only difference being that I will be wearing 40 pounds of body armor and a Kevlar helmet rather than flip flops and shorts. Here's a little synopsis of the past three days that marked the beginning of my first combat deployment:

- 2100 hours, March 3rd, 2005: I begin my journey at the post gym, where I dropped off my two allotted pieces of luggage—one each Army-issued OD green rucksack and duffle bag. It took me about six hours of packing earlier in the day to fit everything I'll need for the next year of my life into a carry-on and two pieces of cargo luggage. I had time during my last day at Fort Carson to eat a final meal at Schlotsky's (a BBQ chicken pizza topped with jalapenos), watch a

7

meaningless episode of *Survivor*, and call Jen and my mom one last time. Then I put my Jeep into the garage, loosened the battery cables, and bummed a ride to the gym from my neighbors Jen and Shane (a helicopter pilot for my unit who is on the same flight) and their four young kids. The gym was already filling up with families and soldiers in one of the saddest scenes I've ever witnessed. Unfortunately, this scene was to last another four hours before the families were told to say their final goodbyes. I was glad that I didn't have to put Jen and the kids through this spectacle as I said goodbye to them two days ago at the Colorado Springs Airport when they packed up to move to her parent's home in Portland.

- 2130 hours: After dropping my bags in the parking lot, I walked a quarter-mile to my unit's Headquarters to have the administration section check my dog tags and ID card and fill out a form allowing Jen and I to collect the $150 monthly Family Separation Pay over the next year. I had my ID card and dog tags, so the soldier behind the desk sarcastically remarked "Congratulations Sir, you're allowed to go to Iraq". The females in the Regiment (there are no females in the three combat Squadrons due to the "no females in combat arms" policy, but many serve in the Aviation and Support units) are ordered to take a urinalysis to see if they are pregnant. I later found out that several females didn't pass, so they got out of going to the sandbox without resorting to the homosexual or conscientious observer route.

- 2200 hours: I made my way over to the arms room to wait in line with dozens of others to sign out my M16 and night vision goggles.

- 2230 hours: I wandered back to the S2 Shop to hang out until midnight, when we were all told to report back to the gym. The four of us lounging around the office ordered a couple of medium pizzas, so the late lunch at Schlotsky's didn't turn out to be my last prized meal. The wife and daughter of one of the soldiers sat around with us, but there wasn't much talking. I emailed Jen one last time to tell her that I was almost in Kuwait, at least based on Army time.

- 2315 hours: I mentioned that it would be nice to be able to sleep and was told that I was snoring and there was drool on my lip. The pizza guy showed up with two large pizzas and a 2-liter bottle of Coke; he figured we weren't going to have pizza for quite a while and upgraded our order for free.

- Midnight: The four of us in my shop slowly made our way to the gym as the blizzard picked up. A long line of soldiers were waiting in the snow and I wasn't surprised to see that we, once again, had to have our ID card and dog tags checked. I still had mine—so I was still on track to go to Iraq. Most of the crying has stopped because nearly all of the wives and kids fell asleep in the bleachers or on the basketball court.

- 0130 hours, March 4th: A guy with a booming voice entered the gym and yelled for all of the soldiers to board the busses and for family members to say their final goodbyes and depart the gymnasium. The movement of people and bags startled most of the young children awake and the crying picked up from where it left off late last night. All of us boarded the busses and moved to another gym about a mile away while the families loaded up their cars and headed home to start their own crappy day.

- 0145 hours: Everyone lined up their bags to allow the Military Police dogs to sniff out the alcohol and porn (after some intense discussion, it was decided that Maxim magazine is not pornographic). Then we lined up for another inspection—having our ID cards and dog tags checked. I still haven't lost mine.

- 0230 hours: It was announced that all knives, bayonets, Gerbers, and Leathermans must be put in an amnesty box rather than being packed in a carry-on. Almost everyone had to tag and bag his knife.

- 0245 hours: The chow line opened up, featuring steak and eggs and strong Joe. The obligatory wise-ass comments appeared: "I need to get my knife back to cut this steak" and "maybe I could pistol whip them with my M9 to persuade them to give me my knife back".

- 0315 hours: Almost everyone in the gym was sprawled out fast asleep on the bleachers and on the basketball court.

- 0500 hours: The Fort Carson Post Commander arrived to deliver an uplifting speech. The group was largely incoherent and slowly lifted their heads to listen. I remember him saying something about a legacy as I drifted in and out. The Regimental Commander spoke after him and another Colonel after him. They selected the wrong time to drive up morale.

- 0600 hours: The speeches lasted too long, causing us to be late for our flight. The old Army adage of "Hurry up and wait" kicked into high gear and everyone quickly rushed to the busses to make the 10-mile drive to the Colorado Springs International Airport.

- 0715 hours: We boarded the Omni International Air charter. At least this charter sounded more familiar than the Planet Air one that I recently took on a training mission. And at least this one didn't have any visible rust on the engines—I still haven't totally erased the memory of the chartered Arrow Air crash that killed 285 101st Airborne Division soldiers who were returning home from their deployment to the Sinai in 1985.

I slept most of the way to Baltimore, and then it was on to Frankfurt on a leg that allowed me to watch three movies. That's a luxury that Jen and I rarely experienced over the past 15 months since Cade and McKenna were born. It was snowing in Frankfurt and we had a two-hour layover. I found out that I still cracked myself up trying to order in German, but, just like back in 1985 when I was a young Private serving in Nurnberg, I still couldn't be understood by the locals.

A few of us were sitting around in the Frankfurt airport joking about how this whole Iraq thing kicked off and how a terrible or short-sighted plan that allowed the insurgency to take root ever came about in the first place (that's easy to say in hindsight, of course). One of the NCO's recounted an old Army fable about how shit like this happens and we end up with "The Plan". It goes something like this:

HOW SHIT HAPPENS: THE MILITARY VERSION

The Plan:

In the beginning, there was the Plan;
And then came the assumptions;
And the assumptions were without form;
And the Plan was without substance;
And the darkness was among the face of the soldiers;
And they spoke among themselves saying,

"It is a crock of shit and it stinketh."

So the soldiers went unto their Platoon Leaders saying:
"It is a pail of dung and none may abide the odor thereof."

And the Platoon Leaders went unto their Company Commanders, and sayeth,
"It is a container of excrement, and none may abide by its strength."

And the Company Commanders went unto the Battalion Staff and sayeth,
"It is a vessel of fertilizer, and it is strong, such that none may abide by it."

And the Battalion Staff spoke amongst themselves, saying
"It contains that which aids plant growth, and it is very strong."

And the Battalion Staff went unto the Battalion Commander and sayeth unto him,
"It promotes growth and is very powerful."

And the Battalion Commander went unto the Brigade Commander and sayeth,
"This new plan will actively promote the growth and efficiency of the Brigade, in these areas in particular..."

And the Brigade Commander looked upon the plan;
And saw that it was good;
And the plan became SOP.

And that is how shit like this happens.

It was on to Kuwait City from Frankfurt, where upon arrival I kicked myself for not using that clean latrine that actually flushed back in the German terminal. It hit me that it was almost exactly 10 years since I was here last—back then I was a Second Lieutenant in the Light Infantry and Saddam was once again toying with us by massing his forces on the Kuwait border. Aside from Sadaam being unable to toy with us ever again, it doesn't look like much has changed. We boarded some civilian busses and three hours later we hit our first base camp in the middle of the desert. Camp Udairi will be our home for the unforeseeable future and it's so far out in the middle of nowhere that mortar attacks or improvised explosive devices (IED's) will be out of the question.

It was 11 p.m. on Saturday night. I mentioned to one of the NCO's that this was the third time I've seen night on this trip. He casually replied, "Yes Sir, it's been a long day".

Nobody knows how long we'll be here, but it will be at least a couple of weeks while we wait for our tanks, Bradleys, helicopters, and other equipment that were loaded onto the ships in Texas over a month ago. In the meantime, we'll go to the weapons ranges and plan our move into the war zone—a move to an as of yet undisclosed location in an as of yet undisclosed role. The guys are excited just to get this thing going. Over 70 percent of the unit was here on the last trip, a mere 10 months ago. Many of them could have changed units or left the Army, yet they chose not to. I feel privileged to go forward with people like this.

MARCH 13, 2005: THE JOYS OF KUWAIT

"Ours is a world of nuclear giants and ethical infants. We know more about war than we know about peace, more about killing than we know about living. We have grasped the mystery of the atom and rejected the Sermon on the Mount."

Omar N. Bradley

A few of us were sitting around the cots talking the other night and unanimously agreed that it wouldn't be too bad of a year if we had to stay at this camp in Kuwait rather than head north. Same combat pay and family separation pay as all of the soldiers in Iraq, but the people stationed here are tooling around in civilian clothes after an eight-hour workday while the forward deploying Army and Marines are rolling around fully-equipped as if they were heading into combat at any moment. There isn't a big military risk here; we carry live rounds in our cargo pocket just in case, but we're in the middle of a vast desert wherein any unauthorized movement is easily detected by the constant helicopter activity overhead. Well, almost any movement—an Arab couple appeared out from behind a sand dune to collect our used brass after the small arms fire range yesterday. In Ranger School we called those people the 'Grits'—locals in the mountains of northern Georgia who silently followed our patrols in the pitch-black nights to collect our brass once we finished a mission. I guess there are Grits everywhere.

The hard part about being stationed here year-round would be keeping off the weight. Camp Udairi has a huge mess hall, the Hole-In-One donut shop,

Burger King, Pizza Inn, Baskin Robbins (7 Flavors), a falafel place, Subway, and the Green Bean Coffee Shop. The only problem with the restaurants, which are housed in trailers the size of a small RV, is that you have to wait in a line outside to order and then eat in the always-present haze and dust of Kuwait (and the downpours over the last few days). The mess tent, on the other hand, is so large that it has four entrances, each one consistently featuring a long line of soldiers with one or more weapons slung over their shoulder waiting to get in. A soldier at the door counts heads with a clicker; I was there at the beginning of lunch and the counter at my door already clicked the thing a thousand times. I haven't seen a chow operation this efficient since my days at West Point when all 4,000 cadets would sit down at one time to eat. It's hard to find a seat with the constant activity and a few of us designated a permanent eating spot because we kept losing each other in the crowd while weaving through the maze to the multiple tents housing the seating areas. I heard one guy today remark that he felt like Herschel Walker when he tried to reverse direction to refill a soda (I don't know why he didn't use a more current analogy—I guess when you're this bored in Kuwait there is plenty of time to think of the perfect comment). There are four meals a day (one is a midnight meal) and they make sure you don't go hungry with a main meal, short order, and deli lines, a soup and salad bar, dessert table, and fridges packed with Gatorade, power drinks, and all kinds of local concoctions (banana milk is surprisingly refreshing). To top off the meal on your way out of the tents you can dip into a selection of freezers housing six different ice cream bars, but the fridge can't quite keep up with the outside temperature and humidity, so the bars always melt in your hands. There are rumors that the place we're moving to south of Baghdad is one of the few remaining FOBs (forward operating bases) in Iraq that has substandard living conditions. The unit currently occupying the place is merely keeping it warm for us as they protect themselves from attacks energized by MRE's rather than a nice home-cooked meal. It may be a good thing that the soldiers are getting fat and happy now.

Other conveniences abound on Camp Udairi. The gym is in another huge tent stocked with a more-than-adequate amount of free weights, treadmills, and bikes and more fridges for the free Gatorade. Colin Quinn hosted a comedy event on the basketball court outside of the tent, but I missed it due to our evening staff briefing. There is a free laundry service run by the TCN's (Third Country Nationals) not far away. It costs three bucks to have your uniform pressed, but I haven't seen anyone vain enough to use that service yet. Haji (this war generation's term for any person of Arab descent, similar to the use of Charlie back in Vietnam—I don't think it is currently considered derisive, but give it 20 years) will even count out your dirty socks and drawers as he places them in a laundry bag.

Our living quarters are even decent, although they get a bit more humid and acrid after each PT (Physical Training) session. The Army PT uniform is unparalleled in its inability to wick away sweat and body heat and quickly bottle and retain that smell when soldiers don't routinely drop them off to Haji in the laundry office. We live about 60 to a tent in just enough space to house a cot, rucksack, and duffle bag. The difficult part about tent life is the physical separation between the tent and the port-a-john, because the large amounts of water consumed throughout the day causes a very early morning trip, which means putting on your boots and uniform. I really miss the comfort of walking five steps to the bathroom back home without a Mini-Mag flashlight guiding me. If you have to go, you may as well get up for the day and go stand in the chow line before it gets too packed. The showers are set up in another trailer and fed by a line of water tanks. You're supposed to take Navy showers, otherwise known as combat showers (a two-minute process where you rinse, turn off, lather up, turn on, rinse off, and call it good), but nobody does and the shower princesses abound. Needless to say, if there is any water left in the tanks it's usually cold.

Our equipment should be arriving any day now and then the time-con-suming work begins—moving all of the tanks, Bradleys, fuelers, Humvees, and helicopters off of the ships at the port in Kuwait City to our camp in central Kuwait. The ships are already a couple of days late arriving into port; I'm surprised they haven't sunk to the bottom of the ocean by now with the amount of armor on deck.

We're in daily contact with the units we're supposedly replacing and they say that things in Iraq are definitely changing for the better since the country's first election. The locals are smiling more often and the police and security forces are slowly starting to unmask and show their faces. They say that the people are definitely prouder and more willing to identify the insurgents. There was a great quote the other day in the *Stars and Stripes* from a Battalion Commander north of Baghdad; he pulled all the local sheiks and tribal leaders into his office a couple of hours after an IED went off on one of his patrols and said, "I have tanks in this hand and money in this hand, which one are you going to choose?" An IED hasn't gone off in their territory since and the lull in action finally gave them a chance to help the people by rebuilding the antiquated sewage and water systems. I'm anxious to see this for myself.

MARCH 19, 2005: LIFE IN THE REAR

"We make war that we may live in peace." Aristotle

Until last night, we thought that the ships toting all of our vehicles to war really did sink. They have been a day late every day for the past week and the first one finally hit land in Kuwait City yesterday afternoon. The detail of soldiers that departed Camp Udairi early yesterday morning to drive the vehicles back from the port has been gone all night, which isn't surprising for a token three hour trip. It's amazing how slowly military convoys move; a 10-mile movement during a training exercise at Fort Carson would easily take two to three hours. Our upcoming convoy into Baghdad is broken up into segments over three to four days, depending on what we encounter along the route. Similar in distance and terrain, my grad school junkets from Phoenix to Las Vegas for a weekend gaming and drinking excursion used to take five hours and that included a stop at the McDonald's in Wickenburg and a traffic jam on the Hoover Dam.

Our recently-arrived boat ended up taking over a month to make it from Beaumont, Texas to Kuwait City. I'm sure the Private and Sergeant we assigned to accompany the vehicles were enjoying the trip. Their only job over the past month was to play cards with the Navy Seabees and count the number of vehicles onboard twice a day to ensure none of them fell overboard. Those two jobs were in high demand. I was thinking that the total inactivity and lack of thought that position required reminds me of a job I had back in 1985 when I was a brand new Private in Nurnberg, Germany—"Rubber Guard". I was provided with a diagram of all of the barracks rooms overlooking the busy pedestrian thoroughfare in the city and ordered to observe any blown up condoms floating down onto the Germans as they scampered to work. My only job was to put an 'X' on the room matrix to identify the source of this hijinx and let the First Sergeant take care of the rest.

Once all of our vehicles make it to camp and the soldiers put them through the paces of the convoy live fire exercises, gunnery, and artillery ranges (both for training and to ensure the salt water didn't rust out the barrels), we'll probably have to wait to head north when the Arba'een Holiday concludes. Arba'een is a Shiite holiday commemorating the massacre of the Caliph Hussein to an overwhelming Sunni force back in 680 AD. Soldiers call this festival the "Flail Fest" (instead of whipping and beating themselves to an unconscious state as they do in Karbala and Najaf, the Shia in the U.S. have a more reasonable tradition of donating blood). Our path to the north will be flooded with a couple hundred thousand pilgrims tooling around beating themselves and it would probably be in everyone's best interest if we worked around that holiday.

From what I recall of my past experiences in Saudi, Egypt, and Israel, I think I'll enjoy this culture once again—the hospitable people, the desire to form relationships before doing business, and the focus on family. I remember that if we were early to a meeting they would think we are trying to hustle them (why else would you be so anxious to get there?), so it was a free pass to be running late. They also believed that people with blue eyes have an evil-eye keeping watch on them. We joke around that all of us should buy some blue contacts and word will spread that there's thousands of blue-eyed guys watching over their every move. And moustaches are a sign of power, virility, masculinity, and discipline. A lot of guys are growing them out, but the decision is made mostly due to laziness (it creates less facial area to shave in the cold water) and their wives not being around to tell them to get rid of it. I tried to grow mine out for a couple of days, but the hair comes in brown, red, gray, and I think there was even a blonde one—not so masculine and it just looked like I had remnants of a juicy burger on my lip. One of the recent cultural taboos, announced a generation earlier than I suspected, is the recently ordered prohibition on the term "Haji". A Haji truck is now referred to as a Bongo truck and a Haji dress is a man dress. I can't imagine how the soldiers will handle this. I just don't see them sitting around their cots at night discussing the tactics of the armed insurgency forces rather than what Haji is up to. When my assistant Intel officer, 1LT Webber, gives updates to the troops he now uses the PC phrase "Bad Guy Bob".

We are taking it easy before moving into the bad sandbox (we're currently in the good sandbox), so I'm basically working a little more than a half-day schedule—7 a.m. to 9 p.m. My sleep cycle is still somewhat erratic and I attribute that largely to waking up a half dozen times per night over the past year and a half to attend to the kids rather than any jet lag. I know I'm still getting a lot more sleep than Jen (and her family now that she moved to her parent's home in Portland). I woke up this morning when I heard some shuffling in the tent, got up, put on my PT gear, and ran to the tent gym. I thought it was odd that only three other soldiers were working out in there because the place is usually packed all the time. I lifted, took a little run, and was stretching out in front of the tent when a soldier on night shift came by and said "Sir, what are you doing up so early?" Since I don't wear a watch so as not to be constrained by time, I asked him for the time. It was only 4 a.m. and I had been up for an hour. On a positive note, it was the first time in over a week that I showered with hot water and without a couple of inches of murky water coagulating at my feet.

I've only had two opportunities so far to use my cool-guy stuff. These activities were: 1) using the mounting scope on my M16 to gauge the range to the laundry trailer and the zoom capability to observe the turn-in line and 2) using the night vision goggles to observe the aforementioned line should darkness fall prior to turn-in or pick-up (this turned out to be ineffective due to the ambient lighting provided by the generator-powered lights lining Eisenhower Boulevard). The Squadron surgeon has been teaching us how to use some more cool-guy stuff of the medical persuasion after the evening staff meeting each night. Our surgeon is a Major, but everyone jokes that Army doctors don't know what that means so they still refer to Captains as "Sir". This guy is pretty good, though. He volunteered to leave the comforts of Fort Carson's hospital to be with a combat unit. Plus, he is currently acting like a personal doctor to all the staff and commanders. He'll even make a house call to your cot to drop off some Motrin, the strong stuff—"Ranger candy" as we used to call it. The most recent medical advice he dispensed, after a flood of upper respiratory colds, was that we all start sleeping head-to-toe in the cramped tents to fend off the virus. We had another 9mm and M16 range and the medics didn't have the litter-carry required to allow us to start firing (they are still in the one missing boat), so they brought along a couple of cots to appease the safety guys and then napped in them the rest of the afternoon while everyone was shooting. I hope the surgeon and the medics will always be this bored.

Apparently, even our embedded journalists from the *Colorado Springs Gazette* are becoming a little bored and encountering writer's block as they try to come up with storylines. They were searching so hard for a story that they wrote one about how our tankers named their gun tubes (the gun barrel on every tank has a nickname stenciled to it). The tankers were struggling to come up with clean cover stories on how they picked names for their weapons—which was understandably difficult with names like "Dicken's Cider" (say it three times fast), "Dry Wall Mauler", "Donkey Show", and "Juanita's Revenge".

A group of our supply soldiers just returned from the north on a recon to one of our future camps south of Baghdad along the Euphrates, the spartan camp that skirts the "Triangle of Death". We are still short on tents for about 300 people, so most soldiers will have to sleep in their vehicles for a while until the KBR contractors can get down there and construct them. The contractors, however, are understandably hesitant about traveling through the Sunni villages that dot the roads and canals and nobody volunteers for that job or any other job that has to do with FOB Dogwood. My section has an M577 (command post armored vehicle) that can uncomfortably sleep two and won't produce too much carbon monoxide poisoning, but I'm hoping that the contractors get a big bonus to entice them to change their mind and do their job. The guys on the recon were all excited about the current unit leaving the Internet café in place. This Internet café thing cracks me up, though. The café part makes it sound like such a nice and pleasant place—I picture people lounging on soft leather couches with a cup of coffee and a wireless laptop. In reality, it is merely a trailer with Internet portals that allow 32 soldiers to gingerly sit shoulder to shoulder, separated only by a small plywood partition curiously void of the soldier graffiti that enhances the character of the porta-a-johns and AT&T Calling Center.

Hopefully, we'll be able to install a phone center with no problems. Jen and I have our phone routine down pat. I call every Thursday and Monday morning at 5:30 a.m., which is Sunday and Wednesday night for her. The line at the Camp Udairi AT&T Calling Card Center has thinned out by then and it's a great time to hear the kids laughing (or crying—either way I'm ecstatic) in the background. Assuming I'm able to maintain this routine where we're going, I'll continue to use the phone calls as a mental countdown. I tell the guys that I'll be going home in 99 calls. Others say, "Since I call home every week, I only have 50 to go" and it ultimately seeps down to the single guy who will call home only once to tell someone where to pick him up when the freedom bird lands back in Colorado Springs in twelve months.

I don't know if the steady phone calls are going to be available in Iraq, but it has been a godsend for us so far and we're still early in the deployment. I'm so proud of Jen for dealing with the abrupt change in our life after we joined the Army, let alone being put in the position to raise preemie twins who still haven't taken to sleeping through the night. Both of the kids just started getting their molars, so the teething phase certainly won't help her rest cycle and until they outgrow their reflux she'll still be up at all hours laundering and folding bibs. I haven't been gone long, but it's been just enough to miss out on Cade's first steps as he started stumbling along the length of the hallway. I was hoping he would walk before I deployed. At least McKenna let me experience that little joy in life when she took her first steps one week before I left.

Over my short time being back in the Army as a married man, I have become amazed at the burden the Army wife has to shoulder—not just with raising the family alone, but also with dealing in the constant unknown. I would come home from work and not know from one day to the next if I was leaving for a couple of days or weeks for training missions or even a year to Iraq as our timelines changed daily. Here's a little poem about Army wives that I came across and find incredibly accurate, as I am fairly certain that Jen is going to have a much longer year than I am:

> "She wakes very early, he's leaving today. She will stand tall and proud as he's walking away.
> He glances back warmly at his children and wife, knowing they will bravely carry on with their life.
> Her strength and her courage only one understands, he's walking away with her heart in his hands.
> For he knows that without it he will be lost, but they both know freedom comes at a cost.
> She walks away holding her children so close, swallowing tears for the one she loves the most.
> This quiet hero does not walk into war; she soldiers on behind her front door.
> She will move through her life the wind at her back, determined to keep her family on track. Her tears fall in silence while she lies in her bed, her fear is right there but nothing is said.
> She asks that no medals be pinned to her chest. Her husbands safe return her only request.
> Few understand her commitment, her life; she is the quiet hero, the brave soldier's wife."

March 28, 2005: Can We Go Yet?

"Never has there been a good war or a bad peace." Benjamin Franklin

I really thought we were immediately needed in Iraq after the Department of the Army moved up our deployment date and quickly pushed us out of Fort Carson. I certainly never envisioned that we would still be sitting in Kuwait for almost a month. I also never thought that I'd be anxious to move into a war zone so I can get out of staff meetings and stop living out of a duffle bag—I can't wait to find some old MRE boxes so I can craft some semi-permanent shelves for my brown T-shirts and socks.

Our units are slowly pushing north over the next few weeks. My assistant went out with the first convoy. He was the only officer on the trip, so he inherited the responsibilities of Convoy Commander. I asked him if he felt comfortable with all of the contingency plans and routes before he left and he said he only has two questions: 1) do I take a right or left at the main gate and 2) where is the main gate? Route-wise, it's fairly straightforward—literally. You take a left at the gate, go 30 miles, take a left on the hardball road, and then keep driving until you hit Baghdad. There are a few places where a convoy can become lost (as in the Jessica Lynch fiasco when they somehow ended up in downtown Nasiriyah), but we have the checkpoints mapped into our GPS systems so they guide you fairly well. The main threat on the first couple of days is human "head space and timing"—either falling asleep while driving or having a negligent discharge while cleaning a weapon or jumping off of a vehicle with the safety off or cutting yourself with your Gerber knife while opening an MRE. One soldier from a communications unit already had a negligent discharge and it happened before they left the gate and even before he was supposed to load the magazine into his weapon. So far our only mishap was a fire that broke out in an armored track that was fully loaded with mortar rounds, detonation cords, and C4 explosives. Luckily, the crewmembers "un-assed" the track when they figured out that they couldn't put the flames out.

A few of us on staff went to the range yet again the other day in an attempt to break away from our home in the tactical operations center (TOC) and the mind-numbing planning process. The landscape was quite bleak, but I did snap a photo of the charred, melted remnants of the destroyed track that broke up the endless field of sand. We passed several herds of camel along the way with a shepherd crouching in the middle next to his new Land Rover. I guessed that camel herding is a lucrative business out here. We made our way out to the range in the TSB, our acronym for the "Tactical School Bus". Legend has it that one of our crusty old supply Sergeants (SFC Sal) bought this bus back in the little ski town of Gunnison, Colorado using a government credit card that had a maximum limit of $1500. The former school bus was used for years to transport skiers to the Colorado slopes from a small resort. SFC Sal not only had to drive the price down under $1500, but he also had to talk the owner of the resort into manipulating the invoice to read "Office Equipment" so it would be an approved purchase. The bus was painted desert-camouflage, given a bumper number for the manifest, and shipped to Kuwait with our other vehicles. The TSB driver is a Specialist nicknamed "Rainman" due to his robotic motions and constant computations translating kilometers to miles (most of them were wrong, but I didn't have the heart to tell him). The sign above Rainman stating, "If you enjoyed the ride, you may tip your guide" was maintained from the old ski days for morale purposes. They checked into putting armor on the bus exterior, but it has never been done before (nor requested) and out of the question. We'll load the thing onto a long-haul vehicle and take it with us into Iraq. There's recently been some talk of removing the seats and making it into a chapel once we reach our final destination.

As for my mundane existence as I wait to be shipped off to battle? Only being tasked with driving the TSB, like Rainman, can surpass the tedious life of a staff officer during the planning process. I would often consider conceding the rolls of acetate and permanent markers to the old days as a Lieutenant leading infantry soldiers, but I'm older now, in much worse shape, and would probably complain more over time about my decrepit physical condition than about the meetings and briefings. My most powerful weapon now is my 2-

Gigabite thumb drive. I work in about a two-foot square area in the operations tent with a handful of others at any given time, which doesn't allow for much personal space.

At night, I give thanks for my little DVD player to break away from reality. I was only able to fit two books into my rucksack for the trip over and I already read those (my bags were packed so tightly that my flip flops wouldn't even fit, forcing me to squeeze in some 89-cent shower shoes that had a thinner profile). The veterans of this same trip just one year ago learned that a small DVD player is a necessity, as is a small rug to place in front of your cot, an MP3 player, fold-out camping chair, digital camera, lots of Gold Bond powder to shower in if water is unavailable, Febreze in case your uniform can't get washed for a couple of months, and various other items. They also learned that you have to bring your own movie collection, so most guys have been pirating DVD's for the past year in anticipation of downtime in the cot. The only DVD I brought is *Napoleon Dynamite*, which I watched three times and is not in high demand. In order for me to efficiently watch an entire movie before I fall asleep, I usually fast forward through the car chases and fight scenes and, in the case of *Spiderman II* the other night, the airborne fights. I can get through a violent movie with little to no character development in about 20 minutes.

In a way, my daily job is kind of like watching a movie based on actual events. I give two briefings a day about specific events happening all over Iraq and break it down quite a bit into what we think will be our future area of operations. And we plan for just about every scenario that can occur when we do get there, wherever that may be. Two days ago we were informed that we might be going to Mosul instead of Baghdad, which would entail an entirely new set of plans. After a night of bitter criticism about the lack of decision-making by higher and the ever-present "good idea fairies", we learned the next morning that the Mosul request was cancelled.

A majority of the attacks happening now are being conducted by the criminal and thug element and financed by the guys we're really after. The police only make $140 a month and an attack against our forces, the Iraqi forces, or the Iraqis themselves can be had from $10 for an amateur shooting blindly at a convoy or laying an IED to $200 for a professional hit, so crime can really pay out here in a lawless state. Kidnappings are a popular and easy source of financing—the Italians reportedly paid $8 million for the release of Giliani Sbreni and the Swedes claim they talked the insurgents down to $400,000 from $4 million for the release of their countryman. Even if the Italians got a steal at $1 million, that money pays for a lot of attacks and only a few have to get lucky to demoralize a fledgling Iraqi unit or even an entire population (Iraqi or American, for that matter).

It's a harsh reality to accept, but I'm a strong believer in a policy of non-negotiation. Paying terrorists and criminals only provides a strong incentive to continue and even increase the kidnappings. Why kidnap an American when you know you'll get no cash and your propaganda campaign may take a hit when you're forced to stick to your word by killing him? I'm anxious to see the specifics about the shooting of the Italian woman upon their return to the Baghdad International Airport. Soldiers in the area where the shooting occurred are constantly attacked from the alleyways and populated areas—IEDs, suicide bombers, mortar attacks, and snipers. Two soldiers were killed there just days ago when a Bongo truck filled with grass blew up at their position. I'm sure all of the soldiers are jumpy, let alone on that road when a vehicle is blazing towards them.

Our lawyer has been busy teaching rules of engagement to the soldiers and he says a lot of the guys are afraid they'll be investigated and court-martialed if anything goes wrong. There is a complex set of rules in setting up traffic control points; assuming that they are all followed, I don't see how anyone would fail to slow down, stop, or just turn around and go somewhere else rather than blowing through the checkpoint like the Italians reportedly did. The military does investigate just about everything now, just to document every incident in case the ACLU sues for information later. Back in garrison at Fort Carson, I would routinely receive phone calls from investigators looking into alleged crimes against Iraqis from the 3rd ACR's last deployment. It turns out that names of certain soldiers (especially linguists and civil affairs soldiers who were often out on the street dealing with the people) were passed around back in Al Anbar Province and the names were later used in an attempt to obtain reparations or give the U.S. Army a bad name in the propaganda game. These soldiers would be accused of committing crimes months after they left Iraq. The investigators said it happened all the time, but they still had to look into every claim.

I woke up early to attend Sunrise Mass on the basketball court on Easter Day. The mess hall was closed for breakfast, but the cooks laid out a huge feast for brunch. The contractors went all-out with the decorations and the menu included roast beef, ham, turkey, sweet potatoes, a salad and soup bar and an assortment of pies for dessert. The Baskin Robbins trailer closed down to support the mess hall with all of their seven flavors. I was happy that Mint Chocolate Chip was one of them, even if it was mostly melted. The feast created a nice break in the workday and the extended hours provided us with a more peaceful eating environment wherein nobody was walking around yelling at the soldiers to hurry up and eat so others can sit down. I'm thinking it may have been one of my last meals before heading north.

APRIL 4, 2005: ON THE ROAD AGAIN

"The wave of the future is not the conquest of the world by a single dogmatic creed but the liberation of the diverse energies of free nations and free men." John F. Kennedy

I thought the weather in Kuwait was too nice to last and I've been proven correct after chewing sand over the past three days. It's been really pleasant most of the time we've been here. There's been more than a few times while strolling to the chow tent at night that I imagined myself on San Diego's Mission Beach, kicking the sand with a cool breeze blowing on my face. However, the scene played out a bit differently over the past few days—now it was as if the beach bully was blasting these fine granulated particles directly into my grill as the god of hot sweltering winds further mocked me and proceeded to shove it down my BDU top. The Shamal season has arrived in all its glory and we were hit by the first of what will be many sandstorms. Visibility was down to about 100 meters and the insides of all the tents were generously coated with the fine dust of Kuwait. My sleeping bag was tightly rolled up on my cot and I'm still trying to shake out the sand. I've learned very quickly that my usually liberal application of Chapstick is not recommended during these times as the dust readily adheres to the wax. The brownouts just give us one more opportunity to live up to the old Army adage of "embracing the suck".

The highlight of my week in Kuwait was using our new toy—the "Phrasealator"—in the laundry tent in an awkward attempt to converse with the laundry guy while learning how to work the device. The Phrasealator allows you to type a question in English and it comes out in Arabic on the speaker. The only drawback is that the Phrasealator only works one way, so it requires a lot of 'Yes' or 'No' questions. Other than sitting around playing with the Phrasealator, discussing the weather, and debating the issue of where the supply guys should stock the 100 fly swatters they brought over (my vote is to hang several over each urinal in the latrine, because that kind of firepower is needed to take out these creatures), we're at the point where you just wait for your convoy date to get here so you can leave. For the soldiers, sitting around and waiting translates into a lot of weapons cleaning. The 9mm is no problem to keep clean—you can toss it into a swamp, pull it out months later, and it will still fire. The M-4's (an M-16 with a short stock—the M-16's nickname is now the "musket" due to its unwieldy length) and higher caliber weapons are a bit more high-maintenance. As usual, everyone is envious of the pilots. Unlike back at Fort Carson, where our envy lies around the multiple four-day weekends they get to take each month, our envy this time is based upon the fact that they can tailor the four-day ground movement into a two-hour flight.

My first order of business when we arrive into Baghdad and settle into the new tents is a no-brainer. I'm going to post a sleeping chart, something we've never done here because we always thought we'd be moving soon. The night shift is always sending a Private to the tent to wake up one of the staff officers for one reason or another throughout the night. The other night I awoke to the messenger scanning my face with a laser pen in an attempt to determine if I was the supply officer. Unfortunately, in spite of a sleep plan I'll still have another eleven months on my cot. Trying to maintain a comfortable sleeping position with a meager two feet to roll around in doesn't work too well; my arms end up hanging over the aluminum siding sometime during the night until I'm awakened by the numbness caused by a lack of blood flow. I'm fairly certain that Cade and McKenna's cribs have more square footage.

Most of the Regiment has moved north already and my Squadron, nick-named Tiger Squadron, is the last one to leave. We still keep movement dates classified, so I can't be specific on the date even though just about all of the Kuwaitis and foreign workers on post will be familiar with it when they see the convoys lining up at the main gate the day prior. Another big indicator for the convoy dates is when the insurgent sympathizers see a huge caravan of armored gun trucks moving along the only six-lane highway through Iraq and call ahead to their buddies up north. There are heads-up fliers advertising the "Pre-Convoy Prayer Service" and "Pre-Deployment Leader's Dinner" taped up all over camp—on the porta-john doors, the donut trailer, the chow hall entrance, probably on the buses caravanning the Kuwaiti, Pakistani, and Indian workers back to their homes in Kuwaiti City. Everyone jokes that Haji sitting on his La-Z-Boy eating a tuna sandwich back on the Euphrates already knows when we're moving through and what our final destination is even before we do so they can plan the chaos during the major movements and transitions.

OPSEC (Operational Security) is made a little tougher nowadays when the *Army Times* and other open-source materials and web sites print out the deployment schedules, organizational structures, tactics to defeat bombs or ambushes in nice color graphics, and even track officer promotions and movements. Our nation's investigative journalists thoughtlessly divulge government agents and programs under the name of liberty and all of the action movies and TV programs show the bad guys how to prevent capture or have their case thrown out if they are caught. These days, you can build a dirty bomb with instructions from the Internet and piece together sensitive weapon specifications and capabilities by reading technical journals like *Popular Science*. There is so much information available through the Freedom of Information Act and on our public domains that open source searches have become a separate slice of our intelligence community and probably make up the bulk of our enemy's intelligence capabilities as they *Google* for field manuals and training doctrine. Embedded journalists aside, we'll definitely improve on the operational security when we're in country and have complete control of our internal movements. Then we'll just be at the mercy of the Iraqi people's extensive early warning systems of cell phone calls or lights flickering on and off as we attempt to move around stealthily in rumbling armored vehicles.

This morning was the last time we were together as a complete Squadron, so we celebrated it with a little run featuring all 1,200 of us in formation. I really didn't feel like getting up to run, but it turned out to be very motivating. Prior to departing on a 12-minute per mile pace that burns the calves more than a 5-minute mile would, the Squadron Commander gave a great speech on the importance of our being here to help the people and assist in starting their own chapter in freedom. The soldiers are in great spirits. At the end of the run, we (the Staff and Commander) pulled off to the side and all of the units high-fived us and let loose as they ran by. Times like this make me understand why soldiers want to stay in; the camaraderie is just amazing and genuine and it really puts itself on display during the difficult times.

Over the past year, a lot of people have asked me what I thought of the war. I'm probably the wrong one to ask, being that I now consider myself a Reagan Conservative. However, since I was once a registered Democrat and still hold some liberal beliefs on the social side (anti-death penalty, pro gays in the military (I was one of two officers out of thirty-five in my basic course with that view—the other one is now a convicted pedophile), and former pro-choice in the abortion debate until I witnessed Cade and McKenna's little hearts beating away at the six-week mark of pregnancy), that made me one of the most liberal guys on the staff or probably in the Army. Like most people, I tend to stray away from political conversations because whatever side you stand on with just about any issue places you in the 50th percentile across the American landscape, which is exactly why our leaders never make headway into any important issue (oddly, they did come together to support our current actions). As diverse as the U.S. is in regard to religion, ethnicity, race, and geographical character, it still escapes me how we're evenly split. Most countries have to control and appease dozens of sides, so we have it pretty easy compared to what the Iraqis are going up against.

Anyhow, the goal of the war when President Bush drafted the Congressional Resolution was two-fold: affect regime change and rid Iraq of WMD. On the first count, I always thought we should've finished the task immediately after Desert Storm in 1990 by supporting the Shia and Kurd uprising instead of pulling back into, and staying in, Kuwait. That became part of the reason the Shia and Kurds don't trust us to stand with them in today's environment. Then I thought we should have enforced each one of the 13 or so UN Resolutions that Sadaam broke over the course of the '90s while we sat idly by gawking at the UN's incompetence. The reason I'm not a big fan of the UN to this day is because of its failure to enforce its own Resolutions and to act promptly and decisively, as was the case with the genocide in Rwanda in 1994 and the UN pullout from Somalia in 1995 (not exactly aided by the U.S. as we cut and ran immediately after 18 of our boys died in Mogadishu). As we now know, our hasty departure from Somalia left a government-free and lawless vacuum wherein a man named Osama Bin Laden was able to resurrect his dying Jihadist group unchallenged. The removal of Sadaam's regime in Iraq was so important to our national security that President Clinton even signed the Iraqi Liberation Act in 1998 that declared regime change in Iraq as U.S. policy. The guy had an undisputed history of reckless aggression, to include developing and using WMD, committing genocide on his people, and making good on his threats to expand into Iran and Kuwait. And what better way to fight terrorism than to make a bold move to replace this despot with a democratic, or even any type of, ally that lies right between the well-known terrorist-sponsoring nations of Iran and Syria?

On the second count, I'm one of those conspiracy theorists who thinks that evidence of WMD will surface; it won't be as obvious as Sadaam gassing

200,000 Kurds, but something will turn up in Jordan or Syria or Saudi or in one of the 90 or so chemical production dumps that were looted and never inspected (unfortunately we will be based near a couple of them). There wasn't an intelligence agency in the world that didn't think Sadaam was either possessing or seeking to develop WMD, to include his own Mukhabarat Intelligence service. It wasn't Bush's or the Senate Intelligence Committee's or any other politician's fault that we were forced to make the decision based on faulty assumptions and loose connections—on the contrary it was Sadaam's fault for forcing us into that position because he wouldn't let the UN inspectors do their job to prove he was clean. Perhaps Sadaam wanted to deceive the world to emanate strength and keep Iran out of his hair or even deter the U.S. from mounting a ground assault someday—which would be the ultimate irony.

Our failure to act decisively against terrorism after the Marine deaths in Lebanon in 1983, the bombs against the Embassy in Nairobi, the World Trade Center in '93, Khobar Towers in Riyadh, Saudi Arabia, and the USS Cole in Yemen over the past decade, along with our quick departure from Somalia, only strengthened an extremist movement who believed that the American public doesn't have the fortitude to support military action and will quickly back away when photos of their dead soldiers make the evening news. We were in a terrible position in which the easy decision would have been to do nothing until something bigger than 9-11 happened. In this case, the risk of doing nothing could've resulted in many more lives lost than those taken at the Pentagon, the World Trade Center, and Flight 93. I'd personally rather play the Jihad Super Bowl here rather than anywhere close to my family and friends. I just wish the whole issue was communicated in an articulate manner; if Reagan or Clinton were President at the time they could've made the case much clearer and emphasized the removal of a madman and murderer from power, the need for a moderate Muslim government and ally in the Middle East (a continent that is so depressed, impoverished, and radical that it makes the perfect breeding ground for terrorists), and the fact that, while we are not positive of the WMD claim, the risk of not taking action is too great should that WMD actually exist and get into the hands of an international terrorist group hell-bent on destroying America.

On more serious matters, the highlight of my week back in the States was hearing that Cade is now wandering the house on his own two feet and he and McKenna actually use the pantry to choose a snack (Cade preferring animal crackers and McKenna selecting either Trix or Lucky Charms) rather than tearing it apart. I told Jen that it may be awhile before I can contact her and hear more stories, but when she does hear from me it will be from inside

Iraq and I should have some interesting bylines from the trip. For one, my up-armored Humvee has a new engine and a new transmission since it died on the trip from the port at Kuwait City and this will be the first long journey to test it out. I told her not to worry, as I'll be sure to situate myself next to the mechanic's wrecker in the convoy's order of movement and I'll always have those damn sandbags under my feet.

April 15, 2005: The Long March to War

"If there must be trouble let it be in my day, that my child may have peace."
Thomas Paine

I was starting to run out of good things to say about Kuwait in my last letter, but I sure miss the place right now. I haven't had a chance to read my *Kiplinger's* magazine or use my DVD player since we arrived in the big city of Baghdad over a week ago. The days here have become a blur as I have been going down about 2 a.m. and returning to the Ops Center five hours later. It seems like this evening has been the first slow period that allows me a chance to ponder the last few days. Friday is typically quiet because the troublemakers are spending the day at the mosque, so I told my section that they can count on this day each week to unwind and "probably for sure" stick to a 12-hour shift. Believe it or not, that was a morale booster. We are actively patrolling all of our new areas south of the city and it has been interesting in light of the coordinated attack against Abu Ghraib last week. The newspapers made it sound like a very successful attack that wounded 50 American soldiers, but I later learned that only six of them required hospitalization and the others were taped up and RTD (Return to Duty). The American military has amazingly accurate data on casualties, because anyone who is hurt in any way out here makes sure it's well-documented for a possible disability claim should they decide to leave the service or promotion points if they stay in. They can even obtain a Purple Heart license plate granting them a front row parking spot at the PX or commissary back home or send their kid to college for free.

As I stated in my last letter, I suspected that the convoy movement from Kuwait would have its moments of excitement; fortunately, it turned out to be uneventful. At 9 p.m. on the night before the convoy, I briefed the soldiers on the dangers we would likely encounter along the route to Baghdad. There was a nervous anxiety during the briefing, especially when I talked about the most recent events that included a vehicle-borne IED (VBIED) that cut in the middle of a convoy and detonated and an IED on the underside of a bridge that blew itself downward onto a contractor's convoy. The guys were all business after the briefing and most of them headed directly to the motor pool to clean weapons and load ammunition.

We were ready to move out by noon the next day. In typical Army fashion, we finally departed at 5 p.m. after moving to three different staging areas over a five-hour period (luckily, all of the staging areas were in walking distance to the chow tent and the Burger King trailer). We pulled out of the gate and followed a large arrow spray-painted on a piece of plywood to a road that would take us to the Iraqi border about 70 miles away. The first leg of the trip is designed to weed out the maintenance problems before the next morning's long drive. That was a good thing, because 10 minutes down the road the lead vehicle started picking up speed and pulling away from my Humvee (which was third in the order of march) at the lightning quick pace of 30 mph. I turned to the driver (SSG Sobers, my Intel Analyst who is usually the pessimist in the group) and remarked that I used to drive this fast on my moped delivering papers as a kid. I also remarked that the last time I smelled this much oil burning was back at Fort Carson when this same vehicle stopped abruptly on a hill after all of the oil leaked out of the drive shaft. He replied that "all Humvees smell bad", which is partly true, but he failed to mention another negative indicator that overshadowed the smell—the fact that he was flooring it to hit 30. The driver directly behind us noticed all of the black smoke spewing from our exhaust and called ahead for the convoy to stop. Even after receiving a new engine and transmission just one week ago, our Humvee failed its sixth consecutive road march. All of the oil leaked out of the rear differentials and the mechanics had to pull it back to the camp in Kuwait, which turned out to be only five miles away. From there, it was placed on a long-haul trailer to Baghdad with most of our gear inside while the three of us riding inside the lemon jumped into some empty seats for the rest of the trip. Twenty minutes later, after my legs went numb, I realized the benefit of sitting in a front seat with legroom rather than propping my feet up on sandbags in the back.

We arrived to our next holding area along the Kuwait-Iraq border outside of Basra in two hours, just before sunset. I thought we were entering into a secured area, but the local Kuwaitis were on top of us within minutes offering to sell DVD's with five movies burned onto a single CD for $4. I bought one that had a bunch of Nicole Kidman movies on it because I wanted to see *Cold Mountain*, but I was more curious to see if it was possible to burn five movies onto one disk and still be able to make out the picture. After cleaning weapons and doing vehicle maintenance most of the guys started bedding down. You could tell who has been here before because they were the ones laying out the camping chairs and REI tent cots between the rows of vehicles while the newbies pitched camp atop an inflexible hood or roof. It was like camping in a big dirt movie theater parking lot. I slept on top of the Humvee on a piece of plywood being used for a roof and fell asleep under the stars while watching my new DVD. The scene wasn't quite as pleasant as it sounds—after all, my legs hung off the roof as I tried to maneuver them around the tied-down tow bars, there was a constant stream of white noise caused by the truck convoys entering and leaving the camp 10 meters away, and a pack of wild dogs barked and fought until about 2 a.m. It was cold, too—only about 50 degrees out, but it seemed colder due to the 40-degree swing from the day's high and the fact we were all sweaty from wearing the body armor and ammo vest all day. I gave my sleeping bag liner to our supply officer, who was shivering in his poncho liner, leaving me with the outer shell that remains nice and toasty in sub-freezing temperatures.

Early the next morning, before sunrise, we sent a few vehicles across the border to patrol the first 10 miles into Iraq. The lead vehicle consisted of three cooks and SSG Sobers, who jumped into their vehicle the day before after ours broke down. SSG Sobers later regaled us with humorous stories of their circus act as the four Sergeants argued about where they were on the map and one of the cooks kept insisting that they take a left at the electric border fence (I sat in on the route briefing the night before and they made it clear NOT to take a left at the fence). A major bridge was blown up on the route two months earlier, so we had to take a couple of bypasses immediately after crossing the border, being extra careful not to get caught up in Basra where the school kids would bring our convoy to a halt in their search for lollipops and cigarettes. Everyone locked and loaded their weapons as we passed the electric fence and we met up with the advance party on the main road that would lead us to Baghdad. For an effective visual of our glorious entry into war, imagine the worst road, alley, or parking lot in your neighborhood and slowly drive across it for 25 miles with your knees pressed against your chest.

We had no problem with traffic around our convoys as the locals would move far out of their way to skirt around us—most of them would simply cross the median to continue their journey on the other side of the highway as there were no cops in sight and probably no cops in existence down here. They would continue to speed while barreling the wrong way on a major highway; if it were me, I would at least stick to the slow lane by the shoulder, but these Iraqis were totally random in their lane selection and I was surprised that there were no major head-on collisions. The first 100 miles into Iraq was pure desert randomly interspersed with swampland. The only interesting thing about the trip was observing the varied mud shanty architecture that dotted the highway and watching the kids and cows cooling off in the marshes. The marshes were once abundant with wild life, but Sadaam had drained them after the Shia uprising in the early '90s and the U.S. was just getting around to revitalizing the swamps, which were once the lifeblood of southern Iraq. The floppy-eared goats, camels, cows, and ox would be lounging around the scrub brush and trying to beat the heat in the marshes. Each of the little mud hut villages we passed featured dozens of little kids out playing in the canals and dirt and they would line the streets and wave at us as we slowly drove by. The innocence of kids out here is amazing—they wave and smile at us everywhere we go, even as their parents are giving us the evil eye. They don't have running water, electricity, or even shoes and their playground is often a patch of water and a mound of dirt, but they still have a great spirit. The mud shacks were impressive structures, but I found myself wondering if they would melt away as the afternoon rains started to drip down on us.

After twelve exhausting hours of driving, averaging about 25 mph along the way, and passing through several Iraqi Army checkpoints and a couple of joint U.S.-Iraqi checkpoints, we finally arrived at our next rest stop. As I later found out, we made good time solely because none of our vehicles broke down, a situation that would have tacked on a couple of hours to the trip for every vehicle malfunction or flat tire. This holding area was similar to the first one on the Kuwait border, like a truck stop on steroids (minus the asphalt and diner) surrounded by huge concrete barriers. All of the barriers were resplendent with graffiti—soldiers seem to be in rare form in Iraq, likely due to the incoherent state they are in by the time they get to this point. I don't know where they got the spray paint, but there was not an empty spot on any of the barriers surrounding an area the size of the Arizona Cardinal's football stadium. There wasn't a spot of shade, either. The parking lot was full of sun-burned soldiers and civilian contracted drivers sleeping on cots and up on the cabs and roofs of their vehicles. There were convoys of all types and nationalities; Poles, Ukrainians, and Italians bellied up alongside the Americans on the military side and the civilian side consisted of Kellogg, Brown, and Root convoys hauling supplies into theater. This was a mandatory nine-hour stop for fuel, maintenance, MRE's, and sleep. Our nine-hour period was to culminate at 2 a.m., so I found myself an empty cot rather than an empty Humvee roof like the night before and slept for three hours before getting up at 1 a.m. to shave and eat a Cajun-spiced rice and sausage dehydrated meal that I hoped would stay in my gut the rest of the day. Then it was time to move out for the last and most interesting 100 miles to Baghdad through a rough area called the "Triangle of Death"—the place we would be calling home for the next 10-11 months. The last piece of graffiti on the way out of the camp said "Thank You, Come Again" and I thought it would have been nice to be on the way to a place called the "Triangle of Happy and Cooperative Arabs".

The trip through South-Central Iraq featured many more Iraqi Army and joint U.S.-Iraqi checkpoints, mostly on the bridges spanning the Tigris River. Apparently, the sound of our convoys awoke most of the guards, who waved meekly at us as we passed in the fog. There were a few of them who looked fairly professional and vigilant and nearly all of them wore full face masks. They say the enemy works banker hours, but it's still an intense journey and my mind drifted into a "Best Of" slideshow of my life as we meandered down MSR Tampa. Everyone puckered up a bit and came alive whenever we would go under one of the many overpasses. We were almost at the final turn on the outskirts of Baghdad when our convoy came to an abrupt halt. A semi-trailer overturned and blocked the road just ahead. This was an interesting situation because we were stopped on the side of the road of one of the most dangerous and notorious stretches outside of the city and would just be sitting there for the next four hours. The line of wheeled convoys and long-haul trailers carrying the tanks and Bradleys strung out for about two miles behind us. Apaches and Kiowa scout helicopters buzzed around on top of us to provide air coverage the entire time. I never knew Apaches were so loud; they are like flying tanks and make just as much noise. It was my first eerie experience in Iraq as it was only 4 a.m., the fog was intense, and we were sitting ducks in one of the most dangerous places in Iraq. The white noise of the helicopters, compounded by my flak vest propping up my head into a comfortable napping position, lulled me to sleep against my wishes. I tried to stay as alert as possible, but felt like a high school senior in a history class.

Later that day, we finally arrived into our new home in the quaint corner of the Baghdad International Airport that the sign on the corner called "Camp Mayberry". The expansive airport once housed Sadaam's animal reservoir, petting zoo, and a big-game hunting reserve that were completed with gazelles, deer, and even tigers (one of Sadaam's last defiant acts of self-defense was to release the tigers from their cages prior to U.S. forces entering the city). The rumor is that our TOC used to be a big kitchen area and my shop's planning office lies in the old dishwashing room. The plumbing, electrical fixtures, and appliances have been looted long ago and left in their places are gaping holes in the cinder block walls and floors. All of the windows are sandbagged, taped, and boarded to prevent a mortar round from spraying any glass remnants on us, even though there's no longer any glass to fragment. The soldiers live in a tent city that resembles *National Geographic* pictures of the ghettos in Brazil or Mexico City. Acres of colored tarps in hues of faded purple, red, orange, and blue cover aging canvas tents surrounded by sand bags, Jersey barriers, Hesco barriers (chicken wire formed to hold dirt and sand), and concertina wire. The showers here are nice because the water runs away from your feet instead of coagulating around them like the ones in Kuwait. Sleep has come easy when I finally have the chance to go down because I'm once again inundated with the constant drone from helicopters, dogs barking outside the wall, and the sporadic firing. You never know who is firing or where it's coming from, you just hear it in the background and assume you're safe as long as you're still alive to make that assumption.

All of us staff officers live in a charming little canvas tent with a faded orange tarp draped over it. We have a frondless palm tree in a pot outside the entrance atop the chest-high stack of sand bags. It reminds me of the flower bed in front of our old home in Scottsdale, in which I tried in vain every month to plant pretty flowers until the sun would consistently melt the petals—I eventually gave in and bought some plastic flowers that Jen would make fun of because we weren't retired older people who bought plastic flowers. Those plastic flowers would look nice out here right now to brighten up the place and they would blend in with the colorful charm of the tent city across the street. I finally found my footlocker in one of the milvans and was able to unpack my sheets and pillow to make my cot more comfortable. Mentally, the sheets make a world of difference as my arms and legs no longer rub on the aluminum and nylon fabric. A lot of the guys mock me over my sheet selection because they are pink with flowers and my pillow case is turquoise with trees (I packed the most expendable sheets I had in the house at the time); fortunately, I'm apathetic about the belittlement because it's such an incredible luxury to have sheets right now. I was initially happy to have our little tent until the eighth guy moved his cot and ruck into our 10 by 20 foot area on the same day that I saw the remodeled Non-commissioned Officer's hooch. The NCO's made great use of an old deep-freezer, to the extent that they had some civilian workers weld bed frames and scrounge some mattresses for them. I envy the fact that their place is big enough to hold a couple dozen frozen sides of beef, but I would be hesitant to sleep on the mattresses that were found in the junkyard where all of the wild dogs sleep.

Soldiers who don't go "outside the wire" out here are referred to as FOB Goblins, FOB Dwellers, Fobbits, Fobelopes, or FOB Darts (after the old Lawn Darts that stuck in the ground). I certainly won't mind the label. For the most part, I'll be doing most of my work in the TOC and only have to go out on large-scale missions or a special mission where we need to capitalize on real-time intelligence and develop it on the spot or get to know a possible informant. My first trip off the base was a helicopter ride around the city and west over Abu Ghraib to Fallujah, in this case to meet up with a Marine unit on our flank to try to nail down a plan to protect Abu Ghraib against future attacks. It turned out to be the most relaxing time I've had since I've been in country—a pleasant ride over farmlands full of families tending to their fields and livestock and kids out playing along the canals. It's an interesting contrast when you leave the green marshes and intricate canal system of the Baghdad area and abruptly hit the vast brown desert that extends out as far as the eye could see into Al Anbar Province. The desert was loaded with trash, junk, and burned-out vehicles, as if all of Baghdad tossed their crap into this open sandpit.

Our Blackhawk crew released some flares that put an end to my day-dreaming and, after a few fake insertions to confuse any observers with evil intentions, we ended up parked on the desert floor on the outskirts of Fallujah. The Marine base here was a pleasant place with lots of palm groves, walkways, old-world rock-lined irrigation canals, and chirping birds. I finally had a chance to walk on a real sidewalk instead of the river rock that was spread across our camps in Kuwait and Baghdad that I've grown accustomed to over the past two months (the final 200 meters to the chow tent at the airport is lined with about six inches of rock which, when combined with the body armor, provides an amazing lower-body workout). In Fallujah, we started discussing some joint operations with the Marines and the issue turned to logistics, specifically feeding the Iraqi soldiers. The guys here last time said that the soldiers would just bring along their own goats in the back of their Datsun King Cab troop carrier pickups and one goat per day would suffice—they wouldn't even ask for water because our bottled water would give them diarrhea in the same manner we get it drinking from their tap.

One thing I was curious about before deploying to war for my first time was the stress level I would encounter. In all of my years in the Army I can only really recall two situations of stress—one being the final exam periods at

West Point each semester when I never thought I could cram so much information into my head and the second on a live-fire range deep into the deserts of Saudi Arabia as a young Infantry Platoon Leader with no communications and an unresponsive, bleeding gunner who the medic claimed was dead after his M60 blew up in his face. In civilian life, however, I can recall the near-daily stress—the difference being that one day I would not have a job and benefits for the family or having to decide if someone else with a family would be fired. So far, each time that I've been out of the wire has been relaxing. I guess it's like anything else in life—stress when you really have to, but until then you just have to worry about the things that you can control. I think my biggest stressor here will be recommending a target to hit or house to raid while wondering in the back of my mind if I unknowingly sent our boys into an ambush or a home rigged with explosives.

With all that we've been through so far, I can't believe that I've only been away from the States for 40 days. It's going to be a long and difficult year being away from Jen and the kids and not sharing experiences together each night at the dinner table. Back home, McKenna learned to hug and what it means. She was trying to hug Cade all day and he finally gave in and let her. She has learned how to mimic several of the farm animals, but the pig's "oink" sound coming from her throat like she is hacking up a loogie is the best I've heard over the phone. Cade, meanwhile, has become infatuated with picking all of the colorful flowers that are springing up around Portland and, sure enough, McKenna goes around copying him but only desiring the flower he picked. Between the flowers and his new Nerf basketball hoop, Cade has been staying on the move rather than eating or napping all day. You know having twins is hard when Jen gets less sleep in Portland than I do in my nappy tent in Camp Mayberry.

APRIL 25, 2005:

A STROLL THROUGH THE COUNTRYSIDE

"You can say that civilization don't advance, however, for in every war they kill you in a different way." Will Rogers

If it's been some time since my last writing I can excuse it because I've been out of town lately. I couldn't believe I was so excited to return to our little corner of the Baghdad International Airport after only eight days—hot meals, hot showers, and generator-powered A/C in the tent never sounded better. I even enjoy walking on the river rocks again. We just performed a "surge" operation wherein almost everyone in the Squadron went out to live among the villages and get a good feel for the area and people. A couple of *Denver Post* reporters are covering our journeys. One of them was on a convoy where the 3rd ACR witnessed its first casualty of war—a young gunner from Yuma, Arizona was killed by an IED as he was on a patrol deep into one of the known hot spots next to Yusifiyah, south of Baghdad in an area that makes up one of the corners of the "Triangle of Death". We call the corners the "Iyah's"—Yusifiyah, Mahmudiyah, and Latifiyah. It's a place that is a mixture of farms, mud and straw homes, and stately mansions stretching from the city of Baghdad down south to the Euphrates River. It's also a place that is totally devoid of all local and national government, police, Iraqi Army, and American forces. The region received a large influx of some 100,000 hard-core prisoners who Sadaam ordered released from Abu Ghraib Prison just days before Baghdad was overrun in the spring of 2003. I've flown over the area several times and it is supposedly the most beautiful part of Iraq—the "Cradle of Civilization" as the Bible says. It's nice enough with all the farms and orchards, the slow-flowing turquoise waters of the Euphrates River, and the extensive canal systems, but I'd still question the source of the hype those thousand of years ago.

Just prior to the operation, our embedded reporters got a taste of one of our many three-hour meetings, this one being the rehearsal for the operation that would include the Iraqi Army and Special Forces, the U.S. National Guard, the Marines, and Air Force. We had about 100 guys circled around a terrain board laid out in front of our operations area for what would be a truly joint operation. Uday Hussein's farm was to be the sight of our main assembly area (Sadaam's son owned several hundred acres in Southwest Baghdad that was smack dab in the middle of our area of operations), or at least his former farm as the place was thoroughly flattened by the Air Force and reduced to rubble early on during the war.

Our movement was scheduled for 11 p.m. on that same evening, so I arrived 45 minutes early for the convoy briefing and took my seat inside a Bradley at the rear of the formation. Sitting in the cramped confines of a Bradley is comparable to being in a tin can without the legroom. I did have the body armor's neck piece going for me and arranged it perfectly into a position allowing me to lay my head back and shut my eyes after having spent a hectic day finalizing our plans. Sure enough, the movement was pushed back past midnight and every 15 minutes word would filter down that it would only be 15 more minutes. Finally, at 2 a.m., we pushed out of our mobile gate (created by removing one of the huge Texas concrete barriers and replacing it with an armored bridge layer, thus cutting three miles off of the drive around the airfield to get out to the streets linking us to the main highway). The 10-mile drive to the farm took us along a couple of roads well-known for IED's and it only took us four hours, highlighted by a wrong turn by one of the middle vehicles that sent half of the convoy the wrong way in *Animal House* fashion. On top of that, one of the bridge layers (possibly the heaviest vehicle in the Army inventory, weighing in at twice as much as a tank) blew a track so the mechanics had to jump out and install a new one while the remaining convoy pulled security in the narrow streets around it.

We arrived in Uday's farm at sunrise and immediately set up security and communications. I walked the perimeter in search of the wretched smell coming from the bushes and, sure enough, noticed that we set in right next to a slow-flowing canal that reeked of raw sewage and became worse with the day's stifling heat. The first day was a tough one for most of the guys as we toyed with our sleep cycle while maintaining an incredibly escalated level of alertness. The units started their cordon and knocks (a nicer way to say "I'm searching your home and fields, but we'll give the kids a soccer ball afterwards so you'll like us") on what would become thousands of homes and farms. I finally hit the cot hard at midnight after being up for 42 hours straight. The mosquitoes and sand flies were pretty thick during the evening hours, so I donned my mosquito head net and passed out on an empty cot next to one of the armored personnel carriers. I slept fully clothed with my flak vest on, partly because I was so exhausted and partly because I didn't know what to expect in terms of incoming mortars or rockets or even a sedan with a Samurai driver blazing through the camp. I was sound asleep within minutes of going down, but quickly jumped up to reach for my weapons when our howitzers started firing illumination rounds to help out a unit to our east. I ended up sleeping with my boots and body armor on for the first two nights, but I chose comfort after that and slept on top of the body armor so I could quickly grab it just in case. I still slept fully clothed for the rest of the time with my BDU pants, top, and head net tightly buttoned-up so the bugs wouldn't eat me alive. Between buttoning up and sucking the sulfur off of the MRE matches, I remained unblemished compared to a lot of the guys who looked like they caught chicken pox.

Everyone smelled ripe after a couple of days in the moist heat, but it wasn't the "burning through muscle kind of ammonia smell" that drives away the mosquitoes and sand flies. It was the "sweaty almost sweet smell" from wearing so much equipment in the hot sun and high humidity. We were eating MRE's the entire time, so most guys lost weight by abstaining from chow even after we started digging into the tasty kosher detainee meals. A Girl Scout troop from Colorado that adopted the unit sent us a bunch of assorted cookies—Thin Mints aren't as enjoyable melted as they are from the freezer or fridge at home, but they were still the first to go.

The biggest medical threat out here, even bigger than an IED blast, is gastrointestinal illness (GI) or rabies from one of the wild dogs. Unless it's a mission requirement (like a Sheik inviting you in for chow), eating at local establishments and Haji stands on the sides of the road is off-limits. I thought the rabies threat was far-fetched until the other night when I stepped out of the operations tent and a pack of wild dogs ran by me. I slept out in the open, so I ensured my 9mm was close to my body just in case because I heard wild stories of packs of dogs attacking soldiers. They look pretty innocent, but there's so many of them lurking around that it makes digging a slit trench in the reeds by yourself quite an eerie experience when you're hesitant to be caught with your pants down. We had a bomb-sniffing dog attached to us—a playful 2-year-old brown lab that the handlers had to keep a close eye on. Despite the informal rules, the GI's (a pleasant name for diarrhea) had set in for a couple of soldiers who were on patrol by the river and accepted some pita bread from the locals as they passed through.

We only had to use the slit trench by the canal (an 18-inch deep, 6-foot wide, 20-foot long trench) for five days before some industrious Fobbits back at the airport found some old wood and toilet seats and built port-a-johns and sent them out to us on a logistics convoy. Soon, there were three Tiger Johns gracing the canal, complete with doors and screens to defeat the mosquito hordes (until the bugs figured out to enter through the 2-foot gap between the door and roof). The Tiger John inventors welded some metal scraps together to make buckets that fit under the seats and filled them with JP8 diesel fuel instead of the blue chemical stuff from a real port-a-john. Urinating into the buckets is not allowed because urine doesn't burn, so you still have to use the slit trench for that function. The morning cleaning detail merely has to pull out the bucket, light a match, and watch it all burn away while slowly stirring the compost. All I can say is that I won't complain about real port-a-johns anymore. I can't even really complain about the Tiger Johns again—like anything else in life, it's all relative. I only noticed a few items of graffiti in the Tiger Johns; I think it's an ownership thing and the best graffiti has to come from the port-a-johns in the PX or alongside a dark, vacant road, where the writer remains anonymous and doesn't get extra-duty if they're caught penning a poem. Some of the stuff is so good that the thought of a port-a-john graffiti book often crossed my mind.

Occasionally, I would take a ride with the Commander to check out our blocking positions and traffic control points (TCP's) and talk to the people. I quickly learned that these trips make for very long, albeit entertaining, days, as he has a well-known habit of stopping random people in the villages and along the routes. Our conversations as we made our rounds would go something like this:

> "Hey Craig, is this a bad guy?"
> "I don't know, Sir. He looks like a farmer."
> "Do you recognize his name?"
> "Not really, they all sound alike to me."

Then we'd pile back in our vehicles and find someone else to check out. A variation of the conversation would center on vehicles we would stop, except there would be more incredulity at the end like, "Wow, I didn't think butchers could afford a Mercedes 300".

You can definitely tell which villages or even neighborhoods are good or bad upon entry. It's always a bad sign if there are no kids out playing or no women tending the fields or groups of people at the market. One day, a nomadic family and their 500 or so sheep moved in and set up camp a few hundred feet from one of our traffic control points. The Troop Commander at the position gave the kids in the tribe some soccer balls and suckers, so they treated him like Santa Claus every time he entered the area. One little boy, no more than knee-high, reached into the Commander's pocket and discretely snagged his lighter. These kids ask for everything and anything, even cigarettes. I'm sure their parents tell them to bring back some American burners because everyone out here smokes and they absolutely love the Marlboros compared to the Arab smokes that fizzle up faster than a dry blade of grass. Pens and pencils are extremely popular—I don't know if they actually use them or just know enough English to get across "I go to school and I like pens". Horsing around with the kids is my favorite thing to do in Iraq so far. They don't hesitate to approach you, whereas the parents usually need a couple of days of seeing the same guys before they approach to ask about things like jobs, water, and electricity and, if we're lucky, provide us with some information about their neighborhoods. At one little farmhouse we stopped by, a set of boy and girl twins not much older than Cade and McKenna came running towards us along the dirt road (barefoot of course) with the cutest bright dresses and pantsuits. I found myself daydreaming that I was coming home and it was Cade and Mac running towards me.

Unfortunately, we experienced the other side of war on the night after the nomads departed the area around the TCP. A lone Iraqi came walking towards our soldiers' position and didn't stop. All of the TCP's are remarkably visible with bright lights and wires strung up around them. After the man failed to heed the Arabic signs, Arabic shouting, and hand signals, one of the soldiers on a tank fired a warning shot with his M-16 when the guy was 100 meters out and another at 50 meters. The tank driver even backed up when the guy was within 20 meters before the gunner was forced to shoot the man in the chest. In a testament to their training, the troops ran up to him, ensured he wasn't wearing a suicide vest, patched him up and got him breathing again, called in a Medevac helicopter, and within 10 minutes this guy was on his way to the surgical unit. Nobody knows what he was thinking and likely none of us will ever know. I heard this entire event unfold as it was reported over the radio.

Three days after the event, our Public Affairs Officer reported that Al Jazeera's coverage depicted the Americans shooting an unarmed man on the highway.

One of my major headaches during our first big operation was processing detainees. Our first detention in Iraq occurred at 3 a.m. on the second day out of the wire. The troops brought in a guy who was caught digging next to a small road during curfew. The farmers love to dig at night when it's cooler and the Arabs believe that the water flows better at night. Water is an issue for all of the farmers, so they just find any main pipe and dig down, insert their own PVC pipe, and they have a water source for their farm. The only problem is that they are usually digging past curfew (11 p.m. - 4 a.m.) and often out on the main roads where the main water pipes lie. Our soldiers on the ground have to investigate each event in case they are digging an IED pit. Another problem is that Iraq has such a strong weapons culture (every male is allowed to have one AK47 as part of the homeland defense from back in the Iran-Iraq War during the '80s) that it's nearly impossible to search a home or person and not find a weapon. If someone only has a few extra AK's and a couple hundred of rounds, it's easier to simply confiscate the excess and give them to the Iraqi Army for their use. It's like the *Cops* TV show—the helicopters spot something and the ground forces give chase and capture the bad guy and collect evidence and sworn statements while the defendant pleads his case of innocence, ignorance of the curfew, ignorance of the gun laws, and love for the Americans. In this case, I could tell the farmer was a nice guy (unfortunately I have seen a lot of dirtbags so far and it has been really easy to peg the ones exhibiting signs of deceptiveness and lying and getting caught in their own stories) and we had no evidence on him. I feebly attempted to make him smile and relax with gestures I'd make to my kids (the only Arabic words I know are the basic greetings, stand up, sit down, put your hands out) because he was shaking pretty badly. He finally ended up smiling, especially when the capturing troops gave him a ride back to the hole so we could see that it was empty and on his own property.

In the second detention of our trip, our soldiers arrested a guy who happened to have the same name as someone on our Black List (our own Most-Wanted List), something that is very common when you're searching for an Abu Ali in Iraq (which is like the John Smith of the U.S.). It was immediately apparent that this old man wasn't our Black List target. The guy's cousin, a taxi driver, even drove him in (followed closely by our Bradleys) and parked the taxi outside of our assembly area in the rubble of Uday's mansion. The cousin was temporarily detained, as well, and both men were blindfolded so they couldn't take mental notes of our positions. Upon release, I ended up guiding the two of them, still blindfolded, back to the taxi, maneuvering around the sand dunes and concertina wire until I found the car hidden far outside the wire in the midst of what I think used to be Uday's indoor pool. I removed their blindfolds and shook the old man's hand, which surprised me when I found out he only had two fingers. He was very thankful (which I guess is normal after being led across the desert blindfolded) and drove away honking and waving. I was further out of the wire than I thought, but took a little tour around Uday's old stomping grounds to marvel at the tiles and marble ruins while thinking that he must have had a lot of mosquitoes at his pool parties. It takes solid and corroborating evidence to process a detainee through the Iraqi courts, which leads to quick releases for a lot of bad actors. Every time we find a home with C-4 explosives or grenades the owner always claims he uses them to fish (which they probably do, at least according to the Iraqi soldiers and interpreters working with us), so we just confiscate the items to give to the IA unless it's a ridiculously large amount. Otherwise, the offender would end up being released and the arrest could end up turning a good guy into a bad guy after he was dishonored.

Despite the humiliating stories about Abu Ghraib and secret CIA prisons in the press, the detainees out here are treated extremely well. The days of being sentenced to death for stealing a car are over; American justice was in town and the criminals were no longer scared. Any detainee we take is reported immediately up to Corps-level so they can account for them and ensure that there is a chain of custody just in case somebody is mistreated along the way. The medics give each detainee a thorough check-up to ensure that they don't have any ailments and fix whatever they can (and almost everybody in Iraq needs something fixed). Most of the people have foot problems—one guy's feet were all bumpy and the medic said he felt rocks under the skin from years of walking barefoot. After they are photographed and the interpreter helps us capture the basic bio-data, they are led into the holding cage until we can transfer them to higher, which has to take place within 24 hours of capture. We're almost always pushing that time limit because we need to rouse a full armored convoy for the escort mission and either pull those soldiers away from patrols or pull them away from their sleep and DVD plan. In the meantime, the detainee is given a blanket, water, and those kosher meals that all of us love to munch on.

Two companies (roughly 200 men) of Iraqi Army soldiers were attached to us for this mission for both a training event and to put the Iraqi face on the operation. The new soldiers worked out really well for the first day and then started to peter out from the exhausting tempo. The two companies were totally different. The soldiers in one company would work for about two hours and then take a break to lie down and eat. The first thing they did upon returning to the assembly area was lie down on their foam mattresses in the shade of their trucks. The soldiers in the other company seemed to have a lot more energy and aggression, but would save most of that for the soccer game at the end of the day, which, for them, was 5 p.m. All of their soldiers would enjoy the house-to-house searches (as long as we had their backs). They would happily meet and greet the locals and grab anything they could eat along the way—raw green beans, apples from the orchards, and the same pita and falafels that gave our boys the GI's. Our soldiers took all of the guard shifts and manned the observation posts around the assembly area, which made me sleep much more soundly.

The Iraqis proved to be a great motivator for the people in some of the remote villages who have never seen the new Army or one of the new Army members who actually removed his face mask. Respect and pride are huge for the people and their Army was one of the few things that Iraqis could take pride in over the years, back when the Iraqi Army was considered to be the most powerful on the continent and proudly fought Iran to a standstill. You could see how excited some of the people were to see their own Army. A pep-rally broke out in one of the small villages when the tribal leader asked the Iraqi Colonel if he was working for the Americans and the Colonel replied, "No, the Americans work for me". That was a great answer and more answers like that could get us out of here earlier. The IA was a great recruiting tool, too. Young men approached the Iraqi patrols and asked how they could join. The IA used their own names for the villages that we couldn't pronounce—one town was dubbed "The Town of Bad Guys" in Arabic and another was the "Town of Security Workers at Abu Ghraib". The "Town of Bad Guys" was one of the only places where both our guys and the new IA felt obvious hostility. One of the males in the town flipped off a patrol and the IA soldiers pulled him into the bed of their pickup truck and started beating him. Our soldiers stepped in to stop the beating and explain that it was wrong, even if they did want to beat the punk to a pulp themselves.

Most of the soldiers seem to have a different outlook on events after op-erating in the area for the past month and experiencing the first death in the Regiment. A common saying now, and one dotting the port-a-johns around camp, is "I'd rather be judged by 12 then carried by 6". It is a great feeling to do something nice for those who are grateful, but most of our activity will continue to be hunting for bad guys with virtually no help from the people who are being hurt or intimidated. I hate dealing with the detainees because they have that look of hatred burning inside of them, whereas talking to a possible informer who is afraid for his family's life and making him feel good because you actually give a shit or giving the kids school supplies, suckers, MRE's, and soccer balls is such a high. One Lieutenant will probably be a grade school teacher after this little trip; he was fired up when his patrol entered a school to meet with the headmaster and one of the teachers brought him in to meet the kids. He taught them "Heads Up 7-Up" and said it was one of the highlights of his life.

It was quite an experience for my first extended time out in a "combat environment". The Iraqis are very resilient people and seem to easily adapt to crappy times, probably because they have experienced so much hardship over their lifetime and it's simply become part of their fiber. Terrible events and conditions just don't seem to faze them. A huge bomb may go off and close off the streets for a square mile, but once the cleanup is complete and the street is open the people are back on it and the market stalls are packed again. The same thing occurs regularly with recruiting lines for the police and Army—a suicide bomber blows himself up in line and the recruits walk around the mess to get to their interview on time. Two of our interpreters were killed less than a week after we hired them—the day after the mourning period ended there were dozens in line to fill the vacant slots. Some of the interpreters stay with us all of the time and take a four-day pass once a month to visit their families and some of them go home every night to downtown Baghdad or one of the surrounding villages. The big saying in Iraq is "Inshallah", which means "God Willing". It's a response for just about any issue and it helps them deal with their grieving or their ability to go home in the face of being killed, because it was simply God's will that the interpreter lost his life at that place and time.

More and more civilians are growing very angry with the criminals and terrorists and are ready to risk their lives by turning them in. One lady flagged down a patrol from behind some palm groves and would only talk to one of our Arab American interpreters, an Iraqi expatriate hired back in Los Angeles. She claimed to have traveled very far when she heard that Americans were in the area and she had some information to share about a gang that was terrorizing her neighborhood down by the river. She gave us names and places (almost nobody here can read a map and the concept of an imagery photo is out of the question, so they talk in general terms like "the man lives in a hut that is a three-minute walk towards the river from the bridge crossing the canal next to the fuel stand"). Another man walked up to the patrol to provide information about the car thieves who ran off the local police and now controlled his village. The gang would steal cars and sell them back to the previous owner; this guy's brother was shot in the leg while they were trying to negotiate a price to buy their car back and he finally had someone he could trust to tell the story. We ended up taking the brother to the surgeon because the wound was obviously infected and eating up the skin on his leg. After so many locals started to provide us with information as we made the rounds through each village, I left with a sense of optimism that things will get better. Maybe. "Inshallah".

I've had several experiences in life in which I've learned not to take the simple and largely overlooked pleasures in life for granted and my experience in Iraq so far is serving as another of those reminders—a very large reminder at that. Getting out of bed and walking on a carpet, flushing a toilet, walking barefoot on a warm sidewalk, hugging and smelling my wife and kids, watching the news, relaxing on a couch, sleeping on a mattress, wearing shorts and flip flops, sitting in the yard and listening to birds and laughter instead of generators, aircraft, and vehicle traffic. When I was single and having a difficult experience, like at Ranger School, I always found myself coming back to the same comforting moment—lounging in my La-Z-Boy recliner eating a Domino's Hawaiian Pizza and drinking a cold Dr. Pepper while watching a full slate of NFL games. Now, I find myself constantly relying on one memory that drives me; it's that time of night just after the kids' baths and before we put them to bed. Jen and I are both exhausted by then and we are lying in the kids' bedroom with Butkus (our golden retriever) at my feet. Cade is babbling away talking to a book he's reading (which is usually upside down) and McKenna is reaching up to the bookshelves pulling down all of the *Disney* collection. Jen just sent me a video of the kids and it was waiting for me when I returned. I fell asleep to it the past two nights—the kids laughing and saying DaDa does wonders for any morale.

We're back to the drawing board as far as our future location and we're currently working on our fifth change of plans in the past six months—"Semper Gumby" as the Army saying goes (Remain Flexible). Last month, we were on our fourth change of plans, which happened to be the same course of action in terms of time and location as the first change (or second original plan). We were working on our third change while we were in Kuwait, which was a change back to our original plan. I still haven't fully unpacked my duffle bags, even though I may have to this evening because the tent developed a leak right over one of them while I was out. Someday, I'll have a chance to build that shelf out of old MRE boxes that I've been dreaming about. I did hear that camel spiders enjoy snacking on the cardboard as much as they do the sand bags, so I'll remain flexible myself and adjust the shelf structure if I can find some old metal or plywood material. I can't say right now where we're going or when until the information is posted in the open source media—usually the *Stars & Stripes*, *Army Times*, *globalsecurity.org*, or perhaps the guys at the *Denver Post* will write about it, perhaps even before I know. Let's just say that the locale should be a bit more comfortable as far as the bad guys blowing up people and a lot less comfortable in terms of living conditions. It's the same old song for us—no American troops have been out there before so it's a black hole for intelligence and there is very little government, police, or Iraqi Army infrastructure. One thing I am certain of is that the supply guys are looking into ordering tents and sand bags. I've been an Intel Officer long enough to recognize that my short-term goal of living comfortably in a trailer or a connex like the TCN's may never come to fruition. One thing I can always expect here is the unexpected.

MAY 11, 2005: IT'S A MAD, MAD WORLD

"War is an ugly thing, but not the ugliest of things. The decayed and degraded state of moral and patriotic feeling which thinks that nothing is worth war is much worse. The person who has nothing for which he is willing to fight, nothing of which is more important than his own personal safety, is a miserable creature and has no chance of being free unless made and kept so by the exertions of better men than himself."

John Stuart Mill

As you have probably been reading back home, it's still a madhouse here in Baghdad. It was odd that we went out for a week and literally parked in the middle of the "Triangle of Death", one of the worst areas in Iraq, and I felt safer than a lot of places in the States. We'd hear explosions throughout the day and night, but they are usually from weapons caches being blown in place, so I didn't realize the extent of the suicide attacks until we returned to the base. We know that every time the new Iraqi government meets there's going to be a few car bombs and suicide bombers around the city and, if they can't get in, they'll drive on the outskirts and wait for a target of opportunity. Usually that target is an Iraqi Army soldier driving around in the back of their Toyota pickups or a crowd of civilians in line for any government job. Unfortunately, there's little to nothing you can do to stop someone who wants to kill himself. The bad guys planting the IED's are likely Iraqis who know the area and have farmed it all of their lives, but it's always the foreigners—usually the Syrians, Saudis, Sudanese, and Tunisians—who have slipped in for the spectacular suicidal splashes and to punch their ticket to see Allah. These attacks have been a huge success publicity-wise and may be helping in their recruiting campaign outside of Iraq, but I think it's hurting them domestically. Tips from locals are flooding in and we're starting to capture a lot of the major players.

The Iraqi civilians weren't the only ones who had a tough week; our sister Squadron up north in Tal Afar lost two soldiers in an IED attack and the day after we returned to base we lost our first soldier to an IED along a small dirt road next to MSR Tampa. SGT Saxton just switched to the gunner position minutes before the bomb went off. He left behind a wife and three kids, including a 3-week-old daughter who he never had a chance to meet. It seems like all of the violence going on would shake anyone up, but I'm amazed at how our soldiers are reacting to it. They are volunteering to go on patrols and missions to do anything they can to clean the place up and will do anything asked of them to cover each other's back. It's a difficult situation for everybody when you're searching for hundreds of John Allen Mohammeds, which took American law enforcement three weeks to do back in 2002 even though it was resourced with thousands of dedicated officers and an intense nationwide manhunt that included the civilian population. The area we're in, on the other hand, has virtually no governmental resources and a local population that, despite our recent informant successes, remains strongly intimidated or more sympathetic to their criminal or terrorist brethren.

Our latest mission took us to the areas directly south of Baghdad in Northern Babil Province. We moved out at midnight on an overcast, moonless night, past the last piece of graffiti on the road out of Camp Mayberry that states "Don't get hit by an IED, it hurts like hell". Our multiple convoys took a route that led south to the Triangle, driving in blackout drive and navigating with night vision goggles. Blackout drive doesn't do anything to alleviate the noise of 40 tanks and Bradleys pulling down the side streets, but it is effective in preventing an observer or triggerman to accurately detonate an IED from a mile away with a cell phone or from around the corner with a garage opener.

The ride was initially quiet, with the occasional report from our scout helicopters breaking the radio silence to inform us about people moving about on their rooftops (which is where most families sleep in the summer in an attempt to catch that rare cool breeze). The silence ceased once we crossed into the first populated area. A casual observer would've thought we met harsh resistance at this point. In this case, I was that casual observer, monitoring the radio in a Bradley in the second convoy just behind the scouts. A loud cry of "Contact, Contact" abruptly pierced the airwaves and white sparks shot up overhead into the pitch-black night. The lights in the town flickered on and off a couple of times, which is usually an indicator of observers signaling the insurgents of our presence. Our radios fell silent and everyone's senses were on high alert awaiting enemy fire when the air scouts announced that they were taking small arms fire to their front and they identified a group of men running out of a mosque near town. Things were becoming very interesting, like we were living in a video game. At the same time, the lead Bradley's driver misread a turn onto the only bridge leading into Yusifiyah and became entangled in the concertina wire that was blocking the edge (luckily for the crew, the wire saved them from plummeting into the canal). As the crew dismounted to cut the wire out of the tracks, the aerial reports continued about multiple armed men in a Kia Bongo truck advancing towards our positions (which is a much-preferred situation compared to being hit with an IED or suicide bomber because their coordinated attacks become an easy way to take out a lot of bad guys with no paperwork or evidence collection for the prosecution at kangaroo court). The lead Bradley cleared the bridge and a scout section darted off to set in motion a 30-second scenario in which the scouts intercepted the Bongo truck, fired a warning shot to stop it, shot the engine block to stop it, and then shot one of the three armed men who jumped out and was repositioning in the culverts.

When the action died down there was one KIA, which anyone listening to the action over the radio would have believed to be an insurgent. However, a group of Iraqi Army soldiers arrived on the scene and quickly pulled away the body without letting us inspect it. The scouts on the ground and in the air both noticed the body was dressed in jeans and a T-shirt instead of a uniform. The guy was apparently an Iraqi Army soldier; we still don't know what they were doing out there that night. Some of the local U.S. forces working the area later told us that they think many of the local IA is working both sides of the war.

At 3 a.m. we arrived to a spot that was picked out during an aerial reconnaissance a few days before. Our assembly area was located on a large farm that appeared to be vacated and sat about 100 meters from the site of the IED that killed the first soldier in the Regiment. It was at this time that we finally heard the real story about the action over the past couple of hours. Aside from the drama that unfolded around the mosque area, there really wasn't too much action at all. The power lines coming into the city of Yusifiyah are so low that the vehicle antennas hit them on the way in. One gunner, who was jolted by the electrical current, thought an RPG hit his vehicle. The real story is that his antennas snagged and dragged on the power lines, causing the town lights to flicker and spark and make his body go numb. He called out "CONTACT" repeatedly over the radio, thus earning himself a new nickname. Over the next 24 hours he had a really quiet voice and spoke in hushed tones, similar to another guy in the unit named "Rainbow". "Contact" is fine now; the medics said he just caught a big zap from the power lines and shouldn't have any long-term effects ("Contact" is skeptical about that assessment from one of the new 18-year-old medics—he thinks he'll be fishing in the bayou someday when he's retired and his wife will be able to spot his glow from the shores when she's calling him in for chow).

We were joined at sunrise by a battalion of soldiers from the Iraqi Intervention Forces (IIF). The Iraqi government has several elements in their security apparatus: the Iraqi Army, the IIF, Iraqi National Guard, Border Patrol, Police, Special Forces, and Infrastructure Security. We've been working closely with the IIF and, occasionally, the Iraqi SF, which seem to be two of the most competent and disciplined groups in their array of forces. They still have a lot to learn, but they are coming along quickly. They are prone to taking off all of their equipment for a quick swim in a canal and their discipline at night is ridiculously lax. The IIF Sergeant Major was excited about briefing our Sergeant Major on their guard rotation for the night. Their plan turned out to be one guy sitting by a fire while the others slept. We were fine with that plan, though—it's much more comforting knowing that we have half of our guys manning the guns around the clock and only one of their guys is awake to have a negligent discharge.

During the day, the Iraqi Operations Officer asked if I could help him to better understand how we operate and asked about which targets we were going after. I realize that they are the ticket out of here and it's my job and in my best interest to train them, but it's hard to totally trust them, especially when you hear the stories about some of the local units rife with corruption, leaks, drug dealing, and shaking down the locals at checkpoints. This guy had some good stories. He said that the police are still the most corrupt outfit; they were even corrupt during Sadaam's era and even Sadaam couldn't control it. Corrupt police have become an accepted way of life over the past 50 years and that aspect of Iraqi life likely won't change. This officer was from Basra and said he was a tanker in Sadaam's army, but Sadaam only trusted his own Republican Guard. Sadaam gave the Guard the best weapons, equipment, and training and the other forces around the country were outfitted with aged T-55 Soviet tanks that couldn't move and they were left hungry and in the dark. I asked the IIF Operations Officer what his soldiers thought of the previous night's death. His quick reply to that question, of course, was "Inshallah".

He must have thought I was incompetent as I was showing him our plan because I was fabricating a lesson about conducting demographic surveys on the fly rather than telling him which homes our guys were planning to cordon and search. The IIF participated in all of the searches, but we never told them all of the specifics until the day of the action to minimize possible leaks. Most of the Iraqis we work with are in the 2nd IIF Battalion and come from all over the country—primarily the big three cities of Baghdad, Mosul, and Basra. I'm a big believer that the geographical separation from their home allows them to avoid the local tribal and criminal affairs and concentrate on their job without the local Sheik or Imam influencing them and their family. I'll feel more comfortable the longer we work with the same guys and it is nice to have them filter out the foreigners in the population and pinpoint things that we wouldn't notice. Right now, they've proven exceptionally adept at pinpointing which homes have the best Chai tea and beef kebabs.

As in every mission when we move out at midnight after working the entire day, I went down hard after about 40 hours of non-stop activity. I set up my cot in a dilapidated home on the outskirts of the farm after clearing the floor of glass shards and cinder block. The farmhouse had no windows or doors, but at least it had a roof to provide shade and the lack of the exterior conveniences allowed a warm breeze to blow through. As happens in every mission, I was sound asleep until jolted awake by mortars and I grabbed my body armor until I noticed the illumination rounds lighting up the sky and realized it was our own howitzers shooting. You'd think I'd be ready for that by now. My new room was located on the edge of our perimeter, but there was enough glass on the floor to hear anyone coming in or out and a Bradley team was pulling security about 50 meters away. I awoke to a constant flow of foot traffic early in the morning, so I got up to see what was going on and realized that the Iraqi soldiers were using the back rooms as a latrine. I quickly moved my stuff out of the house before I caught Hepatitis.

The bugs ate me up fairly efficiently over the course of the night, despite my precautions. Prior to going down I ensured that I was totally enclosed: my BDU top was buttoned at the neck, pants tied at the bottoms, sleeves tight around the wrists, a mosquito net on my head, and Deet sprayed generously over everything. The only uncovered part of my body was my hands and I dreamt that there were spiders crawling on them all night. As I found out in the morning, there was definitely something with four or more legs crawling around—my hands, arms, and even the skin between my fingers were covered with bites. The medics already self-diagnosed their own bites and word spread that the sand fleas were out in force, which was scarier than hearing insurgents were in the wire to me because my neighbor at Fort Carson returned home from his tour paralyzed and in a wheel chair due to the little buggers.

Our Cavalry Troop down by the Euphrates selected a much nicer home to spend their time in. It was vacant, still under construction, and splendidly decorated with marble floors and oak cabinets. A well-dressed Arab approached them after three days and asked when they were leaving so the construction workers could return to work. He was the Sheik of the Caragoli tribe, one of the largest (and reportedly the worst) tribes in the area, which explains why the home was so glamorous and not yet looted. He didn't mind the U.S. soldiers staying there, but he insisted that the IIF leave immediately.

One of our missions was to search a village down by the Euphrates that had been a hot spot for IEDs over the past year. The area is very difficult to get into with the soft-banked, narrow canal roads and antiquated flimsy bridges. This terrain, coupled with the fact that the place is populated entirely by Sunni tribes, made the area a sanctuary for the ex-Fallujah cell members when they were chased out of town. One of our Bradleys was driving down a canal road and the entire road collapsed under them, causing the vehicle to roll into the canal. The crew made it out safely, but the mechanics couldn't recover the vehicle because the roads wouldn't support a wrecker that weighed more than a tank. We redirected our bridge crew to the area, where they created a new schoolhouse standard of extracting a Bradley from a ditch by setting the 30-meter bridge across two irrigation canals to allow the wrecker to gain traction and pull out the Bradley. The scene quickly became quite a show for the locals and allowed our human intelligence teams to converse with them. In typical Iraqi fashion, however, all of the people had the same well-rehearsed story claiming ignorance of any attacks in the area over the last year—they all claim to go in their homes for the night at 8 p.m. and come out at 6 a.m. because they don't want to have anything to do with seeing the bad guys dropping bombs. I guess it's no different than any big city in the U.S. where the locals just want to get on with their life and turn a blind-eye towards the crime going on around them for their own safety.

The IIF was really well received in many villages along the way, with slaps on the back, hugs, and invites to just about every house for tea and food (which prolongs the searches, because the IIF do not turn down any invites for chow). While the IIF is chatting up and eating with the locals, our guys randomly pull out the metal detectors and just start scanning the fields. A mechanic was standing at a blocking position next to a canal and started pulling on a piece of plastic that was sticking out of a berm because he was bored. As he pulled more and more plastic from the ground, he eventually uncovered a huge underground chamber, similar to the one Sadaam was captured in, housing hundreds of mortars, rockets, full mortar systems, old Soviet anti-aircraft guns, RPG's, and small arms. That was a nice boost to morale, especially when we found several other large caches nearby.

The schools in most of these villages are packed with kids of all ages. All of the school kids are usually released from class to watch the spectacle whenever we drive through a town, so the kids are usually excited to see us because they get out of class and usually fetch some candy or MRE's. One school in Yusifiyah seemed to be in much worse shape than the others; it had a great student to teacher ratio with 250 kids and 17 teachers, but their entire annual allocation of teaching supplies consisting of one blackboard and seven pieces of chalk probably dropped the school in the ratings. A chaplain back in Fort Carson sent us dozens of boxes filled with school supplies and one of our patrols returned a couple of days later to hand them out. The teachers and children were ecstatic. Unfortunately, the headmaster pulled one of our Lieutenants aside to tell him that one of his teachers was beaten pretty badly for talking to us the week before. Our impact only goes so far, because it's impossible to be in all of these villages at once and both the civilians and the insurgents know we'll be leaving soon and the status quo will return soon afterwards.

While most of our time out is fairly miserable with the stifling heat and bugs, there are still some good times. Most of them are so subtle that you don't realize that they're the good times until you're back telling stories about them in the mess hall in the rear. One day, we came upon the burned out, melted carcass of a vehicle bomb on the canal road next to one of our positions and one of the guys jumped in the driver's seat, atop the springs, and shot some poses in the sedan to submit to *MTV's "Pimp My Ride"*. Then he followed up with a couple of shots in a vacant straw and mud hut for *Extreme Home Makeover*. Comparing sand flea bites and heat rashes became a popular pastime. Then there was the excitement created each time a helicopter would land amongst the fiberglass waste. That situation was treated like an incoming mortar round as tiny strands of fiberglass became airborne and stuck to your hair and sweaty skin under the body armor. Each morning we'd get a kick out of the Iraqis sneaking onto the supply pad and making off with loaves of white bread and hot individual milk containers. They'd leave the MRE's alone, which says a lot coming from a group of men who eat just about anything placed in front of them. Then there's listening to the stories coming from one energetic, affable, and very outspoken Platoon Sergeant nicknamed Super Dave (after the character of the same name) as he attempts to befriend locals and collect intelligence everywhere he goes. An excerpt of his conversation with one Sunni elder, a man who had eight wives, went something like this:

Super Dave: "Did you vote?"

Sunni Man: "No, I refused. And I don't like the new government. Never should a Kurd be President and lead the Sunni people."

Super Dave: "Hey, welcome to democracy, buddy. We elect people we hate every day. Next time get all your women together and go vote."

I have to admit that it is kind of scary being out there in some of these places. There have only been three times in my life when I can vividly recall being in a situation where I thought something very, very bad could happen to me: running with the bulls in Pamplona when I tripped on the cobblestone and fell into a pile of bodies as the bulls tumbled over us, being strapped to a 140-pound sleep and food-deprived guy's back as he rappelled off of a 150-foot cliff during Ranger School's mountain phase in the Appalachians, and diving off of the top deck of a paddle boat at Lake Pleasant as a kid and being caught upside down in the wheel's undercurrent not knowing which way was up. Traveling through some of these towns hasn't reached that stage emotionally, but it is an eerie feeling each time I go out. You scan for possible IED's, observers, and triggermen, but it looks like every person and every object of trash and rubble along the routes could be one or the other. The entire downtown of Yusifiyah, which is the poorest and dirtiest city I have ever seen in my life, could've held countless IED's and VBIED's in the crowded marketplace as we drove through intently scanning the area against the backdrop of cold stares and dirty wild dogs barking at our trucks. Being in Iraq does make me you start mentally calculating the odds. Tiny odds and destiny can work in your favor or against you: they worked for me one spring day in Phoenix when I met Jen in the airport while she was on a layover and I happened to be taking a flight and they worked against SGT Saxton when his crew pulled off the highway to make a U-turn on that small dirt road. You can try to minimize the poor odds by not riding in the trail vehicle or riding in the seat behind the driver in a Humvee or getting lucky by stopping to talk to someone alongside the road who may be an observer or triggerman and scaring him off without ever knowing that. In the end, though, I think more about the dirt bags who are hurting all of the innocent people and kids without regard for human life and how I would feel if that were Jen, Cade, or McKenna being targeted or intimidated. I think that is the feeling that overwhelms all others among the soldiers, especially when one of your own is taken.

It's nice to be back at the airfield in Baghdad. Even though you can hear gunshots and explosions in the distance, it's a comforting feeling to walk around in a boonie cap and relax with some greasy burgers and corn dogs in the air-conditioned chow hall. I'll miss the comforts of this place. Every night I walk to chow past the TCN's little make-shift village of connexes converted into hardened shelters and I enjoy seeing them laughing and playing volleyball, living the simple life like you'd experience in a summer camp as a kid. A haircut on base is only $3 and the Pakistani barbers throw in a head and shoulder massage afterwards. I used to get a $1 cut and massage back in Saudi in 1994 every chance I'd get, but I've only been able to go twice since I've been here because it seems like we've been out so much. I jumped in the Tiger Tactical School Bus for a ride to the main part of base, where the big PX warehouse and Burger King are located. The trip takes about 45 minutes in the TTSB and winds around several interior checkpoints and in front of Sadaam's old mansions, where the Division staff guys work and swim in the outdoor pool aside the lake. The guy who I replaced is now on that staff after he was fired from his previous job. Watching all the people in the pool playing volleyball and lining up in the softball rings for their intramural games almost made me want to get fired and sent to Division. I stopped by Burger King to relish in the last Whopper with cheese that I may see for a very long time.

We're still planning for our next move to another area of the country. I'm excited about getting out of here, but I think we could've changed this place with some more time. More and more locals are providing information to us each day, which keeps me busy, and the attacks in our direct area have plummeted compared to those against the Louisiana National Guard unit we replaced. We have a quartering party up north in our future home and it sounds like it's going to be similar to the fiberglass-laden farmland with the rubble building that the Iraqis disgraced as I slept. We're stocking up on all the plywood, 2x4's, and rusty, tossed air conditioning units that we could find so we can build a little village out there. I'm starting a small stash of the best MRE's in the Army inventory—Chicken and Salsa and Beef Enchilada. Nobody is looking forward to eating the omelets (referred to as "Spongebob") every morning after having to suffer through that during the last yearlong deployment. I may have to take some of you up on the offer to send some Twinkies and Snickers after I get up there and make a chow assessment.

Back in the real world, I called Jen on Mother's Day as they returned from the kids' first trip to the ocean off of the Oregon coast. I was so happy to hear her voice and the kids laughing in the background and hear the stories of how they loved running away from the waves even when the waves were hundreds of feet away. Cade just bought his first pair of Nike sneakers and McKenna inherited his old ones, which are the only ones she'd wear back when Cade owned them. Just prior to pulling out of Kuwait, back when I had time to watch movies at night and knew where the gym tent was, my Intel Analyst took a picture of me and printed it out on the plotter. The result was a near life-sized cutout that we called "Flat Daddy". I sent it home to Jen, where she had me laminated and mounted to the kids' wall. Now whenever Jen mentions Daddy, McKenna goes to the wall and hugs Flat Daddy. Cade, meanwhile, has recently taken a liking to red flowers. I received several plastic flowers in the mail over the past couple of weeks, so I snapped a shot of me in front of my canvas tent alongside my new colorful pot of flowers to send home to him. On the same day, my Grandpa Poppi passed away in Phoenix after living a long and full life. I'm so grateful that he had the opportunity to meet Cade and McKenna, and that they were able to be held by their Great Grandfather, before going off to heaven. I know he'll be up there with my dad, Charlie, watching over us as we try to make the world a little better place.

Making "Flat Daddy" to send home to the kids while in Kuwait.

The author sits in front of the staff "hooch" at Camp Mayberry in Baghdad.

The author's gunner trying to sleep in the daytime heat during an operation at Uday

Hussein's farm in Southwest Baghdad.

A soldier taking a photo in a burnt-out VBIED (vehicle-borne IED) in South

Baghdad ala MTV's "Pimp My Ride".

On patrol in the Triangle of Death in South Baghdad.

The SIGO (Signals Officer) using his Humvee mirror to shave at

Tiger Base in Sinjar, Iraq.

Our daily T-ration breakfast at Tiger Base.

Tiger Base prior to installing doors, windows, roofs, electricity, and everything else

that was looted prior to our arrival in May 2005.

The Iraqi Army moving out on patrol in Biaj, Iraq.

The remnants of a suicide bomber's face after he detonated in front of Tiger Base

Iraqi Army soldiers searching for caches in the haystacks in a Sunni village north of Biaj

Sitting in my completed plywood room at Tiger Base; just enough room for a cot and

a chair (my Father's Day present complete with the kids' handprints).

A group of Yezidi kids approaching our patrol atop Sinjar Mountain.

The billets for the soldiers of Crazyhorse Cavalry Troop at Tiger Base.

The Tiger Squadron Commander and Staff in front of the Operations Center.

A cordon and search of a village north of the Sinjar Mountains.

The author at the Rabiah Point of Entry overlooking Syria.

The Rabiah base camp's gym.

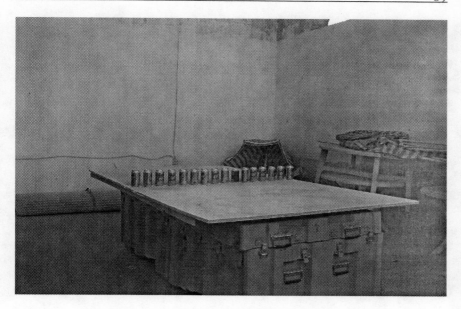

Our plywood ping-pong table at Tiger Base.

A goat grab with the Mayor of Sununi, our Civil Affairs Officer, and our

Air Defense Battery Commander.

Searching a Bedouin tent in the desolate Al Jazeera Desert between

Al Qaim and Sinjar

The berm barrier separating Iraq and Syria.

Plugging the leaks on the roofs after a rainstorm at Tiger Base.

A mounted patrol of Biaj, Iraq.

Voters going to the poll in Domese during the National Assembly elections

Golfing at the Biaj base camp.

Building a soccer field for the kids in Biaj using our old camouflage nets

The Iraqi Army moving out on patrol in Sinjar

Wild dogs canvassing the trash in Biaj

The author's homecoming at the Fort Carson gym with wife Jen, her dad Peter, and twins Cade and McKenna

MAY 25, 2005:

LET THE GOOD TIMES ROLL...TO NW IRAQ

"The quickest way of ending a war is to lose it" George Orwell

In another example of "be careful what you wish for, because you may just get it", I find myself out of the madhouse of Baghdad and into the devastated buildings in the pastures of Northern Iraq. I can't say I really wished for this, but I was really looking forward to a change of pace in another area of Iraq where I could finally stop living out of a rucksack. General Richard Myers, the Commander in Chief, recently stated that the priority mission for the U.S. forces in Iraq is to stop foreigners from entering the country, as they have been identified as the main threat with their attempts to incite a civil war and prevent the government from forming. His statement on CNN was our warning order to start the painful process of moving thousands of people and tons of equipment, food, and supplies on a journey further than our initial move from Kuwait to Baghdad to solve the border problem. The Department of Homeland Security has sent representatives out here to fix the problem and Congress is grilling the top military officials in Iraq on why they can't stop people from infiltrating. I find it a bit hypocritical that we are claiming to be the experts in this endeavor when our government can't even create solutions to deter and document 8000 illegal border crossers daily in our own country, so it will be interesting to see how we'll stop it across a porous border adjoining multiple countries (each with its own agenda), populated by people who have been trading for centuries, and laced with hundreds of smuggling routes developed over those years. The piece we can affect, and what I'm looking forward to, is training the Iraqi Border Police and Iraqi Army to take this place over so we can get out of here.

I was lucky during this move by jumping on a bird and foregoing the tedious 25 mph drive north. I was told to get up there early, before the advance party, to start building the intelligence picture, so I jumped on the first airmobile vehicle out of Baghdad and turned a three to five day (depending on vehicle breakdowns and which routes were safe at the time) journey into a three-hour flight. I rode aboard a Chinook to Tal Afar, a large city in Northern Iraq just west of Mosul. Chinooks are the double-bladed helicopters that can carry a platoon of soldiers or even haul a howitzer underneath it. Soldiers call this bird a "Shit Hook" and it usually gets bad publicity whenever one crashes because of the numerous bodies aboard, but I comforted myself with the knowledge that most Chinook pilots graduate from either the top or bottom of the class, so there's a 50 percent chance that I had an excellent pilot. The operations planner, supply officer, and I were late to the landing strip and forced aboard the trail bird that was stuffed with pallets of duffle bags and supplies. I thought that this ride would be a much-preferred means of travel compared to another long, hot, and dusty convoy, especially since the first ground convoy we sent north hit an IED near Tikrit at 3 a.m. (no injuries, they just blew past it) and experienced a near-fatal accident when a driver fell asleep at 5 a.m. My flight only lasted three hours, but it was painful—it was like two NBA referees sat on either side of me and blew their whistles directly into my ears the entire time. Visually, it was enjoyable as we flew low over rural Iraq with the back ramp down and the moon silhouetting the gunner against a backdrop of farms and small villages. We arrived in Tal Afar at 2 a.m. and hitched a ride (there's always someone driving around at all hours of the night no matter where you go) from the airfield to some vacant tents to get some sleep until morning, at which time we'd figure out how to make it the rest of the way after downing some fresh coffee and eggs in the mess hall.

The base at Tal Afar was pleasant and bustling with construction activity (to include building a set for the following day's Toby Keith concert, which I would not be able to see after just missing him by a day when I left Baghdad). The rolling hills around Tal Afar reminded me of the American Midwest with its wide-open grassy plains and wheat fields. The cool evening breeze while we slept was a nice change, as the nights are about ten degrees cooler than those in Baghdad. After the sun came up I quickly found out that the days are just as hot. It was kind of like having my first day off since I arrived in Kuwait on

March 5th and I wish I could've enjoyed it more, but I had a whopping headache from the Chinook and from inadvertently using the butt of my M-16 as a pillow. I made some rounds to the units on base to see if their Intel Officers had any good targets on the border towns and then wandered out to the huge chow hall in search of an air conditioner. Most of the units were headquartered in the former Iraqi Air Force bunkers, so the depth and concrete construction kept them cool. Soldiers on the base were living four to a mini-trailer; cramped quarters that wouldn't even be fit for prisoners in the U.S., but all of the units had air conditioning and mattresses. The only open tent we found to shack up in last night didn't have anything in it except dust and a greenhouse effect from it's vinyl composition—if it did have A/C I would've slept all day on my first and probably only day off in Iraq.

A logistical convoy from our quartering party arrived just after dinner and the three of us jumped on for a ride to our new home, a future camp that will be aptly named "Tiger Base". It's strange to drive around and not see the constant military and civilian convoys like we experienced on the bustling main highways surrounding Baghdad. I felt safe on the two-hour drive and I arrived to a stunning view of one of the Kurdish Peshmerga-controlled cities on the base of the mountain. The view at night looked remarkably similar to the view from our training base at Camp Red Devil back in Fort Carson towards the lights of Colorado Springs, which sits on the foothills of the Cheyenne Mountains. That's about where the similarities to anything endearing about the place would end. The half moon allowed me to take a quick tour around the barren fields for a first-hand look at the rubble and the devastated, looted buildings that we would be calling home. I don't think Toby Keith will be holding a concert here any time soon.

The 101st Airborne last set up a base camp on these grounds in 2003 and there hasn't been a stable U.S. or Iraqi presence in the area since (sounds familiar, just like our mission in the wild areas to the west and south of Baghdad). As is the case with any vacant building in Iraq, after the 101st departed the buildings were looted right down to the rebar on the roofs (causing them to collapse), but the walls and floors (minus any floor covering like tile and most dry wall) were left somewhat intact to give us a basis on which to build our new homes and offices. Our engineering attachment has been busy trying to build roofs, doors, windows, and an airfield to land helicopters somewhere amongst the clutter. Manual labor hasn't been a big problem, though. A crowd of 100-200 well-behaved men shows up looking for work at dawn each day. Some of the soldiers have been hiring them at the rate of $4 a day to cart away the rubble, trash, and other undesirable objects that weren't worthy of being looted. The Headquarters First Sergeant has been one of the major employers in the region lately, all out of his own pocket. Apparently our paperwork to get any contracting money has been misfiled, so we can't get any funding to build anything until that mess is straightened out (I can't believe the Coalition Provisional Association was so loose with the funds early in the war, but that's probably the reason its now easier to buy supplies and laborers yourself versus going through the arduous paperwork). The first task given to the group of laborers was to clean out the abused bunkers because the Iraqi Border Police and squatters who stayed in the buildings on and off over the last two years used the empty rooms as latrines. Hundreds of flies and the stench of raw sewage filled the air, but I was one guy who was not surprised by that certain hygienic activity after my last stay in a looted house just one month ago down in the "Triangle of Death".

At this time, we have no running water or power except for some small towed generators and our vehicles. Eventually, we'll have all of our generators here and buy some larger ones in the city or up in Turkey or wherever the nearest market is where people don't blow up the customers. We did bring our plywood toilets (those things have seen more of Iraq than most Iraqis) and dug some trenches to urinate in via upside down water bottles taped together to form a pipe leading three feet underground. Our mess hall trailer is set up to serve T-rations twice a day—breakfast and dinner. The best thing going for this place is a platoon of mobile laundry Reservists out of Nebraska who come equipped with a mobile shower and washers and driers. Initially, when very few of us were here, they would have your laundry done in a couple of hours; it takes a couple of days now that most of the unit has arrived, but it's still the biggest luxury around. The shower is nice in that it's a shower, but the water is still freezing and you can't turn around or scrub your backside without rubbing up on the cold plastic. It's about a ½ mile walk to the showers, past 20-30 wild dogs that live in the berms (I actually saw them probing in and out of the holes like the meerkats at the Colorado Springs Zoo) and knee-high grass that may or may not house more canines. I'm wary of them, but I've only seen one growl and that's because she was living with her puppies in a decrepit former guard shack that one of the staff officers was trying to convert into his new room. We don't have any sinks or mirrors, so shaving directly under the nose and along the neck has presented me with my greatest challenge out here so far.

Tiger Base started coming to life as the soldiers made great use of our plywood and 2x4's and the locals mopped and scrubbed their way to earning their $4. The benefit of being here before everyone else is that you get to pick your room. It was kind of like going through model homes with the smell of

freshly cut wood and scrubbed floors. The staff is housed in a concrete building with two windows and an open bay that has been partitioned by plywood
boards into nine rooms, each the width of a small man's arm span and twice as
long to uncomfortably sleep two. I picked the room on the end with a window
that had a limited view of the mountains that lay just beyond the tanker on
guard duty. The rooms that had cement columns in the middle were left to the
Lieutenants (I don't even think they can fit two cots into this floor plan, but
they'll never complain about their old dorm living days again). The building is
only 10 meters from the basement housing the TOC, close enough that I can
run upstairs to my room and roll up the sheets on my cot whenever I see a dust
storm bearing down on us. The downside is the lengthy walk to the shower,
at least that far to the nearest plywood latrine, and a ¾ mile jaunt to the chow
café (there's no room in the tent to eat, so everyone finds a wall to sit against
and it's now an outdoor café).

It wasn't until everyone arrived and I was settled into my room that I realized that my new hooch always smells like puke. I thought the culprit was a
plate of old rice, fish, and onions drying out on the side of the building. After
cleaning that mess up, I found that the origin of the smell still eludes me, but
I'm not in there enough to care about it anymore as our hours have remained
ridiculously long. The first writings of graffiti in the plywood latrines said it all
about our new digs—"For a Good Time Call 1-800-REUP-CAV" and "Ain't
this a Bitch" with a freshly minted reply under it stating "It's not too bad; ever
had field crabs?"

The Iraqi Army is currently moving in right next to us and we'll focus
on training them and taking them on missions with us, as the U.S. is finally
getting serious about putting together and training a real Army. I visited the
Iraqi Brigade's compound a couple of days ago when we were hosting the U.S.
General who commands our troops in Northern Iraq, so the Iraqi soldiers
were on their best behavior and brought us to their finest room. They are very
hospitable and handed out cold Pepsis (which is more than we have, so I gladly
partook) and plates of bananas, apricots, apples, and tomatoes, which only the
flies touched due to our fear of the GI's. I hadn't seen that many flies in one
place since the soldiers on the shit burning detail were an hour late (unfortunately, the shit burning smells good, like chickens on the BBQ—I'll forever
have warped memories at future backyard parties). The Iraqi soldiers seem to
have it pretty good for their $200 a month. They work for 10 days and then go
on leave for 10 (or more, depending on when they decide to come back). I was
reading about Operation Matador in Al Qaim (the big Marine push against

Al Qaeda in Al Anbar Province) and the reason that the Iraqi Army wasn't present during the operation is because they were all on leave.

The IA here has been eating so well that their U.S. advisors choose to eat with them instead of in our chow cafe. The IA Brigade buys fresh bread, fresh meat and vegetables, and cold soda from the town, while we're still eating Spongebob and corned hash beef at every breakfast and T-rats every night. I figure we'll catch up, though, as the plans for the "Oz Market" is in the works. The layout calls for a barbershop, restaurants, theater, game room, and Haji shops. A cardboard "Welcome to Oz" sign on the outside of the future sight is a cheap rendition of something you'd see in front of an undeveloped strip mall in Phoenix. The market will be housed in a building that used to feature jail cells centered on an open courtyard. This sound easy enough; we just have to start with cleaning out the rubble, install doors, roofs, windows and floors, add power and lights, and have a job fair to select the vendors we trust. I'll use the vendors for information, as well, so I can't wait for the Oz Market to be finished so I can spend some time walking its' shops. My best guess is that it will be finished in about eight months when we roll out of here back to Fort Carson and then our work will be looted once again.

While shaving without a mirror is one of my big challenges out here, an even bigger one will be discerning what information is worth following up on. Whereas we were in an information vacuum in Baghdad, we are now inundated with Intel from all types of sources ranging from locals at the gate, people approaching the patrols, the Iraqi Army, Border Patrol, city police, Peshmerga, politicians, and all of their individual sources and source's sources. I hope it's not like chasing Elvis again. We have to dig down into the informant's tribe, religion, and ethnicity, let alone job and career path, and even which Army soldier, Border Patrol agent, or politician is providing it because they all have an agenda. The Kurds say all the Arabs are bad, the Sunnis say the Shia are bad (yet there are Kurd Sunnis who say Arab Sunnis are bad—the Kurds seem to stick together as Kurds), politicians say the police are bad, the police say their city councils are bad, and the game goes on and on. And the stories are long with most lasting a couple of hours before you can anxiously look at your watch and politely break away.

There's such an amazing diversity here that it makes all of the interaction interesting. The Yezidis in the areas closest to the Syrian border have farmed the land since the Ottoman times, but Sadaam confiscated their land during the Arabification campaign since they are somewhat a type of Christian group (the Iraqis call them devil worshippers because they pray to Satan, the fallen angel). The Yezidis isolate themselves from society and speak Arabic to outsiders, but only their own language to each other (our interpreters say it really isn't a language that exists except to Yezidis). There are some historical beliefs that Noah's Ark landed on top of the Sinjar Mountains and that the Yezidis are his descendants. They have more Aryan features than Arabic—some have white skin and blonde or red hair, and they look more like northern Kurds, except with curls in front of their ears and long beards. These people are very happy to see us, as are the Kurds, because they are finally free from persecution after all these years. The Kurds up north, meanwhile, have a great strategic plan for themselves and have capitalized on it. They have been fighting Sadaam for so many years that the Peshmerga, their main militia (the Kongra Gel are still fighting up in Turkey, but they are publicly disowned by the Iraqi Kurds), are well trained and have virtually secured Iraq north of the Tigris River. While they are trying to put Humpty Dumpty back together down south, the Kurds in the north have built a secure community with no attacks. The U.S. advisors here say that the city of Dahuk is like a European mountain community with clean cobblestone streets, plumbing, trash service, and even a shiny new knock-off of Wal-Mart.

With all of these different groups, our interpreters have to speak Arabic, Kurdish, and even Kurjmani. It will likely be safer for them than in Baghdad because most will stay on the camp with us the entire time and others will take vacation in the safe communities up north. In Baghdad, some of our interpreters would go home at night. Just before we left, four of our thirty-five interpreters hadn't been heard from in over a week and we had no means to contact them (most of them are very secretive about their private lives). Nobody knows what happened to them and finding a missing person in Iraq is hopeless. I can only guess what happened to them after hearing all the stories about bodies turning up in the rivers with their hands and feet bound and a round through their skull.

The smuggling activity on the Syrian border is going to be a tough nut to crack, both because of the corruption and graft and because smuggling is the economic engine for most of the small villages out here. It's not our job to stop the little stuff like cigarettes, gas, and tobacco and if we do stop it we can find ourselves creating many more enemies than friends. When the United Nations arbitrarily drew the boundaries for Iraq after WW II, the diplomats didn't fully consider all of the tribes and families that would be split up and become Iraqi or Syrian by edict of the pen. The people continued trading (which became smuggling) since that time, just as they have been for the thousands of years before the boundaries were drawn. They are ingenuous, too. One border patrol agent told us they often catch mules passing over the berm by them-selves—an Iraqi on one side straps a couple of 55-gallon drums full of gas over the mule, throws an invoice in a leather pouch, and slaps the mule's ass. The mule promptly stumbles over the berm into Syria, where the Syrian smuggler slips some cash into the pouch and slaps it on the ass for a return trip. Since fuel on the Iraqi side has been heavily subsidized for decades to keep the people happy (currently $.20 a gallon), many people take advantage of the arbitrage opportunity to make some easy cash in Syria; the easy money became a little bit harder with our arrival, of course. Since the smugglers know the routes and wadis and their cousin or brother is likely guarding the border, it can become very enticing and simple to guide a foreign fighter or move some weapons across in those barrels for a couple hundred bucks.

I can't exactly say I'm looking forward to it out here as life will be extremely uncomfortable and I'm still in Iraq, but I look at it as another of life's learning experiences. There are so many interesting historical events and types of people and we should come across a few biblical ruins out here. My job will keep me busy and I'll likely catch some GI along the way as I will be tempted to dive into the Iraqi chow, but at least we'll be working with some competent Army and police officers and the Peshmerga are great at weeding out the bad guys (or at least the Sunni and Shia Arab bad guys). It's not as populated as the Baghdad area, so it may be easier to identify the troublemakers and intimidators. I have to convince myself that there are some positive aspects to this place, because it is becoming harder and harder to get up and out of the fart sack each day. I've seen some huge centipedes, scorpions, and camel spiders already in the sleep-ing areas and infiltrating the cracks of my sand-bagged window, so I set the legs of my cot in cut-up water bottles to prevent the scorpions from crawling up (a technique handed down from my grandparents in Phoenix). I finally had a chance to watch one of the DVD's I bought way back at the Kuwait border and found out why they are so cheap—they were a bit grainy and then I real-ized that they were being filmed with a tripod-mounted video as several heads of people leaving the theater would cut off a scene and you could hear the guy filming it laughing out loud in the mike. One of the best parts about our little camp is that during the day it reminds me so much of my dad's hometown of Anaconda, Montana, a little smelter town just across the Idaho border. We even have the occasional afternoon thunderstorm, just as I remember from our summer visits to Anaconda while growing up. It supposedly snows up to a foot in the Sinjar Mountains during the winter. I hope the Reserve laundry guys get the shower's boiler working by then.

By far the best thing about our camp is that I now have a huge office in the basement of a decrepit building where I can finally hang my pictures of Jen, Cade, and McKenna. No matter how bad my day is going, I can look up and see them smiling in the photos and that will make any day better, even if that day happens to be in Iraq. Jen sent me a video of Cade going through the phases of walking and he finally has it down. McKenna picked it up a week before I left and she is hilarious as she zips around her brother while babbling in her own little world. Jen said that McKenna just noticed Cade's wiener during their evening bath and reached out to pinch it while he batted her hand away. I sure do miss bath time with the kids. I'm counting down the days until I can get to see them on my mid-tour leave and I'm desperately hoping that nothing gets in the way of that.

JUNE 10, 2005:

BUILDING A NATION ONE SLUM AT A TIME

"The care of human life and happiness, and not their destruction, is the first and only object of good government." Thomas Jefferson

As the writer and philosopher Thomas Paine once said, "Those who expect to reap the blessings of freedom must, like men, undergo the fatigue of supporting it". He hit the nail on the head. I think I'm getting an idea of the problems our Founding Fathers ran up against as we are currently trying to form local governments and police departments, create water, power, sanitation, and phone services, rebuild and supply hospitals and schools, and build the local economies, all while simultaneously providing security to the locals, deterring or killing foreign Jihadists, weeding out the corrupt leaders while keeping them happy so they don't become the enemy, and negotiating agreements between tribes and ethnicities who have hated each other for centuries. Plus, we have two countries on either side of us (Iran and Syria) and an extremist terrorist group who would love to shape and control whatever government eventually forms. We have a ways to go; as one police assessment team newly-arrived from the States put it, "The Iraqi police forces are right where we were about fifteen years before the turn of the century—the 19th Century."

We pushed out on the latest mission late into the night on Memorial Day. We were sent packing with a very nice surprise; real food was pushed out to

Tiger Base for Memorial Day dinner—a hot dog and a cold Coke per man (the buns were as cold as the Coke, but it didn't matter because the dog made up for it). The Oz Market was abuzz with activity and smiles on a beautiful evening. The courtyard had a larger outdoor eating area today, the result of an earlier dust devil that picked up one of the eating tents and sent it over the walls of the Market as the other tent merely did a 180-degree spin and sat back down. The mission tonight was to go take over a town known for harboring insurgents and reinstate the cops and government, both of whom have been in exile for the past six months. It was another pitch-black night with the only movement showing up in the green haze of my night vision goggles being a few packs of wild dogs picking through the garbage lining the roads. Everyone was wide awake for this one; the town was known for its Wild West atmosphere and even Sadaam's Army was shot up every time they entered. For an unknown reason from higher, we were waiting until June 1st to conduct large-scale operations and it was like being a drag racer with one foot on the gas and the other on the brake until we pulled out of the gates.

As is the case nearly every time we've executed a large mission in force, we entered the town without a shot being fired. There's a strong sense of security in bringing a Division's worth of firepower into a town. Once again, we pulled into a vacated farmland next to a granary on the outskirts of the city to set up our operations. The place was like a petting zoo, complete with four squatter families and their turkeys, sheep, roosters, dogs, and chickens. As sunrise hit, the town was cordoned off with the Iraqi Army Battalion, the newly reinstated police, and our guys and the house-to-house search for key targets kicked off. I instantly changed my assessment on the dirtiest and most decrepit city I've ever seen as the conditions in Biaj easily surpassed the little town of Yusifiyah back in the "Triangle of Death" south of Baghdad that we hung out in two months ago. My assessment was initially based on breaking the thin dirt-colored crust of a puddle and splashing the dark-green raw sewage that lay underneath up to my knees. My view was soon confirmed when we passed through the town market: raw sewage running down the streets, donkeys eating the trash mixed in with the sewage, a butcher cutting a head off of and gutting a chicken as the remains ran into the gutter onto a dog sleeping in the mix, and cows meandering up to lick the dirty red puddle. Trash was rampant throughout the city and the little kids playing in the alleyways were filthy and many of them were covered with scars and rashes, either from the poor sanitary conditions or leishmaniasis from the sand fleas. All of the former police stations were bombed a year ago when the police were run out of town by, from what I've pieced together, some teenagers with an RPG. The irony failed to escape me when 200-plus newly returned policemen claimed that there are no bad guys as they ride around town in ski masks and dark glasses in the 105-degree heat. At least the Iraqi Army soldiers were confident enough to take off their masks and let the people see their faces.

A perfect blend of elements engaged us on the first evening in town to create excellent sleeping conditions along a waist-high brick wall lining the stable—the lack of sleep for 40 hours, an evening dipping into the 60s that held the sand fleas and mosquitoes at bay and allowed me to curl up into my sleeping bag, and no mortars or counter-mortar fires waking me up. Granted, there was still the constant sound of helicopters whirring overhead and packs of dogs barking all night and I woke up to a wad of goat hair in my face. The morning wake-up was entertaining; the roosters started crowing at about 4 a.m., followed by the turkeys gobbling and the sheep baahing.

I don't mind going out on these missions because I escape the tedious meetings and planning sessions held back in the moldy basement we call our operations center and I know there are a lot of interesting things to see and people to meet out there. The patrol I was with stopped into some small villages composed of mud huts (they still had their satellite TVs, of course) and every homeowner would invite the group in for Chai tea (which is like sucking a sweet caffeine stick) and bread with cheese (which we politely turn down rather than make return trips to the plywood crapper). The Iraqis engineer their mud huts to stay cool in the days with the perfect amount of airflow, so their antiquated huts were much more comfortable than being back in the granary. Several locals that morning told our patrols that it was the first quiet night without gunfire in years.

We had constant visits over the week in Biaj from high-profile people—U.S. Generals, the top two Generals of the new Iraqi Army, a CNN reporter, and the *New York Times* among others. Apparently, this type of operation hasn't been done before; one where we come in, take over a town known for harboring insurgents, build a base camp, reinstate the police and government, and set up the Iraqi Army to watch over it all (as we watch over them, of course). It could serve as a model (unfortunately there are enough towns like this that a model is needed), kind of like our model using the same specs and resources for building forward operating bases (FOB in a Box) or serving turkey T-rats six days in a row (Thanksgiving in a Box). I hear the new buzzword for the strategy is "Clear and Hold". And, in this case, "Stay" rather than clear the city and then leave as we've seen before. The Iraqi Army performed admirably during the mission. I wish I could say the same for the cops, as I found them very apathetic and obviously intimidated. The IA soldiers were motivated and well received by the locals; it was nice to see the slaps on the backs and hugs on the main streets. We left town after eight days, leaving behind a large detachment of one of our Cavalry Troops and an Iraqi Army Battalion, and rode home along a main thoroughfare that was lined with kids running alongside the convoys, waving the little Iraqi flags that the IA handed out and singing chants that I couldn't understand but at least didn't sound threatening.

In an odd twist, my Squadron's latest casualties in this war didn't come from fighting the enemy. In Baghdad, where we still have a small contingent of our Air Defenders who will soon join us up north, one of our soldiers found an old grenade and it went off as he was handling it, killing him instantly and wounding some soldiers nearby (dated ammunition left over from the Iran and Iraq War in the '80s is bountiful; the engineers on our camp are finding and detonating old mortar rounds daily as we rebuild the place). Even worse, a soldier here at Tiger Base shot himself early one morning. He was just a young man; I think he was 19. I was walking back from chow the other night and a Private walked up to me and just started talking about it, starting with "Sir, I was there the other day". I immediately knew what he was talking about. He slept on the cot next to the dead soldier and he was sprayed with parts of the body. This kid is brand new to the Army and I could tell he just wanted someone to talk to; luckily, I just had to listen because I didn't know how to respond to that.

The only other activity that happened since we've been here was an attack on our gates one morning a couple of weeks ago. I happened to be in Tal Afar for a meeting when three suicide bombers drove up to our two gates and blew themselves up in the middle of a crowd of civilians who were looking for work. The dead and injured were quickly hauled off by their families to the local hospitals and our medics and soldiers quickly responded to seal off the scene; an accurate count of the dead and wounded became impossible, but the best estimates were seven killed and 30 wounded. I returned that afternoon to a totally redesigned entry point, with barriers and berms lining the main street just a couple hundred meters from the perimeter—nothing like three VBIED's to hasten the final designs of a base camp. One of the gates was even pushed forward a bit because some of the shrapnel landed next to our TOC, which is a little too close for comfort coming from just one VBIED. A combat camera crew happened to pick this day to visit us, so they filmed most of the aftermath. On a positive note, the crew also brought some advanced copies of the new Star Wars film and distributed a couple hundred DVD's, so most soldiers seemed more preoccupied by the prospects of seeing a first-rate new release than reliving any of the morning's action.

Needless to say, we had fewer workers show up the next morning and no-body hung out at the gates looking for work, but after the three-day mourning period the people were back as if nothing happened. It's such a fatalistic society. I asked the workers what the mood in town was after the bombings and they almost unanimously replied "Inshallah"—God has a pre-determined path for everyone, so the dead and injured would have succumbed to Allah on that day regardless of where they were or what they were doing.

Tiger Base is coming along quickly, especially now that the security aspects were immediately completed after the bombings. The old rigged water bottle piss tubes have been replaced by PVC pipes with screens (soldiers can no longer clog up the piss tubes by throwing trash down them) and we're making some progress on a shower tent that looks like the one on *M*A*S*H*. We still don't have direct power to the staff hooch, but our nights of reading by chemlight are over since I procured an extension cord long enough to reach a small generator. We should get some air conditioning units into camp soon—the supply guys extend the two-week forecast by one day during every morning's staff meeting, so the units are always just two weeks out. Our problem is still power, however; even if we had A/C units we couldn't run them.

The first store to open in Oz Market, just two weeks ago, was an aptly named barbershop called "The Barber Shop". A cut is only $2 and tipping is discouraged in order to prevent the barber from retiring in a couple of months. The second store to open was the Raad Markt, which sells mostly blankets and some cheap Middle Eastern trinkets. The Raad Markt sells out their crap daily because the soldiers are starved for anything to spend money on. The Supply Sergeant who is coordinating these contracts is the same guy who bought the school bus from a ski resort back in Colorado; he is now unfortunately blessed with the title of Camp Mayor and has to hear the complaints from both soldiers and locals. Everyone jokingly assumes he is getting a kickback like the Iraqis do, but it's worth it because he is the type of guy who can make things happen and finds the items you would think impossible. I was one of the first customers at the barbershop and had a nice cut (he even used the shaving cream and straight blade finish on the back of the neck) in a cramped and dusty room, which is expected when the roof, windows, and doors were missing a few days ago. The barber threw some tiles over the dirt floor (actually wallpaper that looks like floor tiles), covered the walls with flowered blankets to cover the pockmarks, hooked up a generator, set his combs in a tumbler of dirty, hairy water, and opened for business. It was the first time I saw myself in a real mirror since we arrived; I noticed I was getting a bit gaunt in the face, but it's nothing that one

Big Mac Combo a day over a two-week vacation won't cure and I'll be able to regain my belly so the kids can climb around it once again. One room in the Oz Market houses an open-air theater with some lawn chairs and a pirated DVD showing against the wall nightly. The gym, consisting of a bench and some free weights, is next to that (again, open aired) and we finally have an Internet Café after buying a satellite dish and some computers and phones. It's nice to be able to call home again, but the generators broke down on my first night in line and the Café powered down and went dark.

There are several locals who would love to set up a restaurant in the Oz Market. One in particular is a Kurd named Tony who lives in Sinjar and comes to see me daily under the guise of providing information, but ends each conversation with "Try this food" and "When would you like me to set up my restaurant?" I found myself getting bought off and I'm not even on the Oz's business development committee. We have a small basketball court next to the TOC that I mentioned would be nice to play on; the next day he brought me a leather basketball (so far I haven't touched it, but the off-duty soldiers seemed to enjoy it until we set up an overflow sleeping tent on the court to end their fun). Tony showed up at the gate on three occasions with enough lamb, chickens, schwarmas, fries, and pita bread to serve 50 people—if I were on the selection committee we'd have our third vendor tomorrow.

Finding interpreters has been easy, also. We have so many people applying to be interpreters that we can afford to be picky, although none of them volunteer to take the assignments down south in Biaj. We even have a couple of Iraqi doctors who make more money and have more stability as an interpreter and value that over the possibility of getting shot in the back of the head for working with us. The doctors have come in handy several times already; one was coming to work when the bombs went off at the gate and another was with a patrol when they came across a little boy and girl who had shrapnel embedded in them after an attack from a local terrorist group on their village of policemen (now ex-policemen). One of the U.S. hired interpreters brought in from California is an ex-U.S. Marine who is originally from Syria. He loves going out on patrols and always comes back with chow from the local kids (he's apparently been eating well since his Marine days)—twenty greasy little lamb sandwiches wrapped in pita with tomatoes and goat grass for $5 and a case of Coke for $4. My stomach has been holding out well from those snacks. Ironically, the only time I had a case of the GI out here was after a trip to Tal Afar, when I made a beeline straight to the catered chow hall and ate the main meal of roast beef, mashed potatoes, and macaroni and cheese and chased it down with a slice of pizza, a cheeseburger, Dr. Pepper, Gatorade, and slices of chocolate cake and coconut crème pie. I felt worse after that than from any front-gate Haji food and had the GI's for three days.

The detainee restriction is going to be very painful out here because we are so far removed from any real facilities. I had no place to take our first 10 detainees, so I selected a building that is currently being renovated into either a gym or a chapel. The windowless building used to be a sheep stable and still smelled like it after months, maybe even years, of neglect. The local hires had previously cleaned out the bricks, rocks, and sheep shit, but the place still had to be sanitized so a couple of soldiers were mopping out the big room using a strong industrial bleach that changed the smell to that of an indoor swimming pool in a cheap motel. The detainees were led blindfolded into a place that smelled like a chemical-making facility and was permeated with the sound of machineguns blasting away at the new firing range just 50 meters to the south. I initially felt sorry for them, but then I recalled that the physical evidence on these guys showed that they would like nothing better than to kill us if given the opportunity.

Word on the street is that the bad guys want us, rather than the Iraqis, to catch them because they know we'll take care of them, feed them, shower them, not beat them, and then release them for a lack of evidence. Then they can come back to the Civil Military Office and make a claim that the capturing unit stole from them and file for reimbursement. In an attempt to head off any abuses by the Iraqi Army, Police, or Border Patrol, we have to take all detainees into our possession, even if the Iraqis capture them. I've already had several sit-downs with the leaders of those agencies and can't get through to them that it is their new government's standard of evidence that is required. They figure it's the Americans who are requiring the unwieldy burden of proof and every Iraqi official I meet says that they can't win this fight under an American system that favors the bad people. They know they can get people to talk, and they aren't referring to the Lynndey England panties-on-the-head type of way, either. We have a long way to go to teach them and I'm afraid that prisoner rights are never going to rate high on their list of governmental responsibilities.

Back on the home front, Jen is hanging tough doing a wonderful job with Cade and McKenna while wondering where I am when I can't call or email for days or weeks. It's been unbelievably hard for her as the kids have been set back by ear infections and teething and Mac now has to undergo surgery to put tubes in her ears. Luckily, it is Mac who needs the surgery, as she seems to be the tough one who can handle being sick and getting new teeth compared to the overly dramatic Cade. Both kids are growing up like their cleaning-obsessed mom—Jen tells me that they can't stand dirt or trash on the ground and have to stop and pick it up wherever they are. McKenna has taken a liking to eating whole pickles and, on her 19th-month birthday, curiously picked her nose for the first time. Cade is still passionately inspecting all of the colorful flowers blooming in Portland and loves being outdoors. The kids have made some progress in taking walks in the jogger; Cade used to make our walk miserable because he would cry whenever Mac touched him and she would smile and laugh at his agony. We'd have to resort to putting them in backpacks or in their wagons to maintain our sanity. Jen said she peeked through the top of the jogger on last week's walk and the kids were hugging. I'm praying that I have less than a month to tag along on those walks.

June 30, 2005:

All's Quiet on the Border Front

"I do not mean to exclude altogether the idea of patriotism. I know it exists, and I know it has done much in the present contest. But I will venture to assert, that a great and lasting war can never be supported on this principle alone. It must be aided by a prospect of interest, or some reward." George Washington

Finally, a couple of weeks where nothing interesting happened and I only had to leave the FOB a handful of times. I was developing the pasty skin of a Fobbit and it was nice. The lull in activity has allowed me to substantially reduce my hours to 12-14 a day and I even started getting up to run in the mornings. The dirt road that lines the camp's perimeter is 1.4 miles long and it is one of only three "helmet-free" activities allowed; everyone jokes that when you're jogging you can outrun the mortar round that is aimed at your head. In fact, it is really only these three activities that make the day tolerable: running, taking a shower (the boiler maintenance status is a non-issue until winter hits, especially after a hot and dusty morning run), and sitting down for dinner at the Oz Market in the evening under the misting system that the cooks recently installed. The biggest changes we've made over the last couple of weeks have been the completion of a soldier-run PX and the addition of a Reefer Van (actually REFR Van, which stands for refrigerated van). The PX sold out of most products within the first 48 hours with the Mountain Dew, Dr. Pepper, and any chip product moving rapidly off the plywood shelves. The Reefer Van was an even bigger hit, as it now allows us to upgrade our dinner meal most days of the week to A-rations, a form of food just below real food that can be frozen and reheated. This blessing showed up just as everyone seemed to be tiring of the turkey T-rations served over six consecutive days. My experience and desire for fine cuisine is limited, but I can truly say that I had the best salmon I've ever tasted the other night. There hasn't been much progress on the gym in the Oz Market, so we stacked some rocks of varied weights next to the hooch for rock PT in the morning.

The weather here has been hot and dusty, comparable to Phoenix as we top out at about 110 with a low of 80. As always, the supply guys are still forecasting the arrival of air conditioners in just two short weeks. I can't wait for power and A/C to arrive because our rooms have absolutely no airflow. The few windows that do exist are tightly packed with sandbags and the building's concrete composition has been doing a wonderful job of retaining heat during the day and releasing it at night. I slept outside a few nights, but I'm too lazy to move my cot out every evening and resigned myself to the knowledge that my accumulated sweat will cool me down as the night progresses. I can't complain, though, because most of the soldiers have excellent airflow only because they have no doors, windows, or roofs. Their trade-off is a quarter inch of dust coating everything they own at all times. The soldiers down in Biaj (the Wild West town we are attempting to rehabilitate about 20 kilometers south that means "constant storm" in Arabic) are in the worst situation as their tiny camp in a granary parking lot is constantly coated in dirt. The Shamal season (the strong winds that blow up, down, and sideways from Syria across Iraq towards the Persian Gulf) started early this year and we get blasted hard about twice a week. The oncoming storms are visible from miles away, so it gives us about 30 minutes to button up, cover, or zip anything that can close. Our tanks and Bradleys grind the dirt into a fine, flour-like powder that we call moon dust, making the Shamal season extra tough. One night at chow, a Shamal hit one tent and lifted it off the ground; everyone stopped eating their moon dust-topped chili to stand on the sides of the tent as sections of the plywood roof blew off of the cook's billets to add to the dining chaos.

We've had no enemy contact against the FOB since May 28th, when the suicide bombers tried to penetrate the gates. The Iraqis helping to build our camp, mostly locals whose Sheikhs acquire the contract, have enemy contact pretty much weekly in the form of death threats. The only incident close to enemy contact during this time occurred about a week ago when a soldier sleeping in his tent was hit by a stray round in the mid-morning. The round penetrated two inches into his thigh. Luckily, he was sleeping with his pants on and he had a knife in his front pocket that partially deflected the round; he thought it was a scorpion sting. The round came through the top of the tent and we assume it originated from a little village across the street that was being searched at the time. I wouldn't doubt if it came from the IA when they were firing off one of their wild warning shots. Other than that, we've been having a huge success capturing some of the key leadership here and in Tal Afar, but it seems like four or five others from Syria, Saudi, Iran, or Afghanistan pop up to take their places like Medusa's snake. It's still like playing Whack-a-Mole. I always tell people that this is the easiest place to be a bad guy, especially when they are armed with the common knowledge of how hamstrung we are by the rules. If the jails even get too crowded we start releasing people to avoid the negative international publicity of the poor conditions (which, ironically, are better than our current living conditions). One detainee asked me if he could go to the Mosul jail because his friends told him the food is excellent and they get a cot to sleep on instead of just a foam pad.

Our Air Defense Battery finally made its way back to us from South Baghdad. I thought they'd enjoy the change because you don't get that lump in your gut when you drive around up here like you do in Baghdad; their initial assessment is that the IED's blowing up back on Route Tampa are worth it for the superior living conditions and chow in Baghdad (and they arrived just in time for Father's Day Dinner, where we had an orange chicken and rice concoction that tasted like P.F. Chang's and cold Cokes that you didn't have to buy from the Raad Market). It was nice to hear that one of our raids had an impact back there, even though we couldn't keep most of the detainees. Before I left Baghdad, we conducted an early morning raid on some farmhouses and rounded up 10 guys who we suspected were planting and detonating most of the IED's along a rough stretch of Route Tampa. We didn't find any evidence in the homes, so all we had to go on were some informant statements that they made IEDs and detonated them from the intricate canal system alongside the highway. I distinctly remember the two detainees that did go up higher because they were so large that they barely fit into my Humvee when I was taking them to the holding facility and some of their body odor and sweat still lingers on my seats. We told the other men that if there are any attacks in the area they will be held responsible and the ADA Battery, led by Super Dave, proceeded to harass these guys whenever their patrol drove by the men's homes—just little things like stopping by to do maintenance on their vehicles or stopping to eat an MRE in the front yard and stare them down. Since that raid, there have been no attacks on what was considered to be one of the most dangerous stretches of highway in the Baghdad area and possibly in the country.

A reporter from the _Chicago Tribune_ was hanging out at camp for a few days and I gave her my philosophy about this entire situation in the Ninewah Province: "It's all about the Benjamin". You have an economically depressed people (most villages have greater than 90 percent unemployment) who have re- lied on a trading culture and bartering system for centuries before the arbitrary boundaries separated their families and tribes and labeled them either Iraqi or Syrian. It takes little extra expenditure of resources to smuggle weapons and people for profit through age-old commerce routes monitored by a corrupt border police who come from the same family or tribe as the smugglers. The smugglers, through monetary necessity, intimidation, or both, provide foreign fighters with a safe haven where they can move freely and neither of the groups wants a competent government or police force because their way of life will end. The sanctuary that forms due to this relationship causes the foreigners to "headquarter" there and allows them to coordinate actions, a coordination which includes the disaffected former Baathist Arabs who lost their pension and jobs in the new regime. All it takes is three to five foreign Jihadists per day to enter the suicide supply chain, easily slipping across thousands of miles of rat lines from Iran, Saudi, Jordan, Syria, or Turkey, to maintain a steady and deadly volume of spectacular attacks in the big cities. By this point in my diatribe everyone was asleep, so I had to inspire with another of my favorite sound bites, "chasing Elvis". Later, the Squadron Executive Officer was being interviewed and he claims that the only notes on her writing tab that stood out were "It's all about the Benjamin" and "chasing Elvis".

As much as I can barely tolerate this place and situation, I'd hate to pull out our forces any sooner than we have to or it will turn into a civil war and become a vacuum for insurgents like Somalia and Afghanistan before it. I wonder if we would be guarding the front doors of the mall and food courts in Suburbia, U.S.A. instead of conducting flash checkpoints on the road to Tal Afar if that were to happen and our sworn enemy's targeting methodology, venue, and ability to organize in the U.S. improved even slightly. The Iraqi Army has performed well for us and, at the platoon level, they are developing nicely, although their dedication remains suspect and dedication and loyalty is the hardest thing to "train". An entire battalion slipped out overnight and went on leave after our last mission ended. They get their pay and all of them take off at once to their homes spread across Iraq to get the cash to their families—I always say that a banking system where they can directly deposit their checks would be one of the major security improvements in Iraq, as it will keep people on duty, decrease the pay-day corruption, and decrease the banditry as they move cash around. We have to teach the new soldiers fire control, also. Any time the IA hears a gunshot, or even a car backfire, they react by spraying their

AKs wildly, so the locals become agitated as the IA becomes the visible source of the danger. As much as the fledgling Army still has to learn, we would be out of here a lot sooner if we could replace all of the police and border patrol with their Army counterparts. The other discouraging fact about this place is that the people are too expectant and conditioned to receiving handouts, which comes from decades of social welfare and appeasement from the government to buy their peace through "gifts" of food, water, and power. The socialist programs bred very little entrepreneurial spirit or leadership except for the smugglers and criminals who have capitalized on their newfound freedoms. The smartest strategy employed by Saddam, probably in his life, was to release tens of thousands of hard core criminals from Abu Ghraib at the onset of the war—people who will do just about anything for a buck and who will maintain the chaos to survive.

After my recent two-day ground reconnaissance south to Biaj, west to the Syrian border, and back north over the Sinjar Mountains to one of our units' camps in the border town of Rabiah, I arrived back to Sinjar to find out that I was scheduled to go on another border trip in an OH58 scout helicopter piloted by Big Fred, a Warrant Officer in our attached aviation unit who is my neighbor back in Fort Carson and Godfather to Cade and McKenna. Big Fred received his nickname when he was introduced to the unit, replacing a guy named Fred who was much smaller in stature but identical in appearance and the Commander immediately panned, "Hey, you're a big Fred". So that's been his call sign ever since. These little birds we flew off in ping around the cities and mountains like a sports car. They top out at about 140 mph and are so agile that they can land on a speeding truck. They are our big eye in the sky, looking forward for us when we move, watching the borders from afar and calling the ground troops to respond, and flying over target houses during raids to follow the wigglers who try to dash out into the ravines or speed away down the narrow alleyways.

Our flight took us north to the Syrian border and down the Tigris River separating the Kurdish-claimed areas in the former No-Fly Zone from the Sunni farmlands to the south. We had a gorgeous view as we buzzed over the rolling hills with herds of sheep on the Iraqi side and the black plumes of smoke spewing from the oil rigs on the Syrian side and families along the Tigris River washing their autos in the slow-moving turquoise water. One of the more interesting places in our area, called the "Valley of Tiers", lies atop the 1400-foot high Sinjar Mountain; it wouldn't be considered a big mountain anywhere except for Iraq and our little bird barely pushed itself up and over it. I stopped in this same valley earlier in the day on the ground reconnaissance and had a Fanta Orange soda in a little market overlooking the gardens as hordes of kids came running towards us from the mud huts built into the sides of the mountain. The Yezidis, who are known as the "Mountain People", control all the villages up here. In any Arab village we would be offered Chai tea, but the Yezidis were quick to offer up a cold beer (we have to settle for the Fanta due to General Order #1 forbidding the consumption of alcohol). The people cut their gardens into tiers along the slopes and grow tobacco, dates, figs, and nuts. It's like an oasis up there with creeks and green pastures and its about 20-degrees cooler than the rest of Iraq. The Yezidi and Kurd villages are exceptions to the handout mentality, partly because they never received anything from Sadaam, and whatever we can do for them is genuinely appreciated and cared for.

At the very top of the Sinjar Mountain, on the peak where the Yezidis claim Noah's Ark ran to ground, is the 800-year-old Yezidi monument. There's not too much ambience to the small white building; you go in and tie a knot on one of the numerous silk scarves hanging from the rafters while saying your prayer. Those in greater spiritual need can crawl through a three-foot high wooden door and light a prayer candle in the room. The wise and wrinkled Yezidi guard who spoke broken English said he was expecting the red-skinned people with blue eyes to come save them, as their forefathers spoke of in stories handed down over the ages.

One of the things that keep me in good spirits over here is the guys I work with. My intelligence section is a motley crew of characters, each given a nickname by the other soldiers over time. It's some kind of Army tradition to pen nicknames on soldiers and I've had my share over time ("Worm" at Prep School because I wormed out of trouble and "Grandpa" at West Point because I was one of the older guys in the class and "Deuce" every time I've been an S-2—none of those nicknames as unsavory as those given to my old roommates "Pigger", who was a dirty guy, or "Dog", whose breath smelled like a dog's).

Master Sergeant Knowles, aka "Lurch", is our crusty tanker NCO in charge—an ex-First Sergeant who has soldiered for 25 years and itches to get back to the lines to chew some butt. He has the physical characteristics and tone of speech as the old TV character ("You rang?"). He is in charge of force protection for the camp, which is no small task considering the number of contractors, border patrol, police, and Iraqi Army visitors we have to search, badge, and escort daily and the civilians who enter the camp to submit claims against the U.S. or bid on contracts. Lurch's son-in-law is in our Regiment and remained down in Baghdad. He had a scare the other day when a blackout was imposed (no phones or internet) due to a death in the Regiment; word spread that several members of his son-in-law's company lost arms and legs in an IED attack and Lurch was desperately trying to find out the initials on the Medevac report to see if they matched his son-in-law's.

Lieutenant Webber, aka "Metro", is my assistant who has a way with the ladies and claims to have a taste for the finer things in life. He wants nothing more than to get out of the Army and go to Harvard Law, but he is tormenting himself with the question of whether that should be done single or married. Metro is determined to solve the 2003 Biaj bank robbery when the Americans gave the city officials $1 million to start up the bank and the loot was stolen the next day. He's also smart enough to know that if he gets fired he would be moved to a higher echelon where he'll live with air conditioning and fresh food and get to join an intramural softball team. He's hard to motivate because of that, but he's a good guy who does his job and is fun fodder for all of the officers in the Squadron—especially since his girlfriend is serving down in Baghdad with all of the single soldiers clamoring for her attention.

SSG Sobers is "Mr. Gadgets", my primary intelligence analyst who knows all of the cool guy stuff and can rebuild our computers and communications, figure out how to put border sensors together, print out large maps on order like he's behind the grill at Burger King, and is the only guy who really knows where everything is in the shop. He is just back from emergency leave after his 32-year-old brother passed away from a heart attack that shocked the family. He's been in about 15 years and is already looking forward to a job at NSA or some other outfit where he can play with the "high speed" stuff. Some guys call him "Sausage" because he likes to eat sausage and it just fits him.

PFC Brant, aka "Gates", is another intelligence analyst, a Private First Class who is fresh out of training. He majored in photography for three years in a small South Carolina college before dropping out to enlist and he wants to become a combat photographer. He looks like Bill Gates and has similar mannerisms as he answers the simplest of questions with a dramatic pause and reflection, but the nickname actually arose because one of the NCO's always called him Gates, thinking that was his real name, and Gates was too quiet to correct him so it stuck.

PFC Rockford, aka "Rock", is the token Private of the section, a tanker assigned to be my driver and the guy every section needs to fulfill requirements like burning the shit, KP (although the Oz Market now makes people who disparage the chow do KP), pulling guard duty, and changing tires and tracks. He's a military brat, the son of a two-star General, who does anything and everything with little complaining and even asks people if he can clean their weapons. Rock is the kind of guy who makes a statement for never having a draft; he keeps volunteering to escort our supply convoys and man the .50 cal and you'd never get that type of guy unless he willingly signs up.

A couple of other Non-Commissioned Officers were assigned to my section for the deployment. One is a Sergeant First Class with about 19 years in who is waiting to retire. He doesn't have a witty nickname ("Freebo" is just a play on his last name), but he does have the hardest-working third button in the Army (he has lost 30 pounds already and has 70 more to go after living the good life in his last Korea assignment). He is tasked with managing the interpreters, which includes hiring, firing, paying, and listening to their constant complaints, just like a Human Resources guy. He was recently tasked with running a small PX in the Oz Market, so he has to make monthly runs to Mosul to order supplies and submit payments. Partly due to my HR and finance background, I'm basically the scapegoat supervisor in case anything goes wrong. Mr. Gadgets used his Adobe Photoshop Editor to create an "AAFES Employee of the Month" plaque to place above the cash register in the PX. Freebo's picture and name are listed for June; eventually each month is going to have his name and photo captured as he is the sole proprietor, employee, and General Manager of the establishment, which now has a roof and a door that locks to allow Freebo to go and take a piss without finding a Private to guard the place. He was only short about $2600 during his first week in business after most of the inventory sold out; I went through his inventory counts on Excel and corrected some formulas, so it turns out he's only short about $600 and he's currently pondering what he missed. I'm supposed to get a new Roadie (Retired on Active Duty—a guy with a couple of years left who has lost most of his motivation and ambition over the years and is simply hanging in there until he hits the 20-year retirement mark) next week. He'll manage the interpreters so Freebo can concentrate on his inventory count.

I had a nice Father's Day a couple of weeks ago (all things considered), and not only because of the PF Chang-like dinner at the chow hall. Jen sent me a huge box containing a folding chair with Cade and McKenna's handprints, a brown Army T-shirt with Cade and McKenna's handprints, a photo of Cade and Mac in camouflage outfits, and a little stuffed tiger with the kids' laughter embedded on the voice chip in the tiger's tummy. We took a trip to Build-a-Bear in Denver a couple of weeks before I deployed after hearing about the stuffed animals with voice chips from the soldiers who went to Iraq last year. During the trip, we let Cade and Mac choose their favorite animal, which, for a 1-year-old, was a simple process of seeing which one they lunged for and held on to as we slowly walked past the display. Mac selected BaBa, a monkey, and Cade picked a bear he named Sarge and I recorded a voice chip for each of them. Every night before bed they squeeze BaBa and Sarge's arms to hear my goodnight message and now I can do the same. Jen had a great story about Flat Daddy; she heard some grunting from the playroom and discovered Mac trying to climb Flat Daddy on the wall. After seeing Jen give me a goodnight kiss each night by kissing her fingers and pressing them on my lips, Mac wanted to be lifted up so she could give me a kiss on the lips, too. The surgery to place tubes in her ears went well and she's been in great spirits. Cade is anxiously awaiting his first haircut and we're putting it off until I am home on my mid-tour leave, which may be on July 19th (Jen's birthday). I'm praying that things stay sane until then and I can leave because I've never looked forward to anything this much in my life. When I look back over the last two years, it seems like just yesterday I was back in the Tucson Neonatal Intensive Care Unit holding Cade and Mac against my chest to warm their tiny and fragile two-pound bodies. They've come a long way since then.

JULY 18, 2005: OPERATION HOMEWARD BOUND

"Every gun that is made, every warship launched, every rocket fired signifies, in the final sense, a theft from those who hunger and are not fed, those who are cold and not clothed."
Dwight D. Eisenhower

I'm currently sitting in the Dallas airport awaiting my final leg home after a whirlwind trip that took me from the Syria border to Tal Afar, Kuwait, Ireland, and here. Now it's on to Portland in the next couple of hours! The reception in Dallas was absolutely unbelievable; our plane pulled up to the gate under the Dallas Fire Department's water spray salute and there were groups of USO volunteers and passengers lining the corridors and clapping, high-fiving, and hugging us as we headed off to make our connections. It was a rather grueling vacation so far, but the feeling of arriving on U.S. soil gave me an overwhelming and intense feeling of security and comfort.

My mid-tour leave started after an emotionally challenging three weeks in which I was told several times that my vacation would be cancelled due to mission requirements—then those requirements would pass and my vacation would be back on. Every time I read a report about foreign fighters moving into a city near us or an increase in enemy activity in some of our key cities, I would cringe and await the word that we would soon conduct a mass operation. I thought I was in the clear two days ago until we received word to start planning for a mission to be conducted within the next 24 hours, starting on the day my bird was to whisk me away to Tal Afar.

After a hasty overnight planning process and early morning intelligence briefing to all the Commanders, I was able to talk my way out of the mission and ensure them that my section could handle the Intelligence and detainee aspect of it. I jumped on the midnight helicopter shuttle to Tal Afar and awoke early to begin a daylong trip sitting in the web seats aboard a C-130, which is now my least favorite mode of transportation. The last time I rode on a C-130 was back in 1994 when the pilot was forced to hug the rugged terrain along the Yemen and Saudi border as the Northern and Southern Yemenese lobbed Scud missiles at each other. On that trip, one of the soldiers in my platoon barfed and the smell, heat, and turbulence set off a chain reaction. This trip didn't have as much turbulence, but it was just as hot and we had to land and take-off three times before arriving in Kuwait. Every time a C-130 lands in Iraq it conducts a combat landing with excess banking and altitude changes and a fast and hard spiraling landing just in case there might be some small arms, RPGs, or, in the worst case, surface-to-air missiles fired in the plane's direction. Sure enough, one of those landings caused a similar chain reaction after one soldier blew chow in his shaving kit. After starting my journey from Sinjar at midnight we arrived into a sweltering hot Kuwait at 8 p.m. and the administrative soldiers stationed in Kuwait immediately herded over 200 of us into a room for safety briefings and itineraries. Early the next morning we were escorted into customs and sat around for 10 hours in lock-down prior to boarding the chartered aircraft for the next fifteen hours. The Department of Defense pays for a round-trip ticket to the States for any soldier on 12-month orders to Iraq. It's an excellent program, but I'd give up this luxury for the old Southwest Asia deployment rules. Back in 1994, when I was deployed to Saudi Arabia, any soldier deployed over six months received $100 per day for each day they were extended. This policy caused the Army to ensure that no soldier was deployed even one day beyond the six month mark and, sure enough, I arrived home from Riyadh right on time.

Conditions at our base camp have greatly improved over the past two weeks, even though I still can't imagine any other units in Iraq operating in worse conditions than our greatly improved one. Metro's sympathetic girl-friend in Baghdad even sent him a microwave and cookies and chips from their mess hall to help out (unfortunately, when he uses the microwave we have to unplug the printers and turn off the lights and fans or it will blow the circuits). The only luxuries the soldiers really need for an acceptable quality of life is a shower and a hot meal every few days, ice for a cool drink when they come back in from a mission, and power to allow them to play some music, DVDs, or video games to let them take their minds off of life. I think the soldiers take pride in living in squalor, though; you can see it in their faces when we visit Tal Afar in sweat-stained uniforms turned white from a lack of salt intake and dust-caked faces and hair that garners sympathy from the clean, well-rested soldiers on the base.

Major Radford, the Squadron's Executive Officer, hired some civilian drivers with flatbed trucks and took a few gun crews up to Dahuk (in the Kurd Province to the north) to buy some generators and air conditioners earlier in the month. Five days later, they reappeared with the generators, air conditioners, and a few Turkish contractors in tow to install them under the warranty. The contractors don't speak Kurdish, Arabic, or English, so the Camp Mayor is leading them around base and doing a lot of pointing to show them where to install the units. Another surprise was the arrival of a couple of shower trailers, which means my three-quarters of a mile walk to the shower tent every morning may be decreased to about 40 feet—hopefully they will be ready for me when I return from leave. We welcomed another three Turks who were hired to drill a well in the middle of camp. They worked all day and night (by work I mean watching their drill bit go into the ground and changing the bit when it breaks) for five straight days and I finally saw some wet sludge come to the surface the other night. This will greatly aid our water shortage and we'll be less reliant on convoys bringing in potable water, so we may be able to open up the shower trailers. The two air conditioners added to my sleeping quarters have made a significant difference already (significant being from *no cool air* to *a little bit of cool air when you put your head directly under the unit*). The airflow dissipates rather quickly due to the large sealing gaps (the building is completely missing three windows and one door) and the fact that the concrete building sucks up the heat over the day, but it does just enough to turn a stifling hot miserable sleep into a very warm and somewhat miserable one.

I sealed off the sandbagged window opening in my room with some duct tape and I can only hope that it will have the secondary effect of preventing the camel spiders from visiting each night. I thought we had a couple of mice or rats when I saw some figures zooming by me one night, but my roommate claims they are large, fat camel spiders that are feeding off of our Fire Support Officer's open bag of barbeque Fritos. A couple of soldiers have been stung by scorpions and had to be evacuated to Mosul for the anti-venom—one guy was sleeping and the other was putting on his pants. The medics have identified two of the world's deadliest scorpions on our camp, so that is not a reassuring thought prior to bedding down each night. One of the guys who was stung had an exceptionally bad week; he got hit by an IED, spent the night in the Tal

Afar hospital, returned to camp, and was stung two days later and sent to the Mosul hospital for the anti-venom.

Fourth of July in Sinjar was an exceptionally hot and humid 112-degree day as we stood in formation for the Commander's five-minute unprepared speech that was very well prepared and much longer than five minutes. I expected that we would get attacked sometime during the day, most likely during the evening meal. Our 40-day streak of no enemy activity ended on the previous day when several patrols were attacked within a 12-hour period with IED's and a suicide bomber (in which the only death was the suicide bomber, who departed this world to meet his 72 virgins without an entire foot, face, or a penis, which were all left laying on the asphalt). In all of that activity, our only casualty was a gunner who caught some shrapnel in his neck and was able to return to duty the next day. Unfortunately, also on the same day, one of our soldiers was killed when his Humvee rolled over in a traffic accident in the hills and wadis next to the border north of the Sinjar Mountains. SSG Brown was thrown from his vehicle and actually got up and walked around to check on his soldiers before collapsing and dying from internal bleeding. The medics said that his adrenaline took over and allowed him to get on his feet. He was a popular leader and pretty much every soldier who wasn't on guard duty or patrol attended his sunset memorial service; he was a selfless man like so many others out here who pretty much defines the reason I was anxious to come back into the service.

The holiday ended peacefully with the cooks preparing a feast of steaks, hot dogs, potato salad, cold sodas, Gatorade, and chocolate cake. The freshly stocked PX opened at noon and was nearly depleted by dinner; the $20 floor fans were the first to go this time, followed quickly by the Mountain Dew and Red Bull. The Raad Cantina, which sold fries, schwarmas, and roasted chicken and lamb, was prepared to open on the 4th, but delays in hiring some of the workers pushed the Grand Opening until the next day—they are looking for some illegals from Turkey to do the work that Iraqis don't want to do. Raad is the owner of the Raad Markt and he was quickly snapping up real estate in the Oz Market with his engaging personality and "hey, what's up Holmes" catcalls to his prospective customers. I had one of the schwarmas and it was delicious, but the daily visits to the cantina by the medical team just weren't enough to discourage my next visit as the flies pounced on the meat each time Raad turned his back. A week after the holiday, Raad was detained and handed over to the Sinjar Police for attempting to sell drugs from his store and cantina, providing an end to his promising career in restaurant management and retail development.

I went on two reconnaissance trips to the most important towns in our area and along the border over the past couple of weeks. One of the most interesting cities is Rabiah, a border city up north not far from the Tigris River that is one of only two legal crossing points on the Syrian border. One of our Cavalry Troops and our Engineer Company is up here building an entry that actually works, supervising the checkpoint operations so it will actually work, and patrolling the border and city, which consists largely of Sunni Arabs and Wahhabist extremists (also Sunni). Politically, it's not an easy task to exert authority in a city where the Sheik and Mayor are Deputy President Ghazi al Yawar's (the Iraqi government's highest-ranking Sunni) uncle and nephew and it's a task that a State Department official would have difficulty performing, let alone a troop of tankers and scouts. The next closest legal border crossing is down south in Al Qaim, providing us with over 300 kilometers of desert to patrol in between those two gateways.

The most difficult part of running the Rabiah border crossing was to first figure out who is on the Iraqi Customs Department payroll and how many ghost employees exist (phantom employees whose pay goes to someone higher in the Customs chain of command). Next, our guys had to disassemble an organization called the Department of Labor that never really existed—it consisted of people who would do the jobs of the customs officers for a quarter of their pay, so the real officers didn't even have to show up for work. Once they figured out who the real employees were, the Troop Commander instituted shift formations for accountability, rotated jobs to help stop the pervasive bribery, and fired employees and top managers on the spot if they failed to do their job (again, not an easy task when the Mayor immediately asks for their jobs back). Then our engineers built a single-file walkway that forces every person to enter through one point; even if they paid a bribe on both the Syrian and Iraqi sides they cannot merely skirt the lines and meander around the chaos to make their way into Iraq without having their papers checked like the old days. The next step is to stop the black market fake passport rings that seem to pervade both sides of the border. I probably know more about what a fake passport looks like than the Director of the Iraqi Customs in Mosul. The biggest coup at Rabiah has been the introduction of a scanner truck. Word of its arrival quickly spread on the first day (even though it was hidden behind a wall on the Iraqi side) and the daily traffic flow soon dropped in half. In fact, dozens of vehicles simply pulled out of line on the day it was introduced and made a U-turn back to Syria.

Despite the recent improvements, the entry point was still chaotic, dirty, and rudimentary, especially compared to the clean and organized Tijuana, Juarez, and other border checkpoints I've visited back home on the Mexican border (or even compared to the dirty and disorganized Mexican border entry points). One of the soldiers bought some cold Pepsis from a kid sitting alongside the line with his ice chest and umbrella, so our little group ended up touring around the place sipping our sodas through long colorful pink, green, and orange straws like we were at a pool party in Vegas, except that we were in full battle-rattle.

The city of Sinjar, which consists of Kurds, Yezidis, and both Shia and Sunni Arabs, is one of the nicer, safer, and cleanest cities I've seen in Iraq, largely due to the security provided by the Kurds. My recent trip to the city took me to the Kurdish Democratic Party (PDK) Headquarters. Basically, the PDK and PUK (Peoples United Republic of Kurdistan) are like the Republicans and the Democrats and agree on very little except that they both have their sites set on a sovereign Kurdistan. With the Kurds' organization and strong militia, I don't doubt they will get it one day. The city of Sinjar holds over 500 Peshmerga, the PDK's militia that is formally recognized by the Iraqi government as part of the defense structure. Unlike the Iraqi Army, they don't require any training or discipline—they are very experienced after fighting the Republican Guard for decades—and we all know that their loyalty lies on the good side of this fight.

The Peshmerga and local police surrounded the city with checkpoints and obstacles, mostly rock and dirt piles that cause you to slowly weave your way to the city center. At the middle of the dirt piles is the PDK Headquarters, headed by an ex-Peshmerga Division Commander named Sabat who is very arrogant, constantly surrounded by bodyguards, and treated like the Godfather. Sabat was a cult of personality and, unbeknownst to him, his James Bond act proved to be an entertaining show—he would stop talking in mid-conversation, pick up the phone and whisper into it, summon his aides into the room to whisper to them, and stand and open documents in front of us as if what he was about to say would end the war. He had a very nice dimly-lit, completely red office decorated with pictures of his past exploits as a guerrilla fighter, Persian throw rugs, leather couches and, the best part, air conditioning (until the power went out; power only works in the city four to five hours a day, which is an improvement from the past). We sat around on the couches and drank some hot tea and I almost fell asleep to the sound of the A/C purring. Luckily, the highly-caffeinated tea kicked in to wire me up.

After an hour of small talk I was led down to the conference room for lunch, which was the biggest goat grab I've had yet. All of the PDK aides and the Sinjar Mayor's crew were invited to the feast, so my group (a couple of Lieutenants and translators) and 30 or so city elders stood around two large tables covered with lambs and chicken stuffed with rice and surrounded by little potatoes, nuts, rice, raisins, onions, tomatoes, cucumbers, olives, and freshly baked pita. I was the first to dig in and hesitantly pulled on a leg until a large man with rather dirty hands ripped into the chicken and set the meat on my plate as the head Yezidi Sheik proceeded to cup his oily hands, dish up some rice in the middle of the chicken, and dispense it next to the leg. Manners and hygiene are thrown out the window in the goat grabs; you just dig in and stuff your face (with your right hand only, of course, because the left is used for other business in a latrine without toilet paper). I ended up eating three large pitas stuffed with meat, rice, potatoes, nuts, and raisins, skipping the veggies in the hopes of foregoing multiple future trips to the plywood latrines in 100-degree plus temperatures. I was really enjoying the potatoes, nuts, and raisin combination. At the end of our nearly five-hour meeting, Sabat interestingly stated that he hopes we will someday come back to Kurdistan, not Iraq, and he would love to personally host our families in the cool mountains of Dahuk.

I am beyond excited to get home at this point. We are heading to Sun River, Oregon for a mini-family reunion and then I plan to just hang out with Jen and the kids and go to the park, the zoo to watch Cade mimic the walrus, and gymnastics class. Yes, at 20 months, the kids are enrolled in their first gymnastics class. They even have the rings, which I never was able to conquer during Plebe gymnastics at West Point. For now, Cade and McKenna are making a grueling attempt at the donkey kick. If they are anything like me, they will fare very poorly at this sport and decide to run because it requires no coordination or dexterity. The kids are also learning some other important skills—Mac just learned what "poopah" means as she holds her crotch and squats. In the tub, she stood up and announced "poopah" and proceeded to drop a couple of logs. Luckily, Cade didn't notice them the first time, although when she did it the second night they caught his eye as a new play toy. We also have to teach them about looking both ways before crossing the street. During their first lesson, Jen announced, "OK, look both ways for cars" and Mac let go of her hand and ran to a parked car; smiling proudly, she saw another one and ran to it. I'll still keep posted to the tube to see if the 3rd ACR is in the news—as I flew out to Tal Afar at midnight we passed directly over the convoys making their way to the latest operation in a little hamlet supposedly flooding with enemy fighters. If that's true, the bad guys won't be there for long.

AUGUST 16, 2005:

WELCOME BACK TO THE 'RAQ

"It is so well that war is so terrible, or we should grow too fond of it." Robert E. Lee

I finally arrived back to base camp at midnight on the 9th after another brutal journey that took me from Portland to Dallas to Budapest to Kuwait to Balad to Tal Afar and, finally, to Tiger Base. On the final leg, the short 20-minute jaunt via helicopter from Tal Afar, I was drifting off to sleep with the warm wind blasting me in the face when the Blackhawk's gunner violently opened up over a pitch-black Tal Afar, jolting the few of us onboard awake as I thought to myself "Welcome Back to the 'Raq" and drifted back into dreamland. After an amazing (and amazingly quick) two weeks in Oregon with Jen and the kids and spending time with my mom, brother, sisters, and other family at our reunion in Sun River, it didn't really hit me that I was going back until I was buttoning up my desert fatigues at 5:30 a.m. on my final day and went in to stare at and kiss a sleeping Cade and McKenna before catching the early flight to Dallas. At that point, I may as well have been in Iraq getting this thing over with. I was trying to think of positives to look forward to, but came up with very little aside from being around the people I work with. I guess it will be interesting to see how the elections in October and December turn out; other than that, it will be a matter of sticking it out day-to-day and doing the best I can to keep our guys fed with enough information to keep them safe and to keep the bad guys on the run and in extreme danger. I just want to get in there and finish it—train the Iraqi Army, Border Police, and cops, hold the elections, and get out of here so we can let their government handle the bad guys in their own special, albeit respected and efficient, ways.

Arriving in Portland back on July 20ᵗʰ (I missed Jen's birthday by one day) was surreal. I felt like I was in a dream when I saw Jen and the kids walking up the concourse. Cade and McKenna took to me better than I expected as Cade smiled and quickly approached me while Mac smiled shyly and clung to Jen's legs, but they both warmed up by the time we started playfully bounding along the terminal's motorized walkway. Back at Jen's parent's house, it only took Butkus, our golden retriever, a couple of minutes before he started wrestling me to the floor like the old days. After the kids went down on my first night back, I had the opportunity to take a shower that lasted more than two minutes and allowed for a complete rinsing—much preferred over the dainty cold spray on the upper chest and neck area with an inflexible nozzle that I had grown accustomed to. Better yet, I didn't have to turn the water on and off between lathering and rinsing. I sprawled out in a comatose state on the queen-size bed (leaving Jen no room, as she told me the next day) and was out in seconds. It was the first time in over five months that I wasn't confined to my cot's aluminum rods and taut nylon "mattress" with my legs banging into the wooden poles that prop up my mosquito net.

It soon seemed like I never even left home because it was so easy to return to my role as a father and husband and it was extremely easy for me to leave behind the chaos of Iraq. I slipped back into our routine right away with the early wake-ups, changing and feeding the kids, morning activities like gymnastics or the zoo, lunch and nap, afternoon activities like the water park, dinner and baths, reading some books, and putting the kids to bed. I told Jen after my first full day back that there is no doubt in my mind that she has a harder job than anyone I know in Iraq. McKenna had just learned to walk weeks before I left Fort Carson and Cade was still crawling at the time. Now, they are both at the stage of avid curiosity and perpetual motion. Cade has learned to run (although it is more of a race walk that we referred to as goose-stepping) and McKenna's motor never stops as she has developed an effortless gait up on her toes that is worthy of a future half-miler with a deadly kick. I think the kids actually grew an inch or so over the short two-week period of R&R. Cade learned to say the dreaded "no" (although it is in a cute way where he purses his lips to enunciate and draw out the "Oh" ending) and Mac learned to kick out to a handstand when I hold her on my shoulders and properly mimic my squirrel noise

I was happy to see that I didn't think of Iraq over the two-week vacation, unless I happened to catch a glimpse of CNN or read an article in the local newspaper, the *Oregonian* (which was usually a short, depressing article about recent deaths or the failure of the new government to approve the Constitution). Before leaving Iraq, I was concerned as to how I'd react to simple things like driving around—would I be scanning every face and passing vehicle for signs of hostility or passing under a bridge and looking up to see if there was anything strapped to the underside that could blow downward? The most I did think about Iraq was when I thought to myself how great it was not to be thinking about Iraq. Jen and I were also fed the lines at the Army deployment seminars to "expect changes in your spouse", but the only change I really felt was profound giddiness to be back in such a comfortable environment with my family constantly at my side. But I was happy before I left, so even that wasn't anything drastic. No anger, irritability, depression, anxiety, or sleeplessness— just giddy about everything. I could've just sat and stared at Jen and the kids the entire time. It killed me on the night before leaving when I finished giving Cade a bottle and he melted into me and then McKenna burrowed her forehead into my lips for her goodnight kiss. I said goodbye to them earlier that night while reading a bedtime story and said that Daddy has to go help some people and will be back as soon as he can so please take it easy on Mom. Unfortunately, they didn't listen as Jen reported that they awoke with nightmarish screaming over the next four nights and the only thing that changed in their lives was that they woke up one morning and DaDa was no longer next to the crib.

While I was gone, our 3rd Squadron in Baghdad was hit hard. They lost six guys over the two-week period and the unit that replaced us in Baghdad, an Infantry Battalion from the Georgia National Guard, has lost 11 soldiers since we left in May. Even though we seemed to be making headway in that area in the 45 days we were there, I gladly and quickly uprooted to move north. I told Jen that I don't get a hollow, sinking, dead feeling in my gut when I leave the wire up here like I did back in Baghdad. The only thing I read about in our area over my R&R was a suicide bombing incident in the previously quiet border town of Rabiah, where one of our Cavalry Troops is watching over the city and border crossing point. A bomber strapped with a suicide vest detonated himself in a crowd of Army recruits; the snippet in the Portland paper said that 51 civilians died and over 90 were wounded and the U.S. and Iraqi Army soldiers reportedly fired into the crowd. I knew there would be more to that story in a town whose officials have a somewhat antagonistic relationship towards both the U.S. and their own central government. As it turned out, our guys weren't even at the scene and when our teams responded within minutes they reported numbers estimating 10 killed and 20 wounded. As we learned with the suicide bombers at our gates two months ago in Sinjar, it is very difficult to get an exact count because the locals sweep up the bodies in minutes and scatter (our higher HQ actually asked us for a tissue sample from those bombers a month after the fact so they could test for drugs—we didn't have one available as we don't even have a fridge to keep our bottled water cold let alone a sample of human tissue). My shop ended up processing over 100 detainees in the mission that I missed while I was on leave and the operation turned out to be four days longer than the planned eight days. The operation engulfed a small village in the hills north of Tal Afar where we suspected a lot of foreign fighters wiggled to as the Tal Afar situation intensified. As is the case with all of our missions, we rolled in (without me, thankfully, as I graciously traded eight 120-degree sunny and dusty days in full body armor for the pleasant Oregon summer in shorts and flip flops) and the locals waved to the guys and said it was a very peaceful place, at least during the time that they come out of the house during the day. The Squadron soon departed without a shot fired and left the Iraqi Army in place to ensure it stayed that way.

Since I've been back, we've been busy putting on Iraqi Army and police recruiting events, preparing for voter registration, and selecting polling sites. The recruiting has been a hit so far, mostly because there have been no more bombs blowing up on the men in line, but also because the events have drawn thousands of men each day. There's a lot of criticism in the U.S. that the Iraqis are only joining for the money rather than for the love of country, but I quickly discount that because we have the most powerful Army in the world and money and a job is precisely the reason most of our soldiers initially join. I think back to when I first signed up as an 18-year-old kid midway through high school—after years of getting my kicks from running miscellaneous items up the school flagpole and prodding the cops to chase me on my unlicensed, illegal Vespa Scooter, I enlisted as a Scout during Reagan's military build-up in the Cold War primarily for the excitement, closely followed by the opportunity to see Europe, and topped off by the college money. I didn't know or care about any politics or dangers until they set us on the Czech border and said that the Russian hordes would come across at any time. Whatever reasons the Iraqis join, I give them a lot of credit for taking on a job that is extremely dangerous, especially as they are replacing us as Al Qaeda in Iraq's primary target.

We're making a lot of improvements in their military schools, too, but it's still hard to make an accurate assessment of how many units are "trained" and it takes time to get most individuals scheduled to attend. The best quote I've heard on how "trained" the Iraqi Army is came from an instructor who remarked, "It's like eating cotton candy for dinner. Someone asks if you ate dinner and you say 'yes', but the next morning you wake up sick to your stomach throwing up." It's difficult to train an Army when you're in combat. We send our already-trained National Guard and Reserve units to safe bases in the U.S. for half a year before sending them to Iraq or Afghanistan, yet in Iraq we're put in the position to take a group of bakers, farmers, and sheep herders, issue them a uniform and maybe even an AK, and expect them to raid a compound the next day. For the most part, it has to be that way because there is no lull in the action. It's not a far leap in logic to understand why many of them run at the first sign of shooting. Hopefully, the schools and academies that are currently up and running will help identify some badly-needed strong leaders; after their government disallowed anyone who has caused bloodshed in the past from joining, the new Iraqi Army was left with, as one soldier callously phrased it, "an Army full of bitches".

Our efforts put into the voter registration and polling sites should pay off someday—the vote may be for a new Parliament rather than the Constitution, but there will be some type of vote coming up. The Iraqis had less than nine months to elect and form a government and write a Constitution under the constant threat of death; hopefully they can do what the European Union failed to do under a much more organized and efficient setting over the past couple of years in comfy and safe Brussels, although their attempt was for naught when the French and Dutch voted it down. I can't believe we've only been in Iraq for two and a half years when I look at all of the work that has been done; of course the work consists of the mundane stuff like schools, wells, clinics, security forces, and town councils that will never match up to the media spectacle caused by a massive mosque bombing during children's prayer group. I was beginning to think that our departure from this country would help the situation because foreigners wouldn't have a legitimate reason to invade Iraq, leaving the Iraqi government to fight the internal insurgents and thugs-for-hire. I've quickly come to the conclusion that the foreign invaders will still enter and the Sunnis who lost power will still fight—after all, it's not us they're after. They're coming in to incite a sectarian war and maintain a chaotic state by killing the Iraqi police, Army, government officials, and civilians in that order and will take us as a bonus if we're in the area. For the most part, the only time they fight U.S. soldiers directly is if we stumble upon them while patrolling and they have to fire to cover their escape. Other than that, they plant their bombs and hide while planning their next suicide mission and recruiting the poor sap who will partake in it. If ending our occupation was the goal of the insurgency, then the easiest way to attain it would be to cease attacks, causing the U.S. to call it secure and happily (very happily) leave. It's become clear to me that ending our occupation is not their objective.

As for our conditions at Tiger Base (now called FOB Nimr after we converted our naming conventions to Arabic), I unfortunately returned to the same setting as when I left. The first thing I did when I jumped off the bird at 1 a.m. was to search the supply area for some toilet paper and I soon realized that I had to revert to my old option of sneaking into the supply guy's room and gathering some of the double-layered TP that his wife sends him. Jen thought it was strange that the only thing I needed to shop for when I was home were the basic office supplies (paper clips, rubber bands, Scotch tape, some peel-off colored dots to track attacks) that never made it through our supply channels. The biggest improvement on camp is that the cooks now actually cook and serve lunch, making the days of searching for one of the three edible MRE's a thing of the past. The mess tent is dishing out burritos, ham and cheese pockets, individual pizzas, and other easily reheated and tasty items that most of the single guys are familiar with. Another nice change is that the temperatures dipped about five to ten degrees—the days are still a miserable 110, but the 85-degree nights make sleeping bearable once again. I noticed right away that a small mouse who is particularly fond of toothpaste replaced the large camel spider that visited my hooch nightly. My roommate left his shaving kit open on a small nightstand and he noticed there was a rip in the side of his Crest; right when he shook the bag and expressed his hope that a mouse didn't get in, a couple of turds spilled out onto the table. We're going to emplace a trap laced with Cinnamon Crest near the mouse's main avenue of approach to take care of this problem. These traps are industrial, almost cat-size; the spring is so strong that some soldiers are using them as a closing mechanism on the new plywood doors.

The next interesting upcoming event will be the rainy season in October. Apparently, the faded blue line running across the bottom of the operation center's walls, which was painted over when we moved in, was a water line that depicted how flooded the basement gets when the rains hit. Rumors of leeches crawling on cots during the rain season have been making the rounds, too (which would be one of the only accurate Vietnam analogies that I see). Another obvious change is the number of satellite dishes popping up around camp. Groups of soldiers have chipped in to buy dishes for web access and TV (mostly channels from Turkey and Germany) from an Iraqi named "Alf", whose nose, deep eye sockets, and mannerisms resemble the '80s TV character and puppet of the same name, even though Alf happens to be his real name (or at least his real alias). Alf worked for the Squadron in Al Qaim back in 2003 and he was the main man who the soldiers turned to whenever they wanted to buy something on the local economy. When the 3rd ACR turned the area over to the Marines in early 2004, Alf was detained because they figured anyone who openly worked with us and wasn't killed must have been a bad guy. He was released after eight months in Abu Ghraib and returned to his home in Al Qaim, where he lived until we contacted him upon our return to Baghdad. Alf moved to Baghdad to support us and then drove his line-hauler north behind our convoys and opened his anchor store in the Oz Market—his loyalty earned him the prime location as the first store the soldiers encounter when making the turn into the chow tent. Alf recently left us for a short trip back to Al Qaim to pick up his wife—I'm hoping he returns, not so much because I need a fan or a recently-released DVD, but because his luck may be due to run out after all of these years working with the Americans.

SEPTEMBER 22, 2005:

THE ASSAULT ON TAL AFAR—

THE INVESTIGATION TURNS TO WAR

"The art of war is simple enough. Find out where your enemy is. Get at him as soon as you can. Strike him as hard as you can, and keep moving." Ulysses S. Grant

I usually refer to this period in my life as the "Investigation in Iraq" rather than the "War in Iraq". We're preoccupied with gathering evidence to indict the enemy and they rarely expose themselves to us. The way we're forced to fight is frustrating for everyone because our actions are so restricted by vague and constantly changing or non-existent laws, both on the Iraqi and U.S. sides, and there are times when we actually had to wait on a legal review before taking action. We've been acting more like detectives on a police force by investigating crimes and searching for evidence to make an arrest. One soldier even brought a couple of grenades bound in packaging tape to my shop one night, thinking that I could dust them for fingerprints and confirm their use in an assassination on four men on the highway a few days prior. I told him to put some more Scotch tape on those things and get them out of my office before they blow up and we really have an investigation. On another hot summer night, we thought we found some smugglers who bore all the indications of what we refer to as "no shit bad guys"—caught late night in the wadis near the Syrian border with a lame story about farming while they had no equipment, no dirt in the fingernails, and fresh cologne. Further investigation revealed that the two male cousins were merely out on a romantic late night rendezvous. For the guys on the ground, this investigative game is made more difficult with the extensive use of fake ID's and passports and physical descriptions that can write themselves—black hair, thin build, dark skin, dark eyes, and a moustache. We love it when we receive reports of an overweight guy or someone with a peg leg. This game of cat and mouse changed suddenly and the legal rules significantly loosened when we received word to move out on our latest mission, a mission that became the closest thing to a war that we should see.

All indicators pointed towards the 3rd ACR going in to retake Tal Afar, starting with the most blatant when the Iraqi Minister of Defense announced on Arab TV in late July that we were going in to retake Tal Afar. Soon after that, and two weeks before the actual assault, our engineers started building a berm around the city and we simultaneously began moving most of our tanks to the base. The final indicator was when we briefed the war plans and dates of the attack to the Iraqi Army in a tightly guarded warehouse at their Divisional camp up north near the Tigris River. One of the Iraqi Army Colonels even announced, during his grandstanding dramatic speech that is common to all Iraqi staff officers, that "the terrorists know everything; they probably know what I am saying right now".

In the big picture, the "Resistance" (as the Arab media calls our enemy) has been losing control in Northern Iraq since Abu Zarqawi's (the leader of Al Qaeda in Iraq) chief Lieutenant was captured in Mosul in early July. Since that time, the American units in Mosul have been picking off the leaders one by one and we've been effectively controlling the border and outlying villages out west. This made Tal Afar one of their last remaining bastions of control in the north as Zarqawi's forces built the city into a stronghold over the past year. The Resistance also had a powerful emotional rally cry in the northern sector of the city called Quadisiyah, the area of the city where The Battle of Quadisiyah was fought back in the year 800 AD when a small, greatly outnumbered Islamic Army defeated an overwhelmingly powerful Persian invader.

Tal Afar lies just 30 miles to the east of Tiger Base at the heart of the aged trade routes in the north and smack dab in the middle of the Turkic, Kurdish, and Arabic cultures. It's also the perfect place for Al Qaeda to incite ethnic tensions because it is such a diverse city of Sunni and Shia tribes who have a 150-year-old feud, providing the perfect cinder to set off the local civil war. The city is 90 percent Turcoman, with about 70 percent of those being Sunni and the rest Shia. The Turcoman (and Turkey for that matter, which further muddies the politically sensitive waters) feel that the Kurds are trying to incorporate Tal Afar into their autonomous region, adding to their ages-old distrust of the Kurdish people that is even more pronounced after last week's killing of five Turkish soldiers by an outlawed Kurdish Kongra Gel militia in Turkish territory. Meanwhile, the Turcoman don't even trust each other—the Shia Turcoman in Tal Afar had a history of suffrage under Sadaam, which caused them to work closely with the Kurdish Peshmerga in the past, while the Sunni Turcoman in town enjoyed the privileges of high-ranking government positions and generous pension and welfare programs. Al Qaeda capitalized on the conflict, which had all of the elements of ethnic, religious, and tribal fighting and distrust in one place, and moved in with the Sunni's assistance to combat the newly-empowered Shia, who inherited the police and government jobs and used those positions to fight their own internal war. The U.S. was dragged into the fray when we supported the government and police, a stance that made it appear that we were anti-Sunni. Soon, the situation evolved into chaos wherein the Resistance built up a large enough force to evict both Sunni and Shia from their homes and assassinate and kidnap the police, government officials, civilians, and, eventually, even those Sunnis who once supported them and who seemed to be switching sides and wavering towards peace. After three months of fruitless diplomacy and negotiations to bring a truce to the conflict and weed out the Resistance, the stage for an assault was set.

It's an interesting phenomenon when you can motivate soldiers by telling them that they are going to disarm a city the size of Boulder, Colorado (population 250,000) and to expect to encounter Jihadists who will fight to the death in closed quarters and narrow alleyways, but that is exactly what happened when we started our planning. Even if the soldiers don't want to be in Iraq or despite their views of the war in general or the future of the people and country they are saving, most guys get genuinely fired up because they see it as their chance to make a difference in a visible way by ridding the Earth of extremely dangerous and evil people. For the soldiers who signed up in the combat arms branches like the Cavalry, this is what they joined the Army to do, what they have trained to do, what their country sent them out to do, and what brings purpose to their lives. They may not have come to the conclusion that a job catching smugglers or guarding the base was making a difference and it's difficult to tell if their actions are stopping or slowing attacks somewhere down the line, but they were able to immediately see the difference they made in Tal Afar. We all know the people holed up in town are bad because we've seen the dead bodies thrown on the streets, the Mafia-style assassinations on their own people who are trying to make a difference in their new country, the fatherless families fleeing the cities with no belongings, the children seeking medical attention to treat shrapnel wounds after their village was mortared;

everyone has seen enough to make this war personal and want to go in and make things right for people who don't have that ability.

Our soldiers are as equally adept at helping feed and provide medical care to the people, building and contracting infrastructure projects, and training police, border patrols, and the Army as they are at killing evil men. And the people still fighting the formation of the government and stability in Tal Afar are pure evil—when we started attacking in the city, the Resistance started attacking civilians outside of it. Our patrols on the outskirts of the city came across a group of bullet-ridden and burning trucks that were delivering water to the outlying villages. The bodies of the truck drivers were lying in the middle of the highway, still smoldering in a kneeling position. To top off the attack, they kidnapped a 2- and 3-year-old brother and sister from the small village next to the incident so the villagers wouldn't talk. The first vehicle-borne bomb in the Tal Afar conflict exploded against an Iraqi Army patrol; the man who detonated it brought along his entire family. Once the fire burned itself out, the bodies of his wife and two small children were pried out of the passenger seat, melted together as she appeared to be embracing both of them for their last hug before meeting Allah.

In an ironic twist to my little part of the war, we packed up and moved to the most contentious area of Iraq to lay siege to Tal Afar and I actually improved my living conditions. I stayed in a trailer with air conditioning and a foam mattress, had a 20-foot walk to a shower trailer with my choice of hot or cold water, and access to three hot meals a day and a midnight meal if I desired. As a bonus, our Ops Center was well out of reach of any mortars or RPGs. We usually go into a village or section of a city in mass and leave without a shot being fired. This, however, was the largest urban assault since Fallujah in the fall of 2004 and I was safely tucked away at a sprawling former Iraqi Air Force base seven miles south of the city center drinking banana milkshakes and using an air-conditioned toilet. It was strange to think that last year at this time I was watching the NFL Opening Day on *DirecTV's Season Pass*, happily surfing from game to game with a cold Cherry Coke and toasted cheese sandwich (in between changing diapers and reprimanding the kids from crawling on the coffee table). One year later we're surrounding a large Iraqi city to rid it of insurgents, securing it for the safe return of over 100,000 people, and instituting a new police force and government like we did on a much-smaller scale in Biaj a few months earlier. Usually at this time of year, my biggest decision is who to select in the first round of my Fantasy Football draft; now it's advising the Commander on whether or not to use a 500-pound precision-guided Air Force bomb to destroy a group of homes or send our boys up a road alongside the homes that were likely lined with mines (we used the bomb) or whether to lay down the same fire on a known Jihadist-preaching mosque where 10 black-clad armed males who recently fired at our patrol ran into (we didn't use the bomb).

On our first day of operations downtown we lost a great officer to sniper fire as he sat in his tank hatch on one of the main routes. Lieutenant Charlie Rubado joined our unit a couple of weeks before we left Fort Carson. He was fresh out of the Armor Basic Course after graduating from Florida Southern University and was newly wedded to his high school sweetheart. His death hit me hard—really hard. Charlie was one of my favorite Lieutenants. He worked in the operations shop for a couple of weeks at Fort Carson before he was sent to command a tank platoon in one of our Cavalry Troops. Charlie was always upbeat and smiling and nothing could get him down. He couldn't wait to have kids and was one of those genuine types who would ask you how vacation was and then actually enjoy sitting back to hear the stories that a guy with kids likes to tell but would be considered boring to most—stories about time with family and the greatness of the simple things in life, like Cade squatting under a cherry tree and stacking the fallen cherries in a cup or McKenna oohing and aaahing at a bubble coming out of the wand. He was a soft-spoken guy who immediately made friends, to include all the Sheiks and Mukhtars in the villages that he was responsible for. He invited me to meet several of them and we'd go to the goat grabs and enjoy those rare moments of relaxing small talk and hospitality that one usually can't find in Iraq. Those moments will be some of the fondest memories of my time here.

In the same attack, a pilot from the Regiment went blazing in to unearth the sniper and died in a hail of bullets in an ambush that Al Qaeda later claimed credit for. I didn't know Chief Hay personally, but soon heard all about him. He was a real warrior; a former Air Force tactical controller and Para-Rescue who transferred to the Army and was a Ranger prior to becoming a pilot. He was recently accepted into Delta to fly "little birds" in the most elite aviation unit in the world and was going to transfer there when we got home. He lived down the street from us in Fort Carson (as did Charlie and his wife) with his wife, 5-year-old son, and 1-year-old daughter. Jen received word from our neighborhood friends that two government vans entered to inform Charlie and Chief Hays' wives about the deaths, a scene I can't even fathom. Jen said that Chief Hays' son remarked to our neighbor that "the bad guys killed my Daddy and he went to heaven". Their memorials were held together and attended by almost everyone on the FOB who wasn't in the fight in the city at the time. The most chilling part of every memorial, this one being no different, is at the end when the bagpipes play *Amazing Grace*, role call is conducted with the names of the missing soldiers repeated to no answer, followed by the "Volley of Fires" salute from the riflemen, and *Taps*. The memorial was eerily silent with the breeze rippling the flags over the displays of their helmet, rifle and boots, causing their dog tags to tap up against their rifles like wind chimes.

Jen asked if I thought this whole thing was worth losing a life over, just as most people wonder. I thought a lot about that after Charlie's death. I have always thought, and still do, that it's not how you die that is important. After all, death is inevitable. The important thing is how you lived. And people here think what they are doing with their lives is important and fulfilling. Some of the words that were spoken at his memorial helped to clarify it in Charlie's case. Charlie, a deeply religious kid who had already accepted the Lord into his life, was fond of a verse that says "As he died to make men Holy, let us die to make men free". Everyone places a different value on life and some people lose theirs over a squabble over a couple bucks or what color clothes they're wearing, trying to save their car during a carjacking or a wallet during a mugging, trying to challenge themselves by climbing a high mountain or swimming a rough current, or even fighting over who was in the gas line first or who cut the other one off in traffic. Some people knowingly kill themselves slowly over time by imbibing in excessive breathers, drink, drugs, or tasty foods. Some lose their life in a more admirable and noble fashion, like the NYC firefighters entering the burning buildings on 9-11 to give up their lives while trying to save total strangers.

Most of the people in the military, just like most of those in other agencies who take an oath to protect Americans and our way of life, volunteered to put their life on the line for something they believe in that is noble and will make a difference to better the world or, on a smaller scale, their community. I'm surprised that people don't see that we are making that difference with the dismantling of two evil regimes and providing tens of millions of people with the opportunities to live their lives with some hope and freedom from oppression, or at least give them a chance to choose that lifestyle if they decide to take that path. You have to be here to see the gratitude from the people who were oppressed their entire lives to recognize the positive impact. Unfortunately, we've also taken away the good life from the minority Sunni and it's caused them to determine that their lost power is worth losing their life over. Determining what a life is worth is the ultimate personal decision based on circumstance and character; it astounds me how so many people can use the phrases "it's not worth losing a life over" or "let's hope he didn't die in vain" so loosely. You never hear someone say a person died in vain if they are killed in a car crash while rushing to work, but people seem to latch onto that phrase when a soldier who volunteers to do whatever his country asks of him is killed before he hits a ripe old age.

Almost all of the action in Tal Afar took place on the first few days of the operation immediately following the deaths of Charlie and Chief Hays. Perhaps through both luck and training, we were fortunate to have only one more memorial when a medic was killed by an IED in Quadisiyah. It seemed like the troops were hitting IEDs on almost every block in those first few days in early September, as well as RPGs, small arms fire, and shots from snipers. Our guys were in the midst of the fire and operating extremely cool and unfazed. It all starts with the Squadron Commander (SCO)—we were cracking up listening to one engagement over the radio between the SCO and one of the Troop Commanders, talking as calmly as if they were at the mall deciding where to eat lunch. An IED went off behind the SCO and he reported, "I think an IED just hit us...well, maybe not hit, but it was pretty close." Then the Troop Commander interjects with, "...and the building right behind you just blew up." The SCO remarked, "What's that...oh, yeah...wow that's a big one." Likely the bad guy who detonated the first IED had another bomb in that building that was set to the same frequency.

At day's end, the soldiers would come back to the granary (where we set up a small forward area where the most likely danger was a negligent discharge by the Iraqi Army or police commandos stationed there) and laugh and joke about the fighting. All of the Troop Commanders mocked another Commander whose tank hit an IED; his crew was forced out and stood by helplessly while filming the burning hulk of metal. "Mike, why don't you go ahead and take your tank out there on that mission...oh, that's right, you don't have one." One soldier's tank was damaged so badly that the transmission only worked in one gear, so he cruised around the neighborhood in reverse and was still out there blowing up homes where the RPG shots were coming from. It seemed like every part of the city was bad as IEDs, RPGs, and snipers were constantly reported from homes, mosques, cars, and wadis. In one case our guys raided a building and came running out with nausea and burning skin from the chemicals inside (likely immense amounts of chlorine to use in their bombs). The Ordinance Disposal team was sent in, along with some chemical soldiers to test the air; when the disposal team blew up an IED found in the front room, the entire three-story building, rigged with several other bombs, collapsed with it. We were methodically picking off the key leadership, either killing or capturing them and their bodyguards after they shortly gave up the fight. Well over a hundred enemy fighters were killed in the first three days and our soldiers were acting with amazing restraint and only taking out those who were actively engaging us or setting up positions to do so.

One day during the intense fighting, hundreds of locals started marching on the castle downtown (the castle housed the city government and police (now the newly-installed Mayor and a new Police Chief from Baghdad)) and smaller groups joined the march as the mass converged on the government's headquarters. I was watching the movement on the remote viewing terminal with no audio feed, so I couldn't tell if it was going to be a bad demonstration or a good one (in which case, a good one may turn bad if a suicide bomber entered the picture). I saw two of our tanks driving near the crowd and immediately thought back to China's Tiananmen Square, when demonstrators lay down in front of the Chinese Army's tanks. Thankfully, the Iraqi police showed up on the scene and didn't do anything stupid and our tanks slowly backed away. It turned out that the demonstration was pro-U.S. and pro-Iraqi government with a twist—they wanted us to take out the bad people for good and then stay in the city. In this case, unlike in Fallujah last year, we are doing just that and following the same plan that we implemented in Biaj. We are leaving behind new bases in the city and staffing them with police and soldiers from other areas of Iraq who have no agenda or disputes with the locals.

The people in the rally were brave to appear in public like this because the rumor mill, both locally and in the national Arab press, were floating all kinds of sordid, and yet entertaining, stories. The word circulating around Tal Afar at the time was that either the Shia tribesman or Shia police would kill anyone who left town, trekked to our evacuation camps, or took part in public displays. Nationally, at least according to the Arab press, the Resistance in Tal Afar was annihilating the Americans and killed dozens of our soldiers, causing us to resort to the use of chemical weapons (little did they know that we didn't even bring our chemical suits or masks on this trip). Luckily, the press went on to say, the Resistance evacuated the women and children from the town so the innocents would not get hurt in the fighting and their actions saved thousands of lives from the evil American oppressors. The enemy does an amazing job at using the press to their advantage, especially considering the difficulties we had (thanks to these rumors) in displacing civilians to our camps set up in safe areas with food, water, and shelter.

We did have a great showing by the Iraqi forces along the way, but it started out shaky when hundreds of the Iraqi Army from the newly formed Division to the north never showed up for the fight. Apparently, once the unit heard that they were going to Tal Afar most of them took off and never showed up to the next morning's formation. We were concerned about desertion among the IA who embedded with us, but they really pulled their weight with nobody fleeing or quitting and they put on an impressive performance. They aggressively hit every cave, house, or anything else that was pointed out to them. However, when 3 p.m. hits they still turn into pumpkins. Temperatures in the day are well over 100 degrees and our recently issued anti-armor piercing plates added another five pounds, so that is understandable. We gained control of a 1000-man Iraqi Police Commando (IPC) unit from Baghdad a few days into the operation. These guys look like professionals and are noticeably broader in the chest and shoulders compared to the usual 100-pound farmers who are enlisting. They also have a swagger and confidence that is respected by the people. A popular TV program in Baghdad and quickly spreading to the other big cities mirrors our *Cops* and follows an IPC unit named "The Wolf Brigade". It's been a hit with the people, especially young kids who want to grow up and become a Wolf. Media reports stating that we were only using Kurdish Peshmerga for the operation couldn't have been more inaccurate. We used some Peshmerga units, but kept them in low-key operations like searching forests for caches rather than stir up any racial tensions in town. For the most part, our IA and IPC put the Iraqi face on the mission. This went well for a couple of days, until the mostly-Shia Commandos went on TV and chanted about their opportunity to kill Sunnis. We had to figure out a way to either get them out of town or place them in areas where they would do more good than harm. Plus, their Commander felt disrespected after our logistics guys inadvertently sent them pork ribs on their first night here. We figured that the best way to use the IPC was to search the Shia areas and villages on the outskirts, away from the masses and away from the Sunnis. Once these guys were pointed in a direction of attack, they literally swarm the place like fire ants, but the swarm was a little less intense when directed against other Shia.

The IPC's biggest problem is that if we are not physically present they will detain people and beat the hell out of them. In one case, a 17-year-old self-confessed assassin provided us with an amazing amount of information solely because he didn't want to be turned over to the Commandos. The other problem was their lack of disciplined firing. They rarely took their weapons off of "fire", even if they were safely back at the granary; if one of them would trip and fall and spray some rounds the others thought they were being fired at and start engaging the air. Most of the people in Iraq grew up with an AK and still don't know what the front site is used for and it shows. We just had to ensure that the direction of attack we pointed them in was away from us. The IA and IPC were, as always, a logistical nightmare. They are kind of like my dog Butkus in the way they will eat and drink anything placed in front of them—you give them five days of supply and they eat it in one, one day of supply goes in half a day, and not all of those rations may even wind up in the mouths of the Jundis (Privates). I hosted three of the Jundis to show them some mug shots and see if they knew anything about the detainees (when I turned to the first page of the mug shot book one of the guys says (translated) "Hey, that is my uncle"). I sent a U.S. soldier to the chow hall for some burgers, fries, cookies, and Cokes because the Jundis kept motioning to their mouths, which means either food or a cigarette. These dirty Jundis attacked the chow like they haven't eaten in weeks; I counted over seven Cokes for the young one. Then some high-ranking IA officers entered the room, spotted the chow, and molested the burgers like they hadn't eaten in weeks, either. And they were just coming back from lunch at the chow hall.

Although Tal Afar has been extremely quiet over the past couple of weeks and it looks like all of the enemy cells here have been severely decimated, nobody really knows what the future holds here after our actions and, for the most part, the enemy is like a Hydra as far as taking out the top leaders and others popping up in their place. What I do know is that it gave the fledgling IA and IPC tons of confidence and the people in Iraq confidence in them and that certainly can't hurt. Nobody knows what the future holds for Iraq, either, but I do know that a lot of people are going to turn out in the next few weeks during elections to decide it. The conspiracy theorist in me thinks that all of this was in Sadaam's master plan: by invading Kuwait he set off a chain of events that may cause us centuries of conflict with Islamic extremists. Soon after his invasion, Saudi invites us in to help defend their border and Osama Bin Laden (OBL) immediately calls for Jihad against the U.S. for occupying the Holy Land.

We can't really "win" the war here; after all it's harder to kill an idea than it is to kill an enemy in uniform and whatever the outcome may be will likely be construed in the Arab world as a victory to armed resistance, just like Hamas declared after Israel pulled out of Gaza. What we can do is stand up a country that can defend itself and hope that it becomes a moderate voice rallying for the peace that Islam espouses rather than the extremism—build a message that discredits the one embraced by OBL and his affiliated cronies and a message that no other moderate Islamic government seems comfortable in identifying with. The tide is turning as the fighters, whether foreign Al Qaeda or former regime Sunni, are wearing out their welcome with every Arab they kill and are having an increasingly difficult time blending into the population. The only problem now is that a lot of vigilante groups are forming for revenge, to take the matter into their own hands, which plays into the Al Qaeda's master plan as the group tries to drive the wedge between Sunni and Shia and turn Iraq into an all-out civil war. The Shia clerics, joined recently by many Sunni clerics, are remarkable in their calls for restraint and the majority of the people are still listening to them. The only thing similar to a Vietnam in the situation is an antsy American public who make it sound like we are bogged down here after only a couple of years. While it's far from a stable environment and I can't wait to leave here myself for selfish reasons, I would never diminish the importance of what we are doing here. A lot of hard work and progress has been made in Iraq and a lot of American soldiers lost their lives; it would be irresponsible to throw it all away based on the public opinion polls from people who have probably never set foot here or even spoken to an Iraqi to form that opinion. I imagine there could have been thousands of angry people lining the roads to the President's home in Crawford had we not taken this route and then a sarin gas attack killed thousands of Americans; those protesters would be calling for his head for ignoring undisputed intelligence that told us an attack of that nature would happen. People would say that we saw it coming since the early '90s and confirmed in 1997 after Madeleine Albright announced that Sadaam would become the "salesman of WMD".

After almost a month here, everyone's tired and anxious to get back to our border outposts, despite the relative discomforts. Life is a lot more structured at the Tal Afar base since it lies "next to the flagpole" (an Army term meaning the location of higher headquarters, from which most soldiers want to stay clear), as compared to the autonomy and freedom from the crazy military rules back in Sinjar (they even have soldiers pulling "flip-flop guard" here to ensure nobody treks to the shower trailers without a complete uniform). One of our tankers was turned away from the fully enclosed, clean, catered, and air-conditioned chow hall for wearing a sweaty and dirty uniform—this was after he came in after 18 hours of patrolling that included being hit with an IED. Back in Sinjar there are no such rules; in Sinjar, you actually leave the chow area dirtier than when you went in because of the dust clouds kicked up by the refueling helicopters less than 100 meters away.

Things have been relatively quiet in the rest of our area since most of us have been gone. We left enough troops behind, supplemented with the city police and some IA, to take care of any attacks in the cities, but we left the border wide open with the Iraqi Border Patrol (IBP) in charge of ground operations with our boys providing the air coverage. I've been one of the harshest critics of the IBP in the past, but I've been pleasantly surprised. Before we arrived, a teenager with an RPG and an attitude could have forced the surrender of hundreds of police and border patrol. Now, the IBP doesn't hesitate to fight back and they even detained over 40 smugglers one night. The biggest news out west was that a fire ripped through one of our buildings and burned up everyone's possessions. I'm sure it was caused by overloading the circuits with Playstations and DVD players as we stuffed more and more people in there and the plywood roofs surely didn't help to slow the blaze. Fortunately, all but two of the people living in the building were with us in Tal Afar at the time, so they have at least a rucksack full of clothes and equipment with them.

Nobody really knows when we are going to pick up and leave Tal Afar, but it should be soon because we have to get back to secure over 20 polling sites over the next few weeks. I can't wait to break away from this Groundhog Day cycle of work and sleep. I'll soon be able to throw in a morning run and relax a bit at night with a DVD. Mentally, I compare staying here for an undetermined amount of time with being in the NICU when the kids were born. Jen and I couldn't bring Cade and Mac home until they made it four consecutive days without an "episode" (when they stopped breathing) and if one occurred the clock started anew; here, it's like we have to make it four consecutive days without a small arms fire incident or report of anything bad in town before we're released.

Back in the States, Jen, the kids, and Butkus recently left her parent's home in Portland and returned to Fort Carson. She made the move for several reasons, primarily to get there before the snow season hits, settle the kids in before I return, and to mark the halfway point in the deployment to give her a psychological lift. Before they left Portland, Jen's dad let Cade and McKenna each pick a gift out of the Portland Zoo's gift shop (they went to the zoo together every Wednesday over the past six months). Jen said it was hilarious watching two 21-month-olds walking around the shop deciding what to get. Cade ended up selecting a seal pup and McKenna grabbed a frog purse with a ladybug on the side. I know they're going to miss their grandparents and aunt and vice versa. I know Jen is going to miss them, too. I don't know how she is going to make it on her own, especially since the kids still don't sleep through the night. Somehow she is doing it, though. A day after returning to post, Jen had to bring Butkus to the vet and he was diagnosed with tumors caused by stress—you know it's a tough deployment when your dog stresses out. Cade has recently mastered the stairs, so that is one less worry I have. McKenna still slides down backwards on her stomach. She did learn when to say "tank yew" and says it at the appropriate times and says "no, no" when she is caught doing something that she knows is wrong. Every day is going to be a challenge for Jen—even a simple thing like going out in the front to play presents a challenge when the kids break out and run down the street in opposing directions and

I'm really hoping that the "terrible two's" don't kick in until I get home to help. There are some other wives around to help her out and provide company, but she is largely on her own and I'm just as proud of her as I am of the soldiers out here.

OCTOBER 16, 2005:

MAKING ELECTION HISTORY

"The real and lasting victories are those of peace, and not war." Ralph Waldo Emerson

What a treat it's been being back in Sinjar. Aside from reacquainting myself with the mild neck pain and numb arms caused by the tight confines of my cot (I was spoiled with a foam pad for the month in Tal Afar), I was ecstatic to return to the simplicity and quaintness of this place. It's like going back to a vacation home in the country with fresh air and comparatively few worries. Sinjar doesn't have any of the strange smells exuded in the big cities like Baghdad, Mosul, and Tal Afar, where people virtually live on top of each other, and the higher altitude has provided us gorgeous weather with 90-degree highs and lows in the mid-60s. My time spent sweating through the night appears to be over. On my first night back I even resorted to pulling my sleeping bag out of my rucksack to combat the early morning chill. We've been working a lot of long hours every day over the past eight months and I thought about giving the guys in my shop some time off, perhaps sleeping in a couple of hours every other Sunday for both night and day shifts, but after talking this through we all decided that there wouldn't be anything to do if you had time off and you'd probably just come hang out in the office.

One new luxury item that we brought back from Tal Afar was a set of donated golf clubs and 100 used balls. The expansive dirt fields surrounding the landing pads provided us a ready-made driving range. If you pull the ball it may hit one of the parked helicopters and if you slice it then the perimeter guard shack comes into play, but nobody has been able to drive the ball all the way down the center to the Chapel. Whoever hits has to go out and retrieve the balls, but the range lies on the route to the Oz Market for chow so it's not too burdensome. The nicest surprise upon our return to camp was the shower trailers. They were finally hooked up to a large water source and operational, thus cutting almost half an hour off of my round-trip walk to the vinyl showers just in time for the onslaught of a chilly rain season. The trailers are so new that the soldiers put up some signs to keep it that way, stating "Remember not to write on the walls when you leave" (the only graffiti I've seen so far was "The South will Rise Again" with the reply under it saying "Who, Kuwait?"). The two new trailers hold eight shower stalls apiece and are attached to the new toilet trailers, but the set of sanitation wonders have been shut down a couple times already when some Wet Wipes clogged up the pumps. Even though the short walk is nice and you can control the water temperature, I still find myself complaining once in a while. There is very little to no water pressure whenever more than one person turns on the water. As I remarked the other morning, you know there's a lack of water pressure when you can count the number of drops hitting your head as you lather up.

The Oz Market has somewhat slipped downhill since we've been gone. It's like a mall that lost its anchor tenant after Raad was busted for drugs a couple of months ago and his shop and restaurant were evicted with him. The best thing going there now is a small TV hooked up to a satellite dish next to the chow serving line. *ESPN Sports Center* comes on the Armed Forces Network during breakfast on Sunday and Monday, so I can catch all of the scores from the day's college and NFL games and see the replays as long as the sun isn't beating directly onto the screen. I'm back into my routine where I wake up and lift some rocks, do some pull-ups, and then go on a run ending at the chow hall and I try to time my arrival in concert with the cooks lifting the lids off of the eggs and creamed chip beef before the flies pounce on them. Our PX is still operating, but the inventory has been pared down to some tampons (we have about five girls on the camp) and deformed Pepsis that have been priced in half before they explode. It's been tough to coordinate a convoy to Mosul to restock the inventory in the middle of the Tal Afar operations and elections. In the meantime, a new restaurant and store combo opened in our Civilian Military Ops Center (CMOC) by the front gate. The CMOC is the place where the locals come to bid on contracts (one day a woman came in representing the Iraqi Governing Body to Reform Corruption and the next day she apparently quit her job and was making a bid on a well), make claims for damage to their property, or to provide information on someone they don't like and would like us to drive a tank up to their home and arrest them. The Tiger Base Camp Mayor has been driving around in a black Mitsubishi King Cab truck with racing stripes and no plates, courtesy of a guy who threw out an unfinished bomb and ditched the truck during a high-speed chase. I don't doubt that this guy will come to the CMOC to reclaim his vehicle after a couple of months, hoping that we forgot about the incident.

Mike's Pizza Shop opened a few steps away from the CMOC and caters primarily to soldiers (particularly the soldiers assigned to work in the CMOC) because the $5 pizza is too costly for the locals and most of them don't want to be frisked in order to come in and eat. The only sign advertising the joint lies inside the camp perimeter. Mike, the 14-year-old kid who runs the shop and restaurant, is the same guy who always chased me down in downtown Sinjar. He and his brothers would appear out of nowhere whenever and wherever we pulled up and he'd pester me to open a shop. Whenever the staff talked about opening another store I would always put in a good word for a kid who I thought was the most entrepreneurial Iraqi I've met (he's even bright enough to change his name to something we could remember and pronounce) and, after four months of persistence and bugging the right people, he finally received the rights to run a store and a restaurant. I stopped by the other day for a $5 combo meal featuring the lamb kabob and fries. Mike's place is much cleaner than our chow café and one Yezidi is solely devoted to wiping down tables and swatting flies, even when the place is empty. The food was great; it reminded me of the greasy schwarmas I'd eat from the curbside vendors every chance I got back in Riyadh and Dhahran 10 years ago. I went from the restaurant to the store a couple of meters away and learned how loose Mike's pricing structure is when my $16 paid for goods that were individually priced out at over $40 (and Mike's brother even tossed in a cold Coke for my walk back). After eight months in country, I finally had a foam pad to place atop my cot and the blood is once again flowing to my extremities after a night of sleep. As I walked back, my stomach tightened up quite a bit and I found out at the nightly staff meeting that the medics visited a couple of hours prior to my meal and told Mike they were going to shut his place down for substandard sanitary conditions (I did recall seeing the cook cleaning some pans and brushing his white shoes with the same scrub brush). It was still great food and my stomach never completely caved in to validate the medic's claims.

We're getting a lot of new attachments out here as the year drags on. Our last border patrol advisors (basically a bunch of Reservists called up to train the Iraqi Border Patrol) just left and the new guys arrived, wearing the new digitized olive green ACU's (Army Combat Uniform) that are being issued stateside. Then the 101st Airborne Commander and his staff visited as they made their rounds while taking over command of Northern Iraq, also wearing their new ACU's. I'm jealous that they were issued the new uniforms because we'll have to fork over the money to buy them when we return, but I'm not envious of their situation as the new guys. I remember when we first arrived in Baghdad and the worn and ragged guys across the table were on the way out—now we've become those worn and ragged guys. I briefed the new border team prior to their first convoy movement in the area. It's not like a lot of activity is happening out here on a daily basis, but at the end of the briefing their First Sergeant said, "Thanks for scaring the hell out of us". I guess it would be an eye-opener for anyone coming in—a car blowing up here and there, IEDs all along this stretch of road, usually in the gullies and on the first guys driving by in the morning, mortars sometimes landing here or there, a little story about the last time I was on this road we had a flat and pulled off to change it while someone stopped and dumped a dead body right under our noses. We think of this place as Sleepy Hollow, though. If you hear any firing it's probably because some wild dogs are trying to breach the perimeter.

Recently, we've been discussing the redeployment timeline in meetings. It's nice to know that at least it's on our planning plate and there should be enough time to correct any mistakes made by the new movement officer, who is a nice, but not the most organized or competent, guy nicknamed Captain Caveman due to his body hair, poor posture, body odor, and the way he drags his heels when walking (others call him Captain Conrad because he was raised in Russia and speaks incomprehensible English—he has a great movie collection, though, so he is very popular). It will be interesting to see how many soldiers stay in when we return because this is the first unit in the Army to deploy for two complete year-long rotations (the 3rd Infantry Division is back in Iraq, but they didn't stay for an entire year during their initial engagement before being replaced) and it really takes its toll on a person and their families. Surprisingly to me, all of the combat divisions have easily exceeded their reenlistment quotas and, even though the Army is barely missing their upgraded numbers for new recruits, the new guys over the past three years are starting out mentally tougher just by knowing that they are signing up to go to war.

Tal Afar has been *relatively* quiet since we left, aside from the female suicide bomber who blew up herself and five Shia men at an Army recruiting event, another bomber who blew up a car parked in the newly-opened market downtown (killing 30 locals), and a third bomber who blew up at another Iraqi recruiting event (also killing 30 locals). After the nine deaths the Marines experienced in their recent weeklong operation down south by Al Qaim, I'm amazed how our two Squadrons pretty much cleaned up Tal Afar after a month with only three deaths. One battalion of the 82nd Airborne came in to help out during the elections and, even though they weren't ready to participate in the big event last month, they've made a huge difference in keeping the peace since then. The real difference since we left has been in the reporting and cooperation from the locals, both Shia and Sunni, to turn in anyone who is causing problems and there have even been fights reported between Sunni groups as the previously-intimidated are fighting back, even against members of their own tribe or sect. The long-simmering feud in Tal Afar between the Shia Jolaqs and the Sunni Farhats (the Iraqi version of America's Hatfields and McCoys) has cooled down significantly after several weeks of Sheikh meetings to iron out their long-running disputes.

The bitter pill about this war is that the number of bombings targeting the locals increases with the number of locals actively helping to rebuild their community. The remarkable thing about the Iraqi people, though, is that the bombings do absolutely nothing to deter them from living their lives and immediately returning to the markets, recruiting events, or, this month, the polling booths. It's apparent that the operation in Tal Afar had a significant effect on Zarqawi's boys by the number of times he refers to it while seeking his vengeance and he continues to use the city as a case of Sunni repression by the new government—he is a great storyteller and often makes obscure references to history that impassions the Sunnis to continue fighting, like with his recent comparison of the new Iraqi government to the traitor Shia minister in 1258 AD who opened the gates of Baghdad to the Mongols and caused the city's downfall. The Iraqi government's Defense Minister, a Sunni named Saadoun Dulaimi, has been trying to offset those effects and is engaging in a war of words to motivate the Sunnis to fight against the foreign invaders who are killing their fellow Muslims and countrymen.

We returned from Tal Afar just in time to create an election security plan and emplace barriers at 29 election sites spread out over an area the size of Maryland. Election Day was going to be more interesting because it fell right in the middle of the holy week of Ramadan, which historically is a period of a 100 percent increase in attacks because the Jihadists are supposedly blessed an additional 10 times for killing themselves during the holiday (I'm not sure what the multiple is for killing other Muslims, rather than infidels, during the holiday). Our biggest concern was prioritizing which of the 29 sites would be attacked by a suicide bomber (a vehicle bomb was unlikely because we circulated posters instituting a "no-roll" policy, meaning that any vehicle moving inside a village is considered a threat and dealt with as a threat). From that list, we decided which places needed the most concrete barriers and concertina wire and where we would position our medics and troops for casualty evacuations. The priority for security was relatively easy when I made a large list of places that likely wouldn't be attacked, which are the areas that I see multiple reports of smugglers and bomb cell members who wouldn't likely attack their own sympathetic neighbors.

American forces were supposed to be hands-off during the elections process and let the Iraqis handle everything from the security at the sites, the registration and voting, and the delivery and counting of the ballots. Their planning is very "Inshallah" oriented, however, so we had to do some hand-holding along the way and only really got involved once when an official up north in Rabiah claimed that he didn't need a female to search other females because only men were allowed to vote. Our main mission on Election Day was to hang out on the outskirts of the polling sites and respond if needed. The last thing the military needed was an Al Jazeera photo of an American soldier near a polling booth that would be perceived across the world as Americans influencing the vote. Aside from the day we left Baghdad to head north, October 15th was probably the only day since I've been in Iraq that I really looked forward to and that guarded optimism largely arose out of curiosity because it was anyone's guess how well the elections were going to be received and which cities would come under attack. I thought it was off to a bad start when, on the evening prior to the vote, the guards at a polling site in Rabiah reported some small arms fire. Things only went uphill from there, though. On the day of the vote, I visited downtown Sinjar and some of the small villages to get a feeling for the overall atmosphere and people's attitudes. It was uplifting to see the smiling and happy people piling out of the polling centers with their purple fingers in the air and even the reports from Tal Afar stated that the elections were a huge success and resulted in a festive, celebratory occasion. After the polls closed, I was stunned to learn that there were no significant attacks anywhere in Iraq. Just as important as the psychological affect that the freedom to vote has on the people is that it provided another huge boost to the public's perceived competence of the Iraqi Army and police who secured all of the voting sites.

As for the next few months here, it looks like we only have one more hurdle to jump before turning over some of our territory to the Iraqis and that is the December parliamentary elections. I'm hoping that's our only hurdle and I find myself counting the days to convince myself that we can't fit any other big operations in the timeline. One morning on a trip down south, when I took a surprisingly chilly, hour-long flight along the border to visit a new border fort that was built on some salt flats in the absolute middle of nowhere, I found myself seriously calculating the likelihood of us moving down that far to help out the Marines in the border town of Al Qaim—I know most of our soldiers would love to spend some time down there since it's the sight of their old stomping grounds back in 2003 and it would give them another opportunity to kill bad guys in a familiar place. We flew over some brand new water trucks making their way to the fort with a group of border policemen riding on top of the water tanks, barely holding on to their weapons as they bounced along the unimproved dirt road. The border fort was recently built and already in poor condition; the hole-in-the-ground john was overfilling and the numerous flies received a bonus from the leftover falafels and lamb pies tossed around the perimeter from the morning's chow fiesta. I spoke with a couple of the newly-hired border guards who are from Sinjar, neither of whom spoke much English, and came away from the 30-minute conversation with the impression that Tiger Base will receive a lot of flooding next month and then we'll get dusted with snow in December while the surrounding mountains get hit with a foot or so. We've had a couple of the violent, yet beautiful, desert thunderstorms this month and the little rain that did fall quickly filled the wadis. One soldier who grew up farming in Indiana says these people don't recognize the fertile ground they are blessed with—he tossed some watermelon seeds next to the hand-washing pit and there is a nice garden blooming. It's the only fruit on post that the flies haven't pounced on yet.

Meanwhile, while mentally dismissing our next operation, I'm becoming fairly talented at my new hobby here, which is developing visual metrics to count down our time. I have a stash of 53 disposable razors that is slowly disappearing as I use one every other day, a container of 107 multivitamins that decreases by one daily, five more haircuts to use up my last 10 one dollar bills, and there is now the NFL season that I can use to gauge our progress and hope we will be watching the Super Bowl in Kuwait. With the addition of the new latrine and shower trailers and the tasking to the staff officers to clean them each Sunday night, I now have 14 more times to scrub the nastiest toilets that I've seen since my days working at McDonalds as a teen.

Jen and I are anxiously planning our Colorado excursions when I return home, from taking the kids to the zoo every week, riding the train across the gorge in Canon City, climbing Pikes Peak, even down to the simplest picnics at Iron Horse Park on post during my lunch hours. Jen has the kids involved in a full slate of weekly activities from gymnastics to Kinder Music to zoo and museum trips. Mackie (as the neighborhood kids call her now) has hair long enough to put into pony tails and melted my heart when she said "Hi Daddy" for the first time and then once again when she sang "Buggy Buggy" and her and Cade both said their "I love you's" into the phone. McKenna has been talking much more than Cade and has been calling him "Tade" since she really can't put out the "C's" yet. Jen said that one day out of the blue Cade pointed to his sister and spouted out "Sissy", which is now his name for her. The kids turn the big "2" on October 30th. A church in Colorado sent our Chaplain a video camera, blank discs, and a bunch of kid's books, so I had the opportunity to make the kids a DVD of me reading "Winnie the Pooh" for their birthday present. Hopefully, this is the last one I'll miss in a very long time.

November 14, 2005:

A Trip to the Black Hole

"Show me the manner in which a nation or community cares for its dead and I will measure with mathematical exact certainty the sympathies of its people, their respect for the laws of the land, and their loyalty to high ideals." Gladstone

It's like living in a movie out here where a new scene unfolds every day and everyone involved is anxious to see how the show ends. In the most recent scene, it seemed like all of Iraq was getting blown up over the past month and those of us in Northwest Iraq were basking in sweet harmony. I attribute a lot of this to the clearing of Tal Afar and a lot of it to our aggressiveness based on the whole Cavalry mentality. We don't set any patterns and we're constantly going out on missions in force. Allah has been good to the Iraqi security forces recently, too. The latest car bomber only killed himself on the road in front of Tiger Base and the IA soldiers riding in their little white pickup trucks came away unscathed. The week before that, another bomber drove right through an IA tent checkpoint and detonated himself when he reached the far side, thus unwittingly sparing the lives of the eight men inside who escaped with mild concussions. A third bomber went off near the border outside a border patrol checkpoint, wounding several Iraqis and killing one when a wall fell on him, but the detonation spared dozens of men who were eating their lunches less than 20 meters away.

Between the wild dogs scavenging the body parts and the locals clearing up anything metallic to melt and sell, there isn't much evidence left lying around after a bombing. I had one of my more interesting moments out here a couple of weeks ago when we were trying to get a clean fingerprint off of a hand found on the scene to identify the most recent suicide driver. The only problem was that we had no fingerprinting kit, just some pens and magic markers to break open for the ink, a sponge, and blank index cards. One of the ordinance disposal team members was trying to clean the burned and mangled fingers and some of the meat was starting to fall off, so we had to fingerprint quickly while some skin was still intact. The worst part of that ordeal was that we were served Polish sausage for dinner about an hour after getting a somewhat legitimate print. A couple more reporters show up in the past month to try and capture our story out here (one freelance journalist said that we were here for oil rights and I unprofessionally quipped that it would have been a lot easier to take over Kuwait where they have working refineries and a port) and a PBS documentary crew came in and actually asked us if we could introduce them to an insurgent to interview. The sad part is that a couple of guys came to mind right away and I knew when they'd be home.

As part of our efforts to keep the enemy off-balanced and our soldiers busy so they don't grow complacent, we planned an operation in an area self-dubbed the Black Hole, a large swath of desert, grain fields, canals, and wadis northwest of Tal Afar stretching up to the Syrian border. The operation was originally planned for the Eid al Fitr holiday, a period at the end of Ramadan where the people are all dehydrated and irritable from fasting every day for a month and snap out of it with a wild three-day party, a celebration that one of the IA soldiers compared to a three-day Christmas. The Eid begins when the religious leaders spot the new moon (although the Shia and Sunni couldn't even agree on that one and the Shia started a day earlier). We were careful to work around the holiday and mentioned this to the IA Brigade Commander, who said that it would be no problem to search the people's homes during this time and many bad guys may be home for the holidays. He's a Kurd, however, and his staff of Arabs behind him were shaking their heads in a tone that I read as "Bad idea, this won't help to make any friends in these Sunni villages". We decided to put off the operation until after the holiday so we wouldn't show up as the Grinch who stole Eid.

Our latest mission was a little different than the others—for one, we didn't expect any enemy contact in the small villages and, secondly, it was finally chilly out. It actually felt pleasant to walk around in 40 pounds of body armor and ammo in the brisk air and not taking off your vest to expose a new heat rash.

Most of the villagers we met along the way were poor Sunni Arabs from the Shammar tribe. As a Shammari, you're either a winner or a loser in life: there is the President of Iraq who lives in a huge mansion made of marble or the low-level smuggler who loads his donkey down with black market cigarettes and lives in a mud and hay hut with a blue plastic tarp on the roof. There's not much in between. The villagers put on their best game faces when we arrived, acting like they were glad to see the Iraqi Army troops and their American brethren. Most of them have never seen their new national Army and many of the women would initially grab their kids and cower in the corners. By the time we pulled out of a town, however, the kids would be joined at the hip with the IA and the village elders would be asking how their young men could join. It turned into a great PR event and we promised things that we knew we could immediately make good on, things like fuel, generators, new wells, or medical screenings that were easy to provide and would go a long way towards goodwill.

Although most of the homes were built with mud and hay, the small villages were usually clean and devoid of the characteristic shit puddles that line the roads in the bigger towns. Sadaam took care of these guys, too, and we'd see the occasional $100,000 John Deere tractor parked in a courtyard that was a gift from the former regime to buy the displaced Sunnis peace (usually the tractors didn't work due to a lack of spare parts and mechanics, so, much like the equipment we give to the IA, once a tractor breaks it's done for good). At the end of each day, we set up our assembly areas in the grain fields bounded by the canals. The IA initially impressed me when they jumped out with their e-tools (shovels) and started digging holes (in the past, the first thing they would do is lay out their colorful flowered mattresses and bed down). I thought they learned how to dig fighting positions or maybe even trenches to piss in; however, they soon proceeded to pull out their foam pads, lie down, and start huge bonfires in the freshly-dug hole. Since our soldiers don't use any lights at night in an assembly area in the middle of Iraq, I thought at least the enemy would aim their mortars or RPG's at the IA fires rather than at our unobserved positions. That thought was immediately overcome with the reality that any rounds will end up hitting us because the bad guys would aim at the fires, miss, and inadvertently hit the disciplined guys who are silently hanging out in the dark. The nights only got down to about thirty-five degrees, but I bedded down on the hood of my Humvee to capture the heat spilling off the engine while it lasted and wondered how I could be colder here than on the bluffs outside of Colorado Springs during a January blizzard.

Our days consisted of peaceful strolls through the towns, meeting and greeting and speaking with the Mukhtars or Sheikhs in charge of the local area. The Iraqis, whether they are the ones who lay out the bombs or the ones who don't mind you being in their country, are very hospitable and thoughtful when you're a guest in their home. We had a lot of the hot and sweet tea and strong, dark coffee in the 30-plus villages we visited. I still don't totally trust the sanitation of the cups, so I always apply a generous amount of Chapstick before partaking in the drinks. One day, a group of us was sitting in a small café in town chatting with the owner and some turkeys wandered in. I casually inquired as to the cost per turkey and how many people one of them could feed. That night, the thoughtful owner sent us a message inviting us back for a turkey dinner, which I hesitantly picked at while thinking about the bird flu that was recently discovered in nearby Turkey.

I had a memorable experience in one little town when we ran into an ex-Iraqi Army Colonel who had served under Sadaam and fled north when the American forces entered Baghdad in 2003. A group of us (American and IA) sat in his backyard among the eucalyptus trees on a hill overlooking the vast desert leading to Syria in possibly the only grass yard for hundreds of miles. His kids brought out some lawn chairs and Chai tea. I was almost falling asleep in the cool breeze with the sun warming my face and his 4-year-old son kept playfully poking my Ranger tab as if he were an instructor back at Fort Benning and I was nodding off on guard duty. The Colonel and the current IA Commander were telling us war stories and they both knew many of the same soldiers from the former glory days. Our visit brought these two together like a little reunion. As many arm-chair Americans now believe, the Colonel said our biggest mistake in the war was disbanding the former Iraqi Army and the new government should force all of the old officers to come back and serve. If the old officers volunteered then they would be targeted for death, but forcing them back would provide a convenient excuse and allow them to save face, which is the most important aspect of life for most of the people. I didn't want to rain on his parade by mentioning that the old Army demonized 80 percent of the population for 30 years and that these 80 percent probably wouldn't be ecstatic to see the same leaders coming back on the public dole. These old officers were entertaining, though, as they recalled their war stories of how the food was so bad that they'd live on bread and onions and the bread was always full of rocks (to make it look fuller) and worms (because it was so aged). The soldiers used to joke that the Americans would surround a ball of bread thinking that it was a grenade. The Army was Iraq's only source of national pride and it was completely run down since the Gulf War in 1991. As one Iraqi Army officer told me, Sadaam had a difficult balancing act to look strong to Iran and innocent to the rest of the world and the threat of WMD was all that he really had. The Ministry of Defense came out last week and announced that former

Army members with the rank of Major or below will be allowed to return. The Colonel was right, though—a group of 40 ex-IA officers and soldiers trying to rejoin the Army were killed by a car bomber at a Baghdad recruiting site a couple of days after our conversation.

As we closed in on the Syrian border we ran into more diverse and larger towns, occupied by both Arabs and Kurds. I spent a little time at our base camp in Rabiah, a city of about 40,000 that remains a trashy and odd-smelling place that is heavily polluted by the trucks entering from Syria. This is one of those towns that maintain its shit puddles, complete with donkeys, cows, dogs, kids, sheep, ducks, and chickens floundering around in them. Our camp by the border checkpoint is quaint, but small. You could run a lap around it in about a minute and it's close enough to town that a kid could toss a grenade over the walls, but the guys stationed here love it. One day while I was at the border entry point, thirteen trucks full of dead chickens came across and our engineers were called out to dig a huge hole and burn the poultry, thus adding another interesting stench that stretched to the city limits.

Business seemed to be booming in all of the markets across our area. The gas stations lining the roads are particularly amusing. A gas station in Iraq consists of a kid sitting on his father's car with five or six two-gallon jugs of fuel and a one-liter water bottle cut at the top to measure and dispense it (gas is still subsidized by the government and only costs about a nickel per liter, equivalent to 20 cents or so a gallon). I asked one kid why there was a line of a dozen cars waiting for one vendor while the 30 or so vendors within throwing distance had no customers. Apparently, some stations are prone to watering down the gas to increase profits, so reputation is everything in this business. The cheap subsidized gas also causes the locals to take a chance running the border for some quick cash in Syria, where they can get four to five times their price at the risk of being detained or shot by either the Iraqi or Syrian border guards or detained by us. A donkey rents out for a couple of bucks a night and it could carry up to 20 gallons, so another business is created by the guys renting out the donkeys. One little village that has hundreds of donkeys walking the streets is named "Donkey Town" and the tribe, named by the people themselves, is called the "Donkey Tribe". Sadaam's government heavily repressed most of the villages along the border and the only business that ran in their families for generations was trading. Now they are called smugglers instead of traders and it's hard to blame them for trying to make a living, but we're shutting down all their traffic nonetheless and trying to inundate them with civil projects in the place of lost smuggling revenues. The price of sheep skyrocketed in Syria during Ramadan, so the border police would capture thousands of sheep along with the smugglers as they crossed illegally (400 sheep in a herd can fetch a lucrative $80,000). They have a big spread in our joint communications center back in Sinjar every time they make a big catch—I always try to get there first and rip off a handful before everyone sticks their nasty fingers into the meat.

It was pleasant to be out and about with the group of young guys who man the three Humvees that make up our security detail. They even play the old "Doorknob" game that I remember from my high school days—if someone farts the others get to punch him until he touches a doorknob. In this case they call it "Door Latch" because there are no doorknobs out here. These are the same soldiers who are incredibly competent in their jobs and quick-thinking on the ground; one of the guys last month in Tal Afar even told his driver to back over a fence to kill an enemy fighter who tossed a grenade at their Bradley from over the wall. Our medic-turned-translator, a Syrian named Specialist Al who just returned from leave with his new status as a U.S. citizenship (the guys call him "Narise" because of his big nose), is especially entertaining whenever we stop to speak to the locals as he pulls out his "breathers" (cigarettes) to befriend the crowds.

One night we took a trip south to Tal Afar through the mountains and the guys were joking that it was like being in a bad Halloween movie. We were driving down some alleyways trying to find a bypass in a small village called Avgani (a name given by the Kurds that means "Smelly Water" in Arabic) and the ghostly atmosphere provided the perfect backdrop for a vampire or werewolf flick. The worst part about traveling down these narrow, winding mountain roads and through the small towns is that, due to my position as the Intel guy, I always recall where all of the past attacks have happened—each and every roadside bomb and hit-and-run ambush (always against the Iraqis—this enemy is cunning but not very bold). Illumination was near zero and most of the police check points we passed were vacant; those that were manned may or may not have been occupied by cops—just guys with AK's standing on the sides of the road in trench coats and sweat suits and all kinds of non-standard attire. Instead of the usual groups of kids waving at us, all we saw winding along the mountain roads were wild dogs, field mice, and the occasional group of scary-looking men covered with hoods or knit caps peering out at us from behind the decrepit cinder block buildings. Over the past few months, our Regiment's engineers did a great job of scraping the sides of the roads along the 60-kilometer route, making it a little easier to scan the landscape for unusual objects that could be housing an IED. Moving through the market area was a different story, though, as the trash and thick shit puddles could conceal an entire human body, let alone a bomb concocted out of an old RPG round. The highways here (we call them main supply routes) aren't what one would normally envision when you think of a highway—some are simply one-lane dirt roads that barely fit a sedan, let alone a Humvee or Bradley. We safely arrived into the base on the far side of Tal Afar and the biggest disappointment for the guys was that the chow hall closed at 9 p.m., so there would be no cheeseburgers or Baskin Robbins.

The biggest morale killer of the war is an IED. It's just so impersonal, as even the generic name is made into an acronym. You can be as vigilant as you want while driving around in the towns and on the dirt roads, but the bombs are so easy to slip in and detonate that it eventually comes down to luck. The suicide bombers and VBIED's come in a close second and third—while walking around the towns talking to the people and playing with the kids I often find myself wondering when they will start strapping suicide vests on the children and detonating their own relatives from around the corner. We've already seen 10-year-olds throw hand grenades and dig holes for the IEDs, so it isn't too far-fetched to resort to that tactic and pay a family a couple of grand for their grief. We've been doing a great job at finding and destroying huge caches of artillery rounds and that helps, but the best and possibly only way to locate or prevent an IED is to gain the trust of the locals to tell you where they are and that's a bit difficult in a country that has a love-hate relationship with you (they love our money and local security, but hate us being in their country). All of the Kurdish areas remain bomb-free and that's largely because they are the 20 percent who do want us here and freely tell the Iraqi security forces or American soldiers about any suspicious people in their towns. It sure makes fighting the war and rebuilding (or building in most cases, because there was nothing to start with) much easier.

It's just not as fun to kick a soccer ball with the kids on Market Street when you are checking out everyone's chests for bulges indicating a suicide vest and watching the crowd to see who is keying their cell phone pad. I've been lucky since I've been in Iraq, though. Before last week, the closest I've come to being near a bomb was in Baghdad, coming "home" from the Triangle on MSR Tampa when a suicide bomber struck the convoy behind mine. Last week, we were driving along in our three-vehicle convoy and a helicopter pilot checking out the route in front of us clued us in to some suspicious rocks on the side of the road. We passed the area in question and pulled up alongside the rocks to allow the gunners to get a good look through the binoculars. My Humvee blocked the road to the north and the trail Humvee blocked traffic in the south while the SCO's vehicle drove up closer to inspect the mound and then fire at it to knock aside the debris (I had to call my driver back into the vehicle when he was taking a leak just in case the mound detonated from the .50 cal's penetration). The rounds kicked aside some brick and exposed a couple of artillery shells, so we called the ordinance disposal team and then raced off into the desert to question a Bedouin family and search the saddles on their donkeys for a triggering device. The pilot who spotted the IED is now owed a bottle of Scotch by the other pilots as part of their internal rewards system.

The post-election excitement out here was fun to follow. Our province (Ninewa) turned out to be the swing vote state, kind of like the Ohio or Florida of Iraq. It was one of three provinces (out of 17) that voted 'No' to the Constitution, but the 45-55 vote wasn't enough to gain the two-thirds 'No' votes needed to defeat it. Being the swing vote state, it seemed like it was Iraq's "hanging chad" as the claims of fraud were mostly leveled at the Kurdish groups here. The Kurds make up the majority in the province with the Sunni in a close second. The Kurds are more politically organized and efficient and have near-100 percent turnouts. The other interesting dynamic of the vote here was the enemy telling people "vote, but if you vote 'Yes' we will kill you"—not an effective message when the bad guy is unable to look over your shoulder to confirm your selection. Since the Referendum, there have been over three times the number of political parties (225) registered for the upcoming Parliamentary elections compared to last January's elections. I don't doubt that there will be an unbelievable turnout of more than 80 percent in December. The people here really do embrace democracy, even if they don't realize it and still vote the way their clerics or terrorists tell them. There is something special about that purple ink that is used to counter voter fraud. The purple seems to empower and energize them—once the people stick their finger in it after voting they smile and happily show it to us for days until the die rubs off. One of the big changes that the parties learned from the last election is to campaign using their number or symbol rather than their name so that the illiterate will easily recognize the party on the ballot. Whatever new government does arise hopefully allows for some economic progress, religious freedom, non-discriminatory opportunities, and freedom from repression that will create a more difficult environment for our enemy to recruit the mostly young, poor, and uneducated men with nothing in their life except hatred. It certainly can't do any worse in the quest for a less violent world than the past regime provided.

Despite all of the recent fun and amusement, even the most optimistic person out here can become jaded after nine months in Iraq and I've started to see a lot of screen-savers coming on (another Army euphemism that describes the glazed look as soldiers are tuning out). You become numb to the good things and the bad things, like the bombs or trying to get the Iraqis to take responsibility for their actions instead of just saying "Inshallah", start driving you nuts. We have such a revolving door policy with detainees that I think most people believe that even Sadaam is going to get released and returned to Baghdad. The Iraqi government didn't do us any favors when they conducted mass releases from Abu Ghraib over Ramadan that allowed some of our ex-detainees to return home. Basically, the detainees merely had to sign a statement saying that they will become productive citizens of Iraq. The good people become much less inclined to provide witness testimony and statements once they see their indicted neighbors, friends, and relatives return after a few days of detainment.

As for the good, since February 2005 the U.S. has turned over 27 forward operating bases to Iraqi control, either to their Army or to the government, to do whatever they want with them (one of Sadaam's garish mansions in his hometown of Tikrit was just handed over to the people and it will likely become a tourist site). Abu Ghraib will be gone next year and the Iraqis will control their own prisoners. We're doing everything right to get out of here; it just takes time, though, and that's one thing Americans don't like to spend. I'm optimistic about the December elections, but I know there's going to be a lot of assassinations prior to the vote now that the candidates' names are published. We'll see a lot more bombings in a last-ditch effort to undermine anything remotely involved in the political process and stability. In the meantime, we have almost 100 projects under development in our area, mostly schools, hospitals, government buildings, and wells. The job creation from the contracts and hiring of cops, soldiers, border patrol, customs, and other government jobs have started to create a trickle-down expansion as more people have money to shop and eat out, which creates the restaurants, service industries, car dealerships and mechanics, and all of the suppliers for these industries.

As the days drone on I do find myself sitting in meetings where we are discussing how to rid their governments of corruption or talk someone into testifying to put a bad guy away and I find myself not caring as much as I used to. I just keep thinking that in a few months none of this will be my problem and I'll be out playing in a park with the kids and planning our next vacation like hundreds of millions of average Americans. I'll be able to sit on a leather couch and complain that the A/C is too cold and read the paper with a Starbucks with caramel and not have to worry about someone wishing to lop my head off.

The new changes around here have us taking control of more land; we now operate in an area the size of South Carolina and it wouldn't surprise me if someday we find ourselves running into the Marines way down along the Euphrates River in Al Anbar Province. One of our visitors recently commented that our Squadron basically controls all of Northwest Iraq. We still don't warrant any Kellogg Brown & Root support (and the accompanying Thursday night steak and lobster) and it looks like we won't while we're here. So, unlike the big bases, we clean our own toilets, fill our own water from our own wells, burn our own crap and trash, haul in and cook our own food (our cooks are some of the only cooks in the Army who actually do their job), and run our own morale activities like the Internet café and PX. A new theater and gym are taking root in Tal Afar while we just had a contract denied to build a roof over the outdoor chow hall. My roommate, our Signal Officer, just went to Mosul for an X-ray on his head and came back relaxed and refreshed after what turned into a four-day vacation. He said that he went to a movie in their theater one night and it was like being back home in a mall. He couldn't even remember the name of the picture (some new release) because it was so nice to just sit in there for a couple of hours with a bag of popcorn and a cold Coke and just vegetate. The soldiers and contractors waiting for phones there sit on leather couches and watch flat-screen TV's and listen to announcements about karaoke night and the upcoming intramural soccer league.

The amazing thing is that, despite the grumblings here about still burning our shit and eating powdered egg and cheese whiz omelets for breakfast every morning, recent surveys on quality of life issues showed that our guys are happier than soldiers on these big bases. A couple of our mechanics did build a new ping-pong table the other day—it is a piece of plywood painted white set atop some packing crates and adorned with a net made of a dozen Coors Near-Beer cans. We're still waiting for an MWR (Morale Welfare & Recreation) gym set from Turkey that was ordered a couple of months ago. The latest word on that order is the Turkish drivers dropped the load off to an unknown American in a uniform at the border, so someone in Iraq is enjoying the weights and treadmills. Hooch improvement is currently as popular here as kitchen and bath remodeling is in the States. The Camp Mayor put out word to everyone that he had extra waterproof roofs like the ones the pilots nailed atop their plywood. In the next breath he says, "You know...the ones that blew away the other night during the sandstorm". Guys with extra time on their hands build themselves some remarkable rooms. The best ones are called Taj Mal Hooches—high ceilings, carpeting, and brick and rubble walkways. Sergeant Sal, the same guy who procured our Tiger school bus from the Colorado ski resort, built his new room in the extra 100 square-foot space under the guard tower on the operation center's roof. He lined the sides with Plexiglas windows so he could command a beautiful 360-degree view of the valley and the place ended up looking like an upscale condominium. We almost lost our upscale eatery, Mike's Restaurant, last week for continued health violations and I thought I would have to remain content with the catfish-in-a-bag and carrots on Saturdays and processed pork ribs on Wednesdays. One astute young soldier mentioned that our own mess hall wouldn't pass a health inspection with all the flies laying eggs in the fruit that is placed outside on the tables. Mike was given another shot at cleaning his place up and, although it remains an ongoing-concern, they continue to dish out tasty schwarmas.

My sister asked about life at the camp for the few women we have here. I remember when we first arrived in Baghdad and the big news at the time was the ambush of a civilian contractor's convoy east of the city by 50 well-armed fighters. The small group of military police escorting the convoy fought back and killed 40 and captured another eight. Half of the MP squad on the escort mission were women. I thought that would have quelled the discussion of women operating near the "front" lines, but I was wrong and that argument is still alive. As far as I'm concerned it's a non-issue. The great thing about the Army is that everyone is treated and assimilated the same, regardless of sex, race, ability, intelligence, or religion, so life really isn't any different for them. Our camps in Biaj and Rabiah don't have any women; the five females here in Sinjar are all enlisted and have jobs supporting base operations, like water purification, fixing the helicopters, and medical service. The count was six until one of the married women went home on leave and got pregnant, so she was pulled back to the rear in Colorado the day after she found out. The women on camp pull a 12-hour shift doing their job every day like most of the support people, live in the same areas as everyone else in rooms separated by plywood or brick, and use the same shower tents and plywood toilets that everyone else uses. I see them doing their jobs and eating chow and sitting around laughing with members of their squads and the only time I ever thought it would be tough to be a woman out here was when we were still using the piss tubes before the port-a-johns were delivered. One of the five females is a helicopter mechanic married to the SCO's driver and he says the only thing she hates about this place is that the female shower time is limited to a half-hour in the morning and evening. Even though these two are married they still live apart in their separate plywood boxes and have limited private time together.

One thing I really enjoy and find relaxing out here is my evening walk to chow. It's very peaceful when the sun is going down and burning a colorful purple and red picture into the horizon and fires are dotting the camp's landscape as the soldiers light up the day's trash, shit, and classified documents. I'll always remember this walk when I leave here: hop over the concertina wire while balancing on a large pipe, cross the helicopter flight line (looking both ways in case one of the silent Kiowas is sneaking in to land), skip across the large boulders laying across another strand of concertina, walk through 100 meters of crushed buildings and rubble, hop down into a wadi that is becoming a little nature reserve from the well's runoff, pass the water well dug by the Turks, stroll through the outside storage area full of crates containing bottled water and next week's food rations, and finish up along a sidewalk made of crushed brick and former concrete roofs to the alleyway between the medics and the motor pool. The walk is quiet and it's one of the only respites from the constant roar of generators and vehicles. It's also the only time we see birds around here. There are only two trees on the camp and both of them lay in the line of fire of the .50 caliber machine gun in the tower, so most of the birds hang out in the next best sanctuaries of the wadi and next to the boxes of rations that are shaded by the buildings.

We finished our Black Hole operations at noon on November 10th, the day of my 4th wedding anniversary. Jen and I were married over Veteran's Day Weekend in Lake Tahoe, just two months after 9-11. I remember all of the worries that many of our guests had in getting to the wedding so soon after the attacks, back when people were afraid to fly. Those worries sure faded quickly and I hope what we're doing will ensure that Americans never have to be afraid to travel to another wedding again. Jen took the kids to our favorite international restaurant (McDonald's) to celebrate the occasion in Colorado Springs. After spending our 2nd anniversary in the Tucson NICU after the kids were born and our 3rd anniversary apart when I was out training we figure that our 5th one will be great as long I'm home and we can get our Big Mac combos together. It will be fun to be home over a Veteran's Day when we can start a little tradition of taking the kids to a national cemetery wherever we're at and placing flags on the headstones of our country's warriors. Jen went to the Air Force-Army football game at the Air Force Academy last week and said she cried during the emotional halftime show honoring a brigade from the 2nd Infantry Division who just returned from Iraq. These guys spent a year in Korea away from their families and then were sent to Iraq for a year while their families were relocated to Colorado Springs to await their return. Cade and McKenna celebrated their second birthday at Red Robins restaurant on October 30th and were embarrassed when the waiters sung to them and Cade remains terrified of the lady in the bird costume, just as he is with the Chicken Man yelling at cars next to Wings Stop. The kids are growing up very well-mannered and love to share and help each other. McKenna goes upstairs to retrieve Cade's paci (pacifier) whenever he forgets it and Jen said that they were watching my video and she walked up to the TV to offer me her paci. McKenna learned to say her own name (either Kenna or Mackie) and they are currently headstrong into the phase of putting words together—Cade looks up to the moon and points it out saying "moon", then when the clouds cover it he says "where go"? Jen tells him that I'm looking at the same moon.

With Thanksgiving coming up, I'd just like to end with an Iraqi saying wishing everyone a great holiday. "Dahman"—may your table always be full.

December 13, 2005:

Thanksgiving in the Desert

"I exhort you to take part in the great combat, which is the combat of life, and greater than every other earthly conflict." Plato

The big event over the last month was the highly-anticipated arrival of our newly-named replacements as the leadership from a battalion out of the 1st Armored Division made the short flight from their base in Germany to scout out their future home in Sinjar. Not only did their three-day stay increase our morale by confirming that someone higher up doesn't have a plan to extend us, but it also forced us to make some quick quality-of-life improvements so our replacements wouldn't think that we lived in squalor over the past year. A couple of days before the scheduled visit, a convoy of passenger busses pulled up to the front gate and 50 Turks piled out. Two days later, and just a day before the arrival of the 1st AD, eight huge circus tents sprouted up around camp; two for the mess hall, one for the new gym, and the remainder to serve as excess tents to give the soldiers an option to move out of the rubble and under waterproof roofs for the rainy season.

The most dramatic improvement has been saved for the new mess hall. We used to have more flies on the food than seasoning, but the colder weather and tents have changed that a little bit. While the tents don't provide the same serene atmosphere that the outdoor café did, they do keep us much warmer and dryer. The gym is also a huge improvement—now you can actually bench without staring up at the large cement block caught in the camouflage net that surprisingly never dropped. The gym also has two real ping-pong tables (the net never showed up for one of them, but that doesn't stop the soldiers from playing on it), so the old white plywood table with near-beer cans for a net has been relegated to the annals of early base camp lore. The new ping-pong table has been a savior as a mental release and I've honed cat-like reflexes to further intimidate the flies and mosquitoes throughout the day. There was a foosball table in the gym tent, but it was rendered non-mission capable faster than the toaster in the chow hall (which even had a sign over it stating "Do not put ice cream in toaster" to ward off its destruction). Two days after all of the tents were in place we received the first hard, all-night rainfall. This was the camp's first real test and our jimmy-rigged structures failed miserably, to the point where we now walk on pallets upon entry into the Oz Market courtyard to stay out of the standing water. It was like watching a barn-raising the next morning as soldiers occupied every roof on camp nailing down new tarps and canvas or any other scraps they could find to cover newly-discovered leaks. The basement housing the TOC and my office held up fine and the moats we dug out along the interior walls turned out to be unnecessary, at least this time around.

We celebrated Thanksgiving a few days after the big rainstorm. The five frozen turkeys that fed almost 600 people couldn't quite compare to the 2003 celebration when the Outback Steakhouse flew out some cooks and real chow to feed the Squadron in Al Qaim (they even brought the Blooming Onion appetizer with them), but it was a great buffet nonetheless. The turkeys were supplemented with a few real hams and roast beef and served up by the senior enlisted and officers. The officers also pulled guard on the gates and observation posts for a 24-hour period to give the soldiers a well-deserved day off. It turned out to be a gorgeous day and it felt like the closest thing to a weekend that we've experienced since deploying. Our weekly mail convoy arrived early that morning and I had about a dozen packages that were quickly dispensed out under the decorated and lit plastic Christmas tree in my office. Everything was a hit and the Twinkies and Ding Dongs were devoured within minutes. After my late afternoon meal at the designated Headquarters time slot, I donned my gear and took my post guarding the main gate and struggled to stay awake in the warm sun with a full stomach. A group of soldiers played Turkey Bowl II in the dirt lot next to the helipad (the inaugural 2003 football game was played in a rail yard in Al Qaim). Most of the rocks were cleared from the field or became visible after the moon dust hardened from the rain and only two injuries occurred after receivers ran into the barbed wire surrounding the dirt lot. I was reminiscing of the last time I pulled guard, when I was a Private in Germany and the Red Army Faction bombed a disco in Berlin, killing two American soldiers, and threatened to blow up more American bases in Germany. It was during the Christmas holidays in Nurnberg and I sat in my foxhole during a blizzard watching the drunks stumble out of the Kris Kringle Market. I was trying to stay awake back then, too, only this time I had live ammo. It was peaceful being a gate guard, not having to think, and listening to the cheers and laughter from the game. That's what Thanksgiving is all about and it was as much as I could've hoped for in this place. I wish it was laughter from my family, but for some of the guys this is their family. A group of us ended the day sitting on MRE boxes smoking some Cuban cigars (the international cigar trade seems to be thriving here) as the sun went down on the holiday.

As far as the war goes, the entire Regiment has been faring well over the past three months. It was really quiet for all of us until mid-November when 3rd Squadron in Baghdad lost four guys at a traffic checkpoint in South Baghdad after a car bomb attack and 2nd Squadron lost one soldier to an IED in Tal Afar. Our last two deaths, in early December, have been more normal, if you can refer to anything in Iraq as normal. A soldier attached to us from a unit out of Georgia was killed in a vehicle rollover just north of Tal Afar, on the same winding mountain roads that I found so eerie last month. A civilian car was barreling down the narrow road coming the other way and the soldier's Humvee flipped into a wadi after the driver swerved. A week after his death, a soldier in Tal Afar went to the medics with a common case of the 24-hour NVD's (nausea, vomiting, and diarrhea) and was put on bed rest. He died the next day from pneumonia. We have seen quite a few medical evacuations for strange incidents up north in Rabiah and the soldiers in the TOC rolled out a chart highlighting the days and hours since the last medevac to mock the recurring incidents: the roll-up of incidents includes a cat bite, a broken leg from a football game on the asphalt helipad, a cold, and a sprained wrist. I almost had a million-dollar injury myself when I sliced my little toe on a tent stake while walking to the shower in my flip flops, but some super glue cured it.

It's been nice to travel around to the villages and see some sense of peace returning, at least to our little area of Iraq. The activity on Thursday evenings, when all of the weddings are celebrated, is especially enjoyable. It seems like everyone in town is out on the streets and in the markets wearing their best silk clothing and guns and firecrackers are popping off at parties across the desert (nothing compared to the amount of gunfire that went off two nights ago when Iraq beat Syria in a televised soccer game for the West Asian championship—46 people in Baghdad were injured from celebratory fire). Even the smallest towns are plastered with campaign posters that brighten the atmosphere. I always like to chat up the locals when we're out. I asked some people on the street in Sinjar what their favorite shows are now that everyone is allowed to have satellite TV. The three shows that they agreed were the best are *Friends, Dr. Phil,* and *Desperate Housewives.* No more "all Sadaam, all the time" TV on the four state-controlled channels. The best line that an Arab told me is that the crazy Judge Judy should be trying Sadaam. One of the interesting rumors floating around is that the Americans don't want Iraq to be totally safe because we want to keep the terrorists here so they don't move to the States. Conspiratorial, yes, but not as interesting as the former rumors of our sunglasses allowing us to see through women's clothing or our helicopters seeing through the buildings or the "electronic shields" around the Humvee causing their RPG round to miss.

We've been continuing to put the Iraqi face on everything we do, from the non-violent food handouts, school openings, and medical fairs to the not-so-violent raids and cordon and searches. We're relegating ourselves to a backup and logistical role as much as possible. Some things will never change, though, and they depend on us for logistical, maintenance, and communications support. From everything I've ever heard speaking to soldiers and officers in the old Army, none of that ever worked in the past either and if a vehicle battery went bad then it was time for a new vehicle or if a hand mike on a radio went bad then it was time for a new radio. All of the talk in Congress about the failure to move IA units to Level I status is entertaining because I strongly doubt that Sadaam's Army would have met the criteria and they were arguably the most powerful Army in the Middle East. We're at the point where the IA is training the border patrol and the local police and we even had the Sinjar Hospital doctors teach everyone combat lifesaver medical courses. The three departments joined together to secure the 29 polling sites in our area of operations during the Referendum and we just melted into the background. We have 41 polling sites for the elections in two days and the Iraqis are well prepared. Yesterday, the government announced the closure of the border entry points, a nighttime curfew, and a no-roll policy inside the cities, rendering even a moving donkey cart illegal. All of the big bombings during the last elections took place between the time of the no-roll announcement and the day the policies took effect and we're now out of that period. A new change that the government announced, one that made me a very, very happy man, is that the Iraqi Army can take their own detainees and process them through the Iraqi judicial system; I'm sure there are going to be some kinks to this and the U.S. will bear the blame internationally for any future beatings, rape, or torture, but it's a good start to establishing a system of justice that has never really existed. I trust the IA to take care of their detainees—it's the Police Commando units, the wild ones we had to kick out of Tal Afar, who we have to worry about. I wonder if the Sunnis ever thought they'd be complaining to the UN or Human Rights Watch about detainee abuse.

As part of our efforts to train the IA to take over, we let their Brigade Staff plan the recent operation down south, back to Biaj. They named the mission (in Arabic) Operation Perfect Cordon, which didn't have the appeal of our name back in June when we called it Operation Biaj (pronounced "Bee-ahj") Slap. The mission to cordon and search the entire town of 5,000 people was scheduled to take five to seven days. I knew it would be a little condensed when their first draft of the order was a page and a half and basically stated that one battalion would go straight and the others would flank. One evening, our staff walked across the berm separating our camps to help them out with the orders process. Unfortunately, the Kurdish General who leads the Brigade (he's a tough old guy who is missing the tip of his index finger from his earlier days of fighting Sadaam) said he just took his boots off to lie down, so the meeting had to be rescheduled. The planning went much better the next morning, after the initial Inshallahs and a couple rehearsals, and we all headed to the city a couple of days later to put the plan into action. I rolled out with the new Lieutenant who replaced LT Rubado after he was killed by the sniper in Tal Afar. This guy is very similar—a clean-cut, respectful, well-mannered kid right out of college and the Armored Officers Course who is now driving in a tank that the soldiers in his platoon renamed "Charlie's Pride" after their former LT.

The last time I was in Biaj for a mission I slept in an animal pen and woke up surrounded by the smell of fresh manure and flicking wool off of my tongue. This time, we had a secure camp in a farm field next to the granary and yet I still awoke to the fresh smell of manure and wool blown into my mouth. Biaj is undoubtedly the most spartan and smallest of our camps. While it may take less than a minute to run a lap around our camp up north in Rabiah, the closest you can get to running a lap in Biaj is to sprint along a 100-meter straightaway in the moon dust and turn around to run back. The most popular cardio workout here is running up the 16 stories to the top of the grain silo. A small tent city of American and Iraqi soldiers sprung up on the dusty grain field, using the same canvas GP Medium tents that have been standard Army issue since WW II. The soldiers still have MRE's for lunch, but they can now get a hot breakfast and dinner by serving themselves from the mermite cans in a chow tent that seats about 20. The camp is close enough to town that the 5 a.m. call-to-prayer from the nearby mosque serves as an alarm clock and an RPG fired from the village can easily hit the motor pool. The latest leader's dilemma here is whether or not to limit the number of times a soldier craps to every other day so they can dispose of the waste efficiently. One of our new soldiers, a Reservist who just arrived in country as an attachment to collect intelligence from locals, remarked, "Almost three years after taking Baghdad, I didn't think there were still places like this". Despite all of the tough conditions, the soldiers in the Cavalry troop here love it and don't want to be anywhere else.

The operation itself turned out to be an effective and amusing training event. The planned weeklong operation ended up taking less than 24 hours as two battalions of Iraqis scurried house to house. Starting the operation on Friday, the Muslim's day of prayer, caused the biggest glitch in the plan. The locals started moving to the mosques at the mid-morning call-to-prayer and the Arab 2nd Battalion Commander suggested we let them go pray while the Kurdish 3rd Battalion Commander suggested we keep them in their homes. The Kurdish General decided to let them pray as long as they didn't move from a non-searched area to a searched area and the operation continued. The Iraqis did capture four men who were on our Black List and found a large cache of missiles and RPG warheads that surely would have been turned into IED's at some point. And there weren't any Iraqi death blossoms (where they all start shooting wildly once they hear a shot, causing other surrounding units to shoot wildly in response like spectators doing "The Wave" at a football game), which was our greatest concern. All in all, the mission greatly increased their confidence and operational experience without anyone getting killed and I only had to spend two freezing nights in the manure.

The people of Biaj, almost all of whom are Sunnis, are part of the 80 percent or so of Iraqis who don't want the U.S. here, but they are becoming comfortable with the mostly-Sunni IA battalion stationed at the granary with us and that's what matters. Most of the 80 percent who don't want us here know that we can't leave right now, just like most Americans still understand. I think that we will all save face by December 2006 when the UN Security Council Resolution authorizing us to be here comes up for another extension and the new Iraqi government will be pressured to vote against it. Our departure is at the top of the list for most of the Iraqi political parties, but so is security and right now you can't have one without the other. Politics, for the most part, is rarely discussed among all of us at the camp. I guess there are just too many other things to dwell upon and our conversations are more subdued and unimportant. We discuss things like which DVD series is better between the mindless entertainment of the O/C or the intense 24, would you rather be really hot or really cold, single or married, kids or no kids, pork rib or meat loaf T-rats, Carl's Jr. burger or Sonic, and what's going to be your first meal and where you're going on block leave when we return to the States.

Everyone just assumes that if we pulled out of here the fighting won't end and they'll kill each other off like the Croats, Serbs, and Bosnian Muslims did in Bosnia-Herzegovina before the UN finally intervened. There are too many parties that want an invitation to this dance, both Iraqi and foreign. Syria, Jordan, and Saudi will be vying for the Sunni influence, Iran will continue to align closely with the governing Shia, and the Kurds will have to fend off the Turks, Syrians, and Iranians because those countries all have a sizable and restless Kurdish minority to control. Since most of the enemy here are fighters who are resisting our occupation, you would logically think that the easiest way for them to get rid of us is to stop fighting so we'll claim all is secure and leave. The fighting continues, though, partly because some of those countries don't want to become the terrorists' next focal point and they continue to do their part to maintain instability and partly because logic just doesn't apply here. A group of influential Sunni clerics just released a fatwa saying that it is the Sunnis' religious duty to vote and that their actions will hasten our departure from their country; hopefully that will help, and hopefully those clerics have a powerful group of bodyguards to stave off a certain death that will come along with their fatwa.

We are confident and optimistic that the Iraqis will be able to take over in our area very soon. However, the U.S. military, for the most part, is full of optimists. I remember back in Saudi Arabia when my platoon was sitting around one night in the middle of the desert outside of Dhahran debating if our 35-man light infantry platoon could take over Bahrain, which lay just across the causeway (my favorite saying in Saudi was "Allah can't see over the causeway"—thousands of Saudis would travel to Bahrain for booze, dancing, and imported women on the weekends). A couple of months ago back in Tal Afar, our Support Squadron, which consists of mechanics, truck drivers, doctors, cooks, and supply specialists, conducted a raid on a little village outside of the city when all of the combat Squadrons were tapped out with their guys being used elsewhere. The non-combat soldiers didn't even flinch and planned and conducted the mission the next day. That's part of the draw of the military; you think you can do anything or you'll find a way to do it and the attitude sticks with you for the rest of your life. I don't think anyone would be scared or hesitant if we were told to take a thousand guys and conduct a frontal assault on Iran. The running joke is that the guys who are tasked to stay behind in Kuwait and wash vehicles as part of the port detail would even take care of Iran if they were handed the mission.

I'm generally a very positive person, but I'm even tiring of Iraq. We've "had our suck on" (as the famous Army saying goes) since September of 2004 when we started training hard for the deployment. I look back at those long nights and consecutive weeks in the field and wonder why we didn't focus more on spending time with the family, tucking in the kids, and being around for important holidays and events. Instead, we spent months away from the home to train on tasks that we could've perfected in the backyard—things like getting hit by mortars and pulling people out of their sleeping bags at 3 a.m. to drag fake casualties to the fake helicopter, yet I can count on one hand the number of mortar attacks against our three camps and none of their hit-and-run shots have been close enough to worry about. We trained on putting down riots outside the gates and the closest thing we've had to a riot was a surge for jobs when we first arrived and a pro-U.S. demonstration in Tal Afar. We trained at reacting to small arms fire and RPG ambushes, but the enemy is too smart and unwilling to die so they largely stopped those. We trained at getting hit by IED's and it turns out that the enemy is long gone by the time a patrol hits one, so the convoys either blow past it or, if someone is hurt or killed, forms a perimeter to evacuate the casualties.

The intense training is important, but soldiers' personal problems seemed to take the forefront of the leadership challenges out here. One Lieutenant told me that when he arrived in our unit last December his guys were already smoked from the training and that was before the 14-hour days started in January and February to finalize our move. Now, the main sources of his platoon's problems arise from a struggling relationship back home. Freebo, the almost-retired NCO who runs the PX and just got hit by an IED when he went on his monthly inventory run to Mosul, says it best about how much it sucks here when he compares it to a post-retirement job he has lined up—he gets to move to Hastings, Nebraska and will be paid to cut the balls off of pigs on an assembly line. While all of us are getting excited about going home, one of my assistants just arrived on our last personnel re-supply flight. The LT was declared non-deployable for the past nine months due to an irregular heartbeat. He's since provided the place with a nice burst of energy, excitement, and curiosity, kind of like all of us once had back in March. He's a lucky man—he's only here for a month before he has to go back to Colorado to testify in a murder trial from the first deployment when a former Iraqi General died in a detention center. I guess the only time you can refer to someone who has a heart condition and has to testify in a murder trial as lucky is when you're out here.

As we get closer to tasting our own freedom in mid-February, I've found it harder and harder to pull my eyes away from the pictures of the kids hanging in my office and hooch and thinking about how much I've missed. Jen says that Cade has been asking to watch my video several times a day and stands at the TV and says "Daddy, Daddy", even at the expense of watching *The Wiggles*. The anticipation to hold them and let them known Daddy doesn't live inside a TV is just overwhelming. The holidays are going to be bearable just because I know we're close to getting out of here and I'll keep myself busy with the national and then local elections. It's going to be hard missing the kids' first recital on December 16th when their church group puts on a Christmas Special that opens with the 2- and 3-year-old crooners singing *Rudolph the Red-Nosed Reindeer*. Mackie sung me a little taste of *Twinkle, Twinkle, Little Star* on the phone last week and she has it down pat. Last Christmas, not long after their first birthday, they both bawled when I sat them on Santa's lap at our troop party (it didn't help that Santa was our chain-smoking arms room NCO who just spit out his chew and was likely sipping brews in the parking lot before hoisting up the kids). This year, Cade willingly sat on Santa's lap while McKenna scurried up over her mom's shoulders to escape the scary man with the big beard.

While it's been Arizona-like weather here, the blizzards and single-digit temperatures finally hit in Colorado Springs and it gave the kids their first opportunity to walk in fresh snowfall—Cade curiously and slowly made his way through it and was fine as long as he stepped in the fresh stuff, but McKenna wanted no part of it. While Mackie may seem a bit more reserved when it comes to trying out new things, she is still the outspoken, take-charge type around the home. My mom sent me a picture taken during her visit over the kids' second birthday that shows McKenna putting her hand down the back of Cade's pants to check for poop. I posted it on the whiteboard in my shop under the "Current Intelligence" section with the caption "McKenna performing area reconnaissance in Cade's drawers to confirm or deny the presence of shitty pants". Mac remains well-mannered even as she seeks out trouble, like telling Cade "sorry" immediately after slugging him and saying "excuse me" as she makes her way to ransack the bathroom drawers.

JANUARY 10, 2006:

<u>SO LOOKING FORWARD TO A NEW YEAR</u>

"I know war as few other men now living know it, and nothing to me is more revolting.
I have long advocated its complete abolition, as its very destructiveness on both friend
and foe has rendered it useless as a method of settling international disputes."
GEN Douglas MacArthur

Now that we're in the twilight of our tour, many people are a bit more hesitant to go outside the wire for the little things that once may have been important, like driving to Tal Afar for a grilled cheese sandwich or a chocolate milk shake. I've recently turned down the "opportunities" to go VBIED hunting on Election Day and looking for "guys shooting mortars" on Christmas Eve. The recent crash of a Blackhawk helicopter as it approached Tal Afar on a blustery, rainy, and cold late-night flight drives home this hesitation even more. The helicopter accident was the deadliest in Iraq since a Chinook went down in Al Anbar Province back in January of 2005. I only knew two of the 12 men (eight soldiers and four civilians) who were killed in the crash; they were both intelligence officers in the Regiment whom I often worked closely with. One of the officers was a recently-promoted Major who turned down a teaching job at West Point to come out here and the other was a bright, young Lieutenant who pestered me for a job in my shop each time I went to a meeting in Tal Afar. He was the father of three young kids and the type of guy who wanted to be out in the action and desperately wanted to escape the drudgery of Regimental staff work. I always sincerely told him that I would love to have him if it were up to me. Another Captain that was on the bird just joined us from Colorado; he was in country less than a month. The fact that we're so close to leaving makes this type of accident even tougher to take. Granted, something like this could happen at any time, even back in training in the States, and everyone is aware of that, but making it so far into the deployment and having this happen intensifies the morbidity of the whole thing. Everything that happens in Iraq seems to come down to a roll of the dice—like what seat you get in, what route you decide to go down, which vehicle in the convoy, what side or, in this case, which helicopter did you decide to jump on when running up to the landing pad.

Less than a week before the accident I found myself on a Blackhawk, flying around for a couple of hours far south of Tiger Base checking out the dry lake beds, deep ravines, and randomly-placed sheep herds of the desolate desert between here and the Euphrates River. Two days after our reconnaissance flight, we loaded up our vehicles and took off to the same area in a quest to find weapons and fighters living in no-man's land. I thought it would be great to run across any of that, but I was really hoping to come across the ruins of the walled city of Hatras, the Greek city that was built on the main trading routes just after Alexander the Great's time (supposedly it hasn't been looted like everything else that is vacated out here). Either way, I can now say that I am intimately familiar with over one-eighth of Iraq after this latest jaunt hundreds of miles to the south. The days were mostly miserable with either a murky orange or dark gray colored sky providing our backdrop (depending on if the wind was kicking up dust storms or if the rain clouds floated in and hammered us with downpours). The rains broke a four-year drought and at least the water was a blessing to the farmers. The weather was what we call "Army cold"—nothing extreme if you're back at home with some slippers and hot cocoa by the fire, but the kind of weather that makes it very uncomfortable when you're out doing Army things. All of the troops going on the mission fanned out separately across a 90-mile wide swath of land and my three-Humvee convoy was joined by three Iraqi Army trucks carrying 18 of their soldiers, who turned out to provide most of the entertainment for the rest of the trip. On the positive side, the tour was a much-needed respite from the germ-breeding grounds of the cold, uninsulated, and windowless concrete basement where I work and room where I live. To me, if you threw in some camels, sheep, and Bedouin nomads trying to keep warm in their burlap sack tents, it became similar to a heavily armed road trip across the desert from Phoenix to San Diego. We even brought along a BBQ grill (one of the combat engineers created it out of an old tool box and welded some rebar stabilizers so it would hang off the back of a Humvee), steaks, and a cooler with cold Gatorade and Cokes.

On our first stop on the way down everyone got out to stretch and I thought the Iraqi soldiers were all running out to find a place to pray as they knelt down and faced east en masse. It turned out that they just have an interesting method of shielding themselves as they piss in the 40 mph winds. We drove around for a dozen or so hours without seeing any sign of life. The greatest danger out here was probably the threat of being sucked into a deceivingly dry lakebed (especially for the IA's little Nissan pickup truck) or sinkholes like the 100-foot deep one recently found up north. Iraq has a large limestone reserve, which is good for the recently privatized Sinjar Cement Factory (Iraq's newest IPO on the Baghdad stock market), but bad if you're concerned about sinking into a wadi or lakebed. After stopping at a couple of Bedouin camps and walking several ravines, we ended up stopping on some high ground at nightfall to set in a perimeter for the night. The IA soldiers were a little surprised at our stop; something was lost in translation during their planning and they were nowhere near prepared to stay the night and had no food, water, or shelter. We were so far out in the middle of nowhere that we were undoubtedly safer than being back at the camp in Sinjar, so the BBQ was lit and the steaks rubbed down with canola oil and seasoning and the dozen of us Americans gave up a steak each to the gracious Iraqis.

Our camping trip turned into a nightmare around midnight when the rain joined the frigid winds. I covered myself and my double-layered sleeping bag with a nylon and vinyl tarp that looked fairly waterproof and I fought off the condensation build-up inside of my bag for a couple of hours until my socks started soaking up the water and I realized that I had bigger problems. I slowly pulled my feet towards the dry center a little at a time until my body took up only half a cot. It wasn't until 3 a.m., after noting the water beading off of my hair and two layers of sopping wet sleeping bags, when I finally gave in and set off into the darkness to find shelter in one of the Humvee seats that didn't already have a body or gear on it. Most of the seats were already occupied by guys who gave up earlier than I, but I moved some bags off of the driver's seat of the third vehicle I came to, covered my head with the only dry part of my sleeping bag, and caught an hour of sleep while the rain barely dripped down my neck as it filtered through the open gunner's hatch.

My long, sleepless night ended at 5 a.m. when we decided to leave the area before the Iraqi jeeps became vulnerable to the flooding. As bad as I had it, the Iraqi soldiers were worse off and had to resort to spooning together under some tarps throughout the night and then drive back in the same 30-degree, rainy weather for another nine hours in vehicles with no overhead cover. One of the IA Jeeps (Russian Waza trucks that you can buy on E-bay for a couple grand each) had no clutch, so the driver did donuts in the mud to maintain momentum whenever we stopped to figure out where to cross the flooding wadis. Their morale was surprisingly high for people on the edge of hypothermia and when we arrived at the nearest border fort our cooks had some hot coffee waiting that made their day. Two of my photo-ops on this trip describe the experience the best: one was a photo of me holding up a dead camel's leg in a ravine during a fruitless search for caches and another one showed one of our combat engineers igniting the JP-8 fuel on his pup tent at 5 a.m. after it caved in on him after a heavy night of rain.

Other than the trip south and a few meetings in Biaj and Sinjar, I haven't been out too much over the past month. I did have a chance to make what may be my last visit north of the mountains to Sununi, one of my favorite villages, to meet the city judge and finalize some plans to build them a courthouse. On the way to the village, our patrol happened upon a car wreck with four Iraqis sprawled across the asphalt, a scene that is unfortunately very common in a country where there are no rules of the road, no speed limits, stop signs, or even licensing requirements. One of our drivers was a medic who talked the injured men out of shock, taped them up, stopped the bleeding, and calmed down the wailing women. An interpreter and I walked down the line of backed-up cars to find someone with a station wagon to transport the four guys to the nearest hospital. In this area, I hoped the injured were Kurds so the hospital would treat them.

A short 30 minutes later, when the chaos calmed and the roads opened back up, our convoy continued to the town clerk's simple home on the outskirts of the city. The clerk's wife and daughter humbly set out our lunch, one of those amazing five-course goat grabs that was made a bit more difficult here because we sat on the living room floor Indian-style in a precarious position where you tried not to make the cultural mistake of showing your heels while attempting to lean over a lamb carcass and pull off a piece of hot greasy meat with both hands. One thing I really like and will miss about the people here is how well they treat their guests; even the poorest families will go out of their way to treat you like a king simply because you are a guest in their home. After the meal, we boarded our vehicles and traveled through the crowded downtown street market to tour the existing courthouse, which took about 10 seconds to peek in the door of an unfurnished room the size of a coat-closet. Then the Civil Affairs Officer and I went back out to the market and hung out, sitting on some lawn chairs with the police chief, Mayor, and judge drinking RC Colas, waiting for a local contractor to bring us a bid on the new courthouse, and hoping that nobody was going to use the poor man's nuke on us (i.e. blowing themselves up). Even in the cities that we are pretty sure are safe, it's still a little nerve-wracking when the crowd gathers around and we all find ourselves constantly scanning every hand and set of eyes, to include the police. It's interesting to listen to the city leaders chat and make fun of the Arabs about how they blindly follow their leaders—one of them (a Yezidi) said that the Arabs torture themselves by fasting for 30 days every year whereas the Yezidis only do it for three because the Arabs misinterpreted Mohammed and added a "0" to his fasting edict.

Most of our days remain largely uneventful, long, boring, and nothing close to what I ever envisioned a war to be. Each day seems to get even longer as our time in country draws down. We can go for weeks without something happening and being lulled into complacency and then an IED, car bomb, or mortars will go off and we investigate, meet people to collect information and evidence, and try to talk locals into being a witness until the case ends up cold and we find ourselves in another lull and the cycle repeats. We get lucky now and then when a bomb goes off on the people emplacing it and then the objective turns to countering any rumors circulating that it was the Americans who emplaced the IED. It's a tiring cycle and I often wonder if the Iraqis get as worn out from it as we do.

The best news that came out over the past few weeks was word of the new streamlined procedures to leave country, which no longer consist of sitting in Kuwait for a month cleaning vehicles and attending seminars on how to become a productive citizen when you arrive home. Now, it's as easy as flying home on leave with a 24-hour stop in Kuwait to clear customs to ensure you're not hauling out any war trophies or native fruits and vegetables, like the three-foot high deer made of fig that the Squadron Commander was recently given by a gracious farmer with a new well. Most of our equipment is being left in place for incoming units to quickly fall in on, so only the tanks, Bradleys, and helicopters have to be cleaned by the 10 percent of the semi-volunteers who stay behind for an extra couple of weeks (the big draw is to stay a couple of days into March so they can collect an additional month of combat pay and tax-exempt income). Another great thing about the new process is that we forego a weeklong grueling road march across the entire length of Iraq. Even though we would have seen much cooler weather than Allah granted us on our ride into Iraq last April, its one less hazard to contend with and my legs won't fall asleep after endless hours propped awkwardly on the sandbags lining the floorboard. The last convoy home for most of these guys, back in 2004 when they returned to Kuwait from Al Qaim and the deployment was all over by most accounts, was marred by a freak accident when a Lieutenant tank commander was killed as two U.S. convoys passed each other on a small road. His memory, along with events like the helicopter crash the other day, keeps everyone's head in the game.

The elections on December 15th were definitely a high for everyone, both Iraqis and Americans. The only attack against our polling sites was a small RPG hit-and-run against one of the remote sites that was guarded by the IA on the night before the election. The only attack in Tal Afar consisted of some mortar rounds directed at the Shia from a nearby Sunni neighborhood and the voters didn't even leave their lines as the rounds splashed around them. The Sunnis still think that they make up at least half the country, so anything less than half the seats in Parliament can only mean a fraudulent election to them. Hopefully the government will be announced soon so the people maintain their optimism for a happy ending—if there is one thing I've learned in life it is that optimism and hope often become self-fulfilling; the hard part is keeping that optimism and hope alive (we're even reading about that optimism and hope slipping away back in the States as the anti-war momentum picks up).

Back on Tiger Base, we had two separate incidents over the past month that could have been devastating to our own morale. In the first one, all of the ping-pong balls were lost or broken and the paddles severely disabled. Soldiers are famous for breaking things—one Sergeant Major says that "You can send Joe across the street with two ball bearings; by the time he gets across he'll have lost one and broke the other". Then the next day our suck truck broke for the second time in a couple of months, sending us back to the old days in the shower tent and plywood crappers until the truck was fixed or a replacement was found. Tony, the local Kurdish contractor and restaurant owner, quickly rented us a water truck that he "converted" into a suck truck and we were temporarily saved. I always tell people that they better use bottled water to brush their teeth rather than the water from the sink in the shower trailer because you never know how many times these supposedly sanitized water trucks were reconverted for other uses. They use the water trucks to haul anything if it makes money—after the government announced the hike in fuel prices we saw water trucks carrying around fuel. With a little bleach it can become a water truck again and without bleach it can once again become a suck truck.

Just like the entrepreneurial Kurd, a lot of soldiers are looking to capitalize on some sketchy investment opportunities before we leave by buying up thousands of dollars in Iraqi dinars in the hopes of wild appreciation. Locals have told me that home prices in the little villages outside of Tal Afar have jumped 2500 percent over the past year to cause a local housing bubble and I'm sure some guys would jump into the housing market if they could. The Roman coin business is booming, too, with the local 'terps and shop owners taking advantage of the demand to drive up the price of old coins that they claim the Romans left in the area during their dynasty, but the coins I've seen look awfully new for being so old. One thing that will never change in life is soldiers trying to make a buck—I remember back in Ranger school I sold an oatmeal cookie bar from my one MRE a day for $20 and was kicking myself later than night for it. Soldiers who get a four-day pass to Qatar are issued a dozen alcoholic drink coupons upon arrival and, rather than coming back bragging about the beautiful Persian Gulf beachfront or the new Chili's franchise, they come back and brag about how much they got for their drink coupons (or how little they stiffed another soldier for his).

The holiday period didn't exactly enliven the drab atmosphere. The weeks surrounding Christmas and New Year's consisted of cloudy, rain-soaked days with chilly breezes and dreary skies, the kind of days we used to call the "Gloom Period" back at West Point when the first sleet hit and everything would be depressing and gray all around campus—the walls, the uniforms, the sky, the river, the mood. Soldiers were walking around in a zombie-like fashion, doing a lot of daydreaming, and hacking up the "crud" caused from either the flu symptoms hitting due to the recent cold and wet streak or just from sucking in a year's worth of dust and fuel exhaust. We tried to brighten up the mood, though. The XO took a group up the mountain to chop down a Christmas tree and came back with a very large Christmas bush that was lit up outside the Oz Market and the mother of one of the mechanics sent a large plastic snowman in a bubble that inflates using a generator's back-blast and blows the snowflakes around. The highlight of my days has been watching a little shaggy gray puppy that has been playfully bounding around camp barking at the people and trucks. We're not allowed to feed or play with the wild dogs, but he's such a comfortable picture of innocence and energy out here.

Christmas itself turned out a little less than spectacular when I tossed up my Christmas Eve spaghetti dinner in the wadi while walking back from chow and went downhill fast after that. I wasn't even feeling well enough to fully appreciate Sergeant First Class Sal coming down from the rooftop a few hours later (partly because he lives on the rooftop, but it still had its appeal) wearing a Santa outfit embroidered with "S. Claus" and "U.S. Army" name tapes and dishing out candy from an Army-issue green OD laundry bag. I went to bed somewhat early that night with the chills and woke up at 1 a.m. to Gates standing over me with a red-lens flashlight asking what to do with a detainee who was just captured; he said it was snowing out and the bird that was going to fly in to pick the guy up became grounded. So, in effect, I woke up to an early white Christmas (although it melted off and turned into thick mud later that afternoon).

There were a few activities planned on Christmas Day, to include a soccer game pitting a group of our soldiers against the Iraqi Army soldiers on a dirt field about 100 feet away from where the car bomb went off when we first occupied the camp. I opted for the ping-pong tournament at the gym tent, which was on the way to the medic's building where I could find enough drugs to overwhelm all of my flu symptoms. Fortunately for me to hasten my trip to Doc's hooch, I drew a "local national interpreter" (meaning a guy from the area who can speak anything remotely close to English and isn't afraid to work with us) nicknamed Kenny in the tournament's first round. My ping-pong training at St. Joseph's Youth Camp when I was 12 wasn't enough to withstand his spin moves and I made my way to the medics while Kenny and another 'terp moved on to the semis. A few hours later I found myself spending Christmas Day drugged up in my cot shivering under two sleeping bags and a blanket.

Iraq, or more specifically our little concrete and plywood dungeons, is not an accommodating place to be sick and it seemed like there was nowhere to warm up. Rather than feeling sorry for myself, I actually felt bad for the guys coming in to take our place knowing that they have to endure a miserably hot sleepless summer and then the cold desert nights in the winter for an entire year. I ventured down to my office a little later in the day and felt well enough to browse through some old emails from home and photos accumulated over the year; it was nice just to reflect on the last year and think about how great it will be to get home and live once again. I was supposed to cap off my Christmas Day with a 2-6 a.m. guard shift up on OP3, a bland name for the tower sitting on top of SFC Sal's room on the roof that the soldiers call the "Eagle's Nest". KGB (the Russian-American Captain formerly known as Captain Caveman) felt bad for me and graciously pulled my shift. One of our soldiers passed away a couple of weeks ago after being on guard up at the Nest; he was a young Sergeant who thought he was having a stroke, was quickly evacuated on a bird, and we later found out that he had a brain aneurysm and died the next day. You just can't take anything for granted out here after incidents like that and last month's death in Tal Afar when a soldier with a cold ended up losing his life to pneumonia.

I felt a little better come New Year's Eve when the sun finally popped out to dry the camp and the heater in our building started working again. Other than that, it was just another day like any other out here. We still had our nightly targeting meeting to discuss what bad guys to get and what town projects to kick-start and shift changes went on as usual. Later that night, I fast-forwarded through an old Richard Gere movie and fell asleep just after midnight as the skies over Tal Afar, about 30 miles to the east, and Biaj, fifteen miles to the south, were lit up by the illumination rounds fired by the "gun bunnies" (artillery soldiers) in celebration of a new year. On our camp, we had some leftover fireworks that were brought in from Turkey back on the 4th of July and they made some noise, but largely fizzled out due to their age and shoddy storage conditions. The celebratory howitzer fires were a nice touch, even though the intense Earth-rocking sound of each round likely makes every local shudder and the soldiers had to go out the next morning to find all the illumination shells so nobody can make IED's out of them. We're also going to melt down all of the used shells and make spurs out of the metal for our Welcome Home ceremony—the spurs, along with a Stetson, have been a Cavalry tradition for centuries to acknowledge a "Cav" soldier's time in combat.

As we near our redeployment, everybody is talking about their plans when we return home—stay in, get out, move with the unit to Fort Hood, stay at Fort Carson and join a new unit, try to get stationed somewhere else? Whatever the case, it's time to burn this book and start a new chapter for just about everyone. We still have to take care of a lot of administrative things before leaving, like taking the physical fitness test (push-ups, sit-ups, and a 2-mile run), qualifying weapons at our little range, and firing weapons at night with gas masks on (although most people have a hard time even finding their gas mask at this point). At least we don't have to do the gas chamber before leaving, although the chamber continues to be the most efficient way to clear up chest and nose congestion when you're fighting a cold. There was a rumor going around before we deployed that all a soldier had to do to get out of going to Iraq is to say "I smell bananas" while trying to fit his mask in the gas chamber. Supposedly, this act would make it appear that your face was so distorted that a mask would never properly fit and if the chemicals scented to smell like bananas seeped in now then they surely would seep in during a chemical attack in Iraq. The PT test will be interesting, too. Guys started putting on some weight once the convoys of greasy pizza pockets, sodas, Gatorade, cookies, and chips started arriving to Tiger Base, to complement the greatly-appreciated and obscene amount of junk food mailed from the States. The sauna-like summer heat acted as its own weight loss program, but the winter weather isn't doing anybody any favors. Mail will be shut down in a week or so, putting an end to the import of high-quality treats, and a lot of soldiers started working out when the new weight equipment showed up a couple of months ago. It's like the month before

Spring Break back in college when everyone starts going to the gym and running so they'll look good when they get home.

As we begin to pack up to move south, people are finding stuff that we've been looking for over the past year, like hard drives, printer cartridges, and maps. When we left Fort Carson back in February it was like going on vacation where you pack everything and anything just in case. I even brought a footlocker full of laundry detergent and Febreze to cover both ends of the spectrum; if I lived somewhere really nice we would have washer and dryers and if I lived somewhere really miserable I could just Febreze my uniforms once in a while in lieu of a wash. We ended up somewhere in the middle—when our water was scarce before the well was built the laundry team reused the water and our clothes came back smelling musty and in need of a whiff of Febreze.

Right now we're at the stage where I don't know who worries more, me about Jen or Jen about me. It's so nice to know that my days of watching the kids grow up on film and in pictures is going to end soon. 'Welcome Home' banners should start popping up on garages in post housing as our advance parties begin trickling in and Jen made a paper chain-link counter so Cade and McKenna can detach one link daily as they await my return. Jen sent me the tape of the kids' Christmas concert and it arrived on December 29th, the day before my birthday. That was the best present I could've gotten, followed up by the best birthday song ever sung to me when I called home on the 30th. Cade was finally sleeping while fighting off a bad virus, so Mackie took over and sung "Hap Bay To You, Hap Bay To You". The Christmas concert was amusing to watch as it opened up with an intense moment wherein Cade and McKenna, at just over two years of age being the youngest in the church program, were separated by three other kids. Just prior to *Twinkle, Twinkle* kicking off the program, McKenna spotted Jen in the audience and burst into hysterics. As if on cue at the other end, Cade started in. The producers pulled it together and nobody bolted from the stage as several other kids started crying through *Twinkle, Twinkle* and *Jingle Bells*. Mac was still trying desperately to overcome her heart-breaking sobs where she is trying to catch her breath and she managed to pick up the bells to ring during *Jingle Bells* while Cade just stared straight ahead with his first case of stage fright. They made it through the first recital of their lives.

Even though the two of them have totally different personalities they are quickly developing the twin bond. McKenna makes Cade hold her hand (he lets her about half of the time) whenever they cross the street or walk around the neighborhood and they help each other out and share without hesitation.

One of the greatest pieces of the tape shows Cade sitting on the steps while Mackie goes back and forth to the play kitchen, making him a play sandwich and not letting him eat it until she put play catsup on it. Cade is still the focused, curious, and anal one; he held a pen from the start like an adult and still gets upset when he gets dirt on his shoes or on the floor and likes clean and sparkly things, like his new ruby-red sparkly Dorothy shoes that he just had to have. McKenna is still the daredevil whose motor is always running and she can hang on the gymnastic rings longer than some soldiers I know. She's been the first to walk and talk and has started to put five-word sentences together, like "look at that choo-choo Mama". She recently took a trip to her favorite store, Target, to pick out some yellow ping-pong balls stamped with a smiley face to ship off to me. Watching the kids on the tape made me think that even though I've missed half of their life so far and they've come a long way from the day I left, back when Cade was still crawling and McKenna just started to walk, they are still very much the same wonderful personalities and I have a lot of growing up together to look forward to.

FEBRUARY 11, 2006:

SEE YOU ON THE HIGH GROUND

"You know the real meaning of peace only if you have been through the war." Kosovar

I won't soon forget January 29th, 2006. It was the day my personal heroes arrived, in the form of our replacements from the 1st Armored Division out of Germany. It took me about 20 minutes to show the nine guys in their Intelligence section around the muddy camp while a light snow fell and then they spent the rest of the day poring over the work we've done since May. After about eight hours of studying data and maps in the basement, one of them said, "It's going to be a long year". That was just before we walked through the thick and sticky mud to finish off the meatloaf and carrot T-rations in the mess tent and the same guy remarked, "It's going to be a really long year". Hundreds of soldiers arrived over the following week and the gym tent, and even the chapel, closed down to accommodate the overflow. To conserve the small amount of water we have, their soldiers aren't allowed to shower until we leave, so they are as anxious for us to go as we are. I spoke for four hours during our overview of the entire area to their Commanders and Staff and it was very refreshing (for me at least, everyone else had to stay awake on the metal folding chairs) because it was like my brain was downloading information as I spoke and clearing up hard-drive space for other things in the very near future that didn't involve the Middle East. At the end of the daylong presentation it was announced that a bunch of Congressmen were going to visit during their "tour of bases with austere conditions"—nothing like that to make the new guys feel welcome. Their soldiers apparently were well-briefed on the place prior to leaving Germany—I asked one new Private at chow what they heard about the camp and he said, "They told us it really sucks."

A couple of days later, the Congressional delegation from the States arrived, consisting of Congressmen from California and Connecticut and two Congresswomen from Florida. The cooks laid out a spread of sandwiches and a platter of cut-up fruit and vegetables and soldiers from the visitors' districts were invited. One of the extra-duty soldiers (he was caught with alcohol bought in a Yezidi town) even painted the in-ground urinal upstairs for the visit. I appreciate visits like this because it's the only time we get club sandwiches and Dr. Peppers on ice, let alone a freshly painted urinal. Even though it was a visit to austere bases, the delegation ended up only seeing the walk from the helipad to the conference room in the TOC. The Congresswoman from Miami made the mistake of wearing high heels and tripped up in the river rock and along the plywood that the soldiers laid out over the mud; it was a good thing that their lunch was waiting for them so she didn't have to navigate the pallet walkway to the mess tent.

I was surprised at how simple the discussion was and how little they knew of the situation in Iraq—it seemed to me that they thought we just went in and killed people who we thought were bad and then took off looking to kill more bad people rather than the reality of putting most of our time into actually building a country and training, equipping, and emplacing the Army, Border Patrol, and police. They asked the leaders of those three Iraqi agencies what they thought the U.S. did poorly and the leaders unanimously agreed that we let detainees go too soon and we are too nice to them. The Police Chief mentioned that Iraq's court system is corrupt and some judges sell lists of witnesses to the bad guys. One of the Reservists attached to my shop, an Atlanta cop, whispered, "Sounds just like the U.S.". A Congressional aide asked me about the issue of body armor shortages as they were putting on their lightweight flak vests to re-board the helicopters. I told him that over 60 percent of the soldiers in Iraq, the ones that have to "pay the bills" just to support us being here logistically and administratively, only leave the FOB four times in their 12-month tour—entering Iraq, going to Kuwait on leave, returning from leave, and going home for good. We were issued extra shoulder, side, and groin armor, but soldiers don't want to plod around like the Michelin Man and wisely give up the extra protection for the mobility, so it largely goes unused unless a unit makes it mandatory.

The weeks leading up to the new unit's arrival were uneventful and dragged a bit. *The Stars and Stripes* newspaper came out for a visit and did an article on Alf, the Iraqi who worked with our unit in Al Qaim in 2003 and now lives and runs a shop in the Oz Market. Alf was not amused to find his smiling mug gracing the cover of the Mid-East edition the next day to go along with his quotes berating the cowardly enemy fighters on page two. Despite the coverage, he still makes his weekly jaunts to and from Baghdad and Ramadi and returns in one piece. We had a Somalian interpreter who vanished while on leave in Kirkuk and a Ministry of Defense representative who was working with us from a nearby town went missing for a month. Upon his return, the ministry official told us that he was imprisoned by the Kurds in Dahuk and our continued probing into his detention actually served to free him—finding a missing person in this land, even a good guy, is usually for naught so I was very surprised that we saw him again. Things have changed dramatically since the fall of Baghdad in March 2003, back when soldiers were curiously wandering the shops in Baghdad and driving in Al Anbar Province with plastic doors on their Humvees, and guys like Alf are invaluable. He'll likely stay on with the new unit and continue to provide quality Iraqi products to the soldiers. My cellmate bought a "Rolex" watch from Alf for $20 after his first two watches broke. The new timepiece is really shiny, but the date is forever stuck at "18" and the time fell 40 minutes behind within the first 12 hours of use. Plus, he has to carry it in his pocket because the wristband snapped.

We've been spending a good amount of time training the Iraqis to man their own TOC and it's working out well so far. Granted, they power down all the radios, turn off the lights, and disappear when the sun goes down, leaving behind a couple of Jundis playing cards. Whereas the drink "Burn" keeps our operations center going (one radio operator set a record by downing 22 of them on Election Day), the Iraqis are powered by the sweet Chai tea. Visitors are highly recommended to bring their own glass, though, because they have been passing around the same three unwashed cups for eight months now. We are all hoping that this entire area can be turned over to the Iraqis within the next six months—they are almost ready as a group (Iraqi Army, Police, and Border Patrol). Unfortunately, base camps around Iraq that have been turned over to their forces have been found looted soon afterwards, to include Sadaam's Palace that was turned over in November and was sans windows, doors, roofs, baseboards, and wiring a month later. U.S. engineers currently building camps for the Iraqis minimize the use of nails and wires because they are the first products to be lifted for resale or hoarded for later use.

The Kurds' militia, the Peshmerga, would be ready to take over the area tomorrow, but their presence is becoming a politically sensitive subject now that the word "militia" has been polluted by the Shia Badr Brigade and Mahdi Militia down south. The Kurds are taking advantage of their relationship with the U.S. to fight their silent non-lethal war where they are slowly extending their reach to the south, as far down as their former lands in Kirkuk; they are building schools that only teach in Kurdish, funding projects in towns with Kurdish-elected officials, and letting people move into towns only if they join and claim allegiance to their political party. They are well-managed, well-financed, and efficient—even the two old rival political Kurd parties recently joined together to leverage their Parliamentary seats and one of those parties is historically aligned with Iran. Complaints from civilians up in Dahuk are that the city, while it is safer than any major U.S. city and cleaner than most European ones, is basically under authoritarian rule with dissenters imprisoned, civil liberties curtailed, and free press and free speech "highly discouraged"—so it's like the old Iraq without the genocide. The only discouraging thing about getting rid of the Peshmerga is that these guys are by far the most effective group in Iraq in creating security and stability for the future. After we kick them out of the area and "encourage" their return to Dahuk, we'll surely see events and reports being staged to make a call for their return (which I won't be around to hear as I will be playing with my kids in Iron Horse Park with my mind free of all things Iraq).

About three days before our replacements were due to arrive I thought to myself that there is absolutely no way we have time to do another operation. I inventoried and packed most of my gear and cleaned and packed one of my two pairs of boots, the ones that were thoroughly soaked down south in our last Operation Manifest Destiny trip. Later that night, one of our tanks down by Biaj hit an IED (and not just a normal cheaply-made, hastily thrown together IED; this one was a "no shit professional IED") and we immediately met to plan another weeklong search of the city starting the next morning, this one being so secretive that several of our own officers asked me where we were going as we boarded the vehicles to move out at 3 a.m. Knowing that I only had one pair of boots and the ongoing rains were causing the mud and sewage to mix together into the middle of Biaj's streets, I intended to step very gingerly in town whenever we got out. However, once we dismounted and started to walk down the alleys, the very first puddle I stepped in contained the dark green sludge of Biaj's finest raw sewage, something I never expected to experience ever again in my life. As much as we did for the Sunnis in Biaj over the past year, it remains a tight-lipped closed tribal society that will never change. Our arrival in and around the city did turn out to be a surprise and even the Iraqi

Army Commander, who we awoke upon arrival, thanked us for not telling anyone about it (to include himself) because this was the first time word of an impending operation didn't leak out.

The streets were quiet for the first two days as the people were told to stay in their homes until they were all inspected. The only movement on the muddy dirt streets and alleys were the packs of wild dogs, donkeys, and cows, which were having a great time eating all the turnips and onions left unattended at the vegetable markets alongside the usual piles of trash. There are very few paved streets in the city and the locals chopped up the only concrete sidewalk in town to tile their homes. We ended up finding a couple caches of RPG rounds in some "gardens", which were actually junkyards filled with trash and tires that covered up the weeds used in dinner salads. On the third day, the town Mayor announced that the markets would re-open and our Civil Affairs team paid the local fuel czar to refill the town's benzene tanks, an action that caused thousands of locals to flood the streets with their fuel-toting donkey carts and hundreds of kids rolling 55-gallon barrels to the gas station to fill up.

People were out in town all day just watching our engineers and their massive cranes install barriers on Market Street next to the Rasheed Bank (still closed since the robbery in 2004, but it may open again soon). One of the tracks on a maintenance vehicle, the largest track vehicle in our inventory that can pull tanks out of canals (as we witnessed in Baghdad), blew out driving down Market Street and it took four hours for the drivers to fix it in front of a crowd of at least 2,000 people. The only other excitement in town was when the Iraqi Army Jundies physically beat one of their own men after he was accused of stealing money from a house during the search. Our guys stopped the fighting and found and returned the money and the soldier was later jailed in the Iraqi's little canvas detention tent before being kicked out of the Army. I guess that accounts for progress.

Even though the nights were cold and the rains pounded us, I had the privilege of staying in a dry tent this time (the water did rise up under the plastic and vinyl flooring, making it feel like we were walking on a waterbed, but it never did make it inside). The camp in Biaj is by far the dustiest place to drive into in the summer and the muddiest to drive into in the winter—the mud becomes so thick that even the track vehicles get stuck on the short 200-meter trip from the front gate to the motor pool. After four days in town, I left with the thought that I can now safely say I'll never experience the dark green sludge of Biaj ever again, "Inshallah".

It's due to places like Biaj that make me discount the talk of a large-scale civil war in Iraq. From all of my travels throughout the country, I've come to the conclusion that the main problem is apathy—so many people have lived such a hard life that they could care less about the big picture or the future, for themselves or the country they live in. They build walls around their property and only what happens today is important. Inside their walls, they keep a reasonably clean house and yard and decorate their dirt floors with colorful woven floor rugs. They sweep all of their trash outside the walls to the common areas and install pipes to allow their water and sewage to run out to the same alleys and streets. Nobody cares about the common areas as long as everything within their walls is fine. Even if we buy the town trash dumpsters, place them on the streets, and start up a sanitation department, the people will still toss their trash into the gutters even when they are standing right next to the new dumpster.

There may be a low-level civil war breaking out in Baghdad, but the reasons above are why I don't think a full-scale civil war will occur here; not enough people care enough to fight it and most will just accept the hand that is dealt them. The people make their decisions based on their tribal elders and clerics rather than what the law, government, or police dictates, so whatever system comes into play will continue to be based on nepotism and corruption and graft develops as each tribe does what is best at that time for its own people. We won't see the masses picking up arms to fight a sectarian battle because they don't want to control land or a government; they just want to live on their little piece of property or tribal village without anybody getting into their business. Nobody can predict the end result in Iraq, but federalism is a likely outcome and each province can easily turn their militias into legitimate Armies. As much as we'd like it to be black and white, this is the most gray and convoluted place I think the historians will ever study.

I don't know if I could look back over the past year and say that any single event had a positive significant impact on me or my future, but I can definitely look back and say I am proud of what we accomplished. It's a difficult war to fight and it's going to take a lot more than just the U.S. military to win the cultural war of words and ideas, one so fragile that a political cartoon or rumor of a Koran in a toilet can ignite tensions and hatred worldwide. Having a few Army Armor and Infantry Divisions and a Marine Expeditionary Force on your doorstep does wonders to effect policy change, though. I am amazed at how much has changed in the Middle East in less than three years: in Iraq, we deposed a brutal dictator and regime that committed genocide on its own people, held three national elections where women finally voted and over 250 political parties participated, saw the first-ever Constitution ratified and two National Assemblies set in place, witnessed the growth of over 170 newspapers that could freely express their views, built thousands of schools, hospitals, water distribution and agricultural projects, sewage plants, and electrical grids in places that never had any of that in the past, and observed a growing economy that runs on more than Sadaam's former state welfare programs. In the outlying areas, Libya dismantled their nuclear weapons program, Syria withdrew from Lebanon, allowing the Lebanese to form a government of their own volitions, the Palestinians attempted to hold an election (until some masked gunmen showed up) and was successful in holding a second election (in which the Hamas, with 10 women candidates, took power—but at least it will force them to play the political game and we have a state to blame should Hamas ever claim a role in future terrorist attacks), Egypt held elections (the Muslim Brotherhood quadrupled their number of seats on Parliament, but, again, at least they are coming out of the shadows and entering the political arena to seek legitimacy), a woman was actually elected to a city council in the Wahhabist city of Jiddah, Saudi Arabia, and the authoritarian governments of Jordan and Egypt announced a movement to a free press and independent judiciary systems. We lost over 2,350 soldiers in Iraq and Afghanistan over those three years and most of the people not clamoring for our withdrawal are the guys on the ground making the sacrifice.

In my readings about the philosophy of war, there are some scholars who say that war allows complete self-sacrifice and brings us to the true nature of man and essential relationships where man willingly and without thought dies for someone whom he may not even know. It became apparent early on, right after the first IED in Baghdad injured one of our soldiers and his buddies were volunteering to take on extra missions, that the guys are fighting for each other rather than trying to make sense of the big picture. I don't know anybody who thinks it's an immoral war; after all, freeing people from an unjust ruler was one of our clearest goals. And nobody really cares about the ongoing arguments back in the States about the war because it shows that people are passionate about it one way or the other, which is much preferred over the possibility of being forgotten by an apathetic and ignorant nation like the Vietnam veterans experienced.

We're helping others to be free, which isn't a bad thing and it does represent the ideals America was founded on, but it is a hard sell to say that we are fighting for the freedom of Americans. After all, the average American can still wake up in the morning, go to the diner for a coffee and paper, watch a game with tens of thousands of other spectators, plan their trip to Europe or the

Bahamas, or drive their SUV to the beach on unbelievably cheap gas without any fear of having their head lopped off or a suicide bomber detonating in the theater. There are few, if any, hardships or national sacrifices, like gas rationing, tax hikes, a draft, or even a push for savings bonds to support the war effort. It's easier to say that we are fighting to maintain the quality of life and freedoms that we do love and expect and the fact that people can wake up every morning without those fears and not change their daily routine makes the Global War on Terror a success thus far.

Freedom these days doesn't necessarily mean that we're in harms way of being overthrown; it means that we will be free to enjoy the quality of life that we're used to without fear of attacks, intimidation, or a disruption to our accustomed lifestyle (which, unfortunately means cheap gas). It is the freedom to prosper, get a good education and job, buy a home, provide for your family, travel and move freely; our nation's high standards of living and prosperity depends on access to free markets, cheap goods, cheap oil, and continued growth in stable economies worldwide so people will buy our goods and we'll create more good jobs to feed their markets and the cycle of freedom continues for our children. The freedoms that come from creating a growing and safe world not only ensure that Americans are not laid off and that we can buy a low-priced flat-screen TV at Best Buy or take that 14-day cruise to Greece, it also ensures that we remain protected from the people who want to harm us. It takes sacrifices to ensure that these freedoms are protected and to support governments who cooperate with us to keep Americans free from worrying about those who want to kill them and their families and permanently damage our interests worldwide. Whatever the reason the guys do their job, if it's for their buddies, for their nation, or just because it's their job and they took an oath to do it, they are damn good at doing what they do and I know they'll be protecting my kids' freedoms long after I'm gone.

Thinking back on my time here, I am very fortunate to leave without any serious problems, whether that is an injury, mental scars, or problems at home caused by a long absence. I came to Iraq with the realization that death in a war is just an increased probability of death any other time, except for the shock-effect and brutality of it happening in a hostile place far away from the people I love. I also knew that the chance of being killed or wounded here was slim; in fact, I only knew of one Captain serving in my position (Battalion/Squadron Tactical Intelligence Officer) who was killed since the war started and he was fragged with a grenade by a soldier in his unit (a Muslim in the 101st Airborne Division) while sitting in the operations tent in Kuwait. Even today, the probability of being physically hurt remains amazingly low (over

600,000 Soldiers, Marines, and Airmen rotated through Iraq and we've had 2,260 killed and 16,600 wounded, over half of whom were returned to duty within 48 hours—less than a three percent chance that I would fall into one of those categories). I did, however, know that we would be heading to the "Triangle of Death" south of Baghdad and this was one of the few spots in Iraq that offers up multiple opportunities for death to quickly and expeditiously snatch any of us away.

There were days at the beginning of the deployment when we used to sit around and joke about what we would lose to get out of here—a finger, a knee, a flesh wound? I was also a little leery of our force protection at times. At the large FOBs across Iraq, the biggest danger is spilling your Cinnabon coffee and burning your hand; the camps are well guarded by combat units and contractors whose sole function in life is to keep everyone on the FOB safe. When we moved north and built our own camps, force protection became an important extra-duty to go along with the normal patrols. When we first arrived in Sinjar, picked some land, and started lining it with a berm and concertina wires we were hanging out there alone for a few months at a time when we didn't know what to expect in terms of attacks and didn't have a lot of soldiers here to stop them if they did happen. One day early on, some school kids even broke in and stole a couple packs of bottled water and MRE's from the motor pool. On Christmas Day, when the officers pulled guard for the enlisted, my cellmate returned to the hooch after an isolated early morning shift and said he was glad nobody attacked because he had no idea how to shoot the .50 cal that he was manning.

Once the entire unit arrived, the security situation greatly improved and all of the towers were easily manned around the clock. My only complaints after that were when we hoisted an American flag over the command center and lit it up with a floodlight at night and when we set a brightly-lit Christmas tree on the roof next to that flag over the Christmas Holiday. Who knew that when I came to this war I would never draw my pistol or aim my M-16 in anger or fright and that I would be able to count on one hand the number of times I even felt insecure enough to chamber a round (two times in South Baghdad, one in Tal Afar, and one late-night walk to the Iraqi compound by myself when I diligently watched the shadows).

Last week, we had to fill out a six page medical questionnaire to help identify any of the mental and physical problems we've experienced over the year or think we're going to experience someday. In typical Army fashion, we have to fill out one of the surveys prior to Kuwait as a condition to leaving the

Middle East and then another copy of the exact same form at Fort Carson when we arrive. The form is entertaining—it asks if you've ever experienced the following symptoms during deployment: coughing, headache, irritability, feeling tired with little interest in things, sore muscles, numbness, weakness, indigestion, and diarrhea. Pretty much everything that can be attributed to sleeping on a cot with no A/C or heat depending on the time of year, living with the same guys in a small enclosed area, eating MRE's and T-rats and then shifting midway to frozen foods, shitting on a tub of diesel fuel and flies, and being in a desert for a year sucking up dust and fuel exhaust.

We are rewarded with a 48-hour pass upon return to the States that will allow us some time to assimilate back into society and adjust to family life, so that will be a nice gift after a year of a minimum 12-hour day for 355 straight days. Everyone is hoping that their flight doesn't land in Colorado on a Friday, because you'll have to be back to work on Monday like everyone else who didn't deploy. It will be refreshing not to have any more midnight helicopter landings outside of my room, not seeing my breath in the morning in the winter and air-drying my cot to rid it of sweat in the summer, not hearing the grating sound of the plywood door being kicked open by people coming and going at all hours throughout the night, not hearing the continuous blast of the generators in the background day and night, and not immediately mentally cross-referencing a wanted list whenever I hear an Arabic name. I remember the feeling of getting on the freedom bird over six months ago when I went on leave—the exhilarating feeling of freedom when everything was better, looked better, smelled better, tasted better, sounded better.

Emotions ran the gamut over the past year; fear, adrenaline, suspense, apprehension, tension, anxiety—and that was for both Jen and I. A lifetime of experiences is what you draw on to either rise to a challenge or be crushed by it—when I get back home I expect the enormity of what we've both been through to rain down on us and the weight of the world to roll off our shoulders. We're both completely worn out (Jen by far more than I) and ready for this to end and our lives to begin again. While I've been patiently waiting to leave, Jen is still faced with the daily struggles of raising a couple of 2-year-olds who are becoming more curious and mobile by the day.

I was wondering when the kids first big accident involving a trip to the ER would happen and I thought that the first one would involve McKenna and her wild and spazzy ways rather than the more reserved Cade, but he ended up falling off of a chair that he was standing on and smashing his nose on the edge of a table. It turns out his nose likely wasn't broken, but he did end up with two black eyes that may be healed by the time I return home. A few days before that, Jen was downstairs picking up their messes while the kids were upstairs stuffing a roll of toilet paper into the toilet and flushing, thus flooding the bathroom floor. Dealing with all of this would make anyone curse, but the closest Jen gets is "Gosh darn it", which McKenna quickly picked up on and uses on her play phone (Cade's newest word is getting on the phone to say "I-raq" when Jen asks him where Daddy is and they both say "Dada Iraq—home soon"). Then there was the chaos of McKenna's first vomiting experience, which turned into five separate episodes. The first two episodes frightened her before she calmly settled into the pattern. Jen was cleaning the vomit off of her sheets and clothes before Mac blew all over the floor. While Jen was cleaning the floor, Mac threw up on Butkus, who proceeded to run out back and roll around the dry grass.

The kids do have their moments of trying to help out, like climbing up on the changing table to grab a Baby Wipe to dust the floors or following behind Jen with their little play vacuums, and they recently started getting up and out of bed on their own and running in to pounce on and wake up Jen each morning. They moved to their separate twin-size beds and each one of them picked out their sheets, Mackie selecting Pooh, Piglet, and Tigger and Cade going for various sports balls. Somehow the gender-specific thing works out, even considering Cade's proclivity for the sparkling red high heels and purses.

I don't know if I have really changed over the past year—perhaps I'm a little wiser, compassionate, and more appreciative of life. I also don't know what my future holds, but I do know that I'll be in safe hands with guys like the people I've served with watching my back. I've always lived by the simple advice of making my little corner of the world a better place—whether that is a community, neighborhood, or even as small as a home, or if it's as big as Northwest Iraq. I'm just going to decrease the size of my corner for a little while so I can focus back on my family. I've had a lot of people tell me and the other soldiers that God will grant us entrance into Heaven for all the good that we've done, so I have that going for me.

I know there will be a day when Cade and McKenna ask me about Iraq and the military and I'm anxious for them to understand it all. I know there aren't a lot of people anymore who are willing to serve their country merely for patriotism, like the old days, but if either one of them ever approaches me with an interest in serving then I'm certainly not going to be one of those parents who chases them away. I'll sit and discuss the missions of each service, if they want to go in enlisted or officer, what jobs they may like—I guess, after all the times I thought "why didn't I join the Air Force", that I'll probably talk up the Air Force lifestyle a little more than the other services. I'd be proud of them if they even consider the military because it's such an amazing experience and tool for personal growth—they will be blessed with discipline, leadership, positive experiences, and an appreciation for their country and other people around the world. A lot of our culture seems to be turning inward, surfing the web, playing video games, glued to Ipods, and watching reality shows at the expense of experiencing the world around us. Nowadays, more Americans know the Runner-Up on the first season of *American Idol* than the location of Iraq or Afghanistan.

We do have a big decision to make on getting out or staying in and a lot of that will depend on what my next assignment may be. There are so many positive aspects to finishing out a career in the Army—I need nine more years to retire with a comfortable pension and health benefits, we will get to visit other parts of the country and world and expose the kids to beautiful and horrible places, the people I work with are of an amazingly selfless and spirited group, we will make friends from all over the world, the salary and benefits are comfortable enough that Jen will be able to volunteer at the kid's schools, Cade and McKenna will attend good schools with low student to teacher ratios and involved parents, they'll be able to play in the front streets without worry of crime or kidnappers, I'll have lots of vacation (when I'm authorized to take it) and new jobs and challenges every year so I'll never be bored of my work.

The only negative? Another year in Iraq.

It's going to be a tough decision.

FEBRUARY 17, 2007:

REFLECTIONS ONE YEAR OUT OF THE SANDBOX

"We will have peace with the Arabs when they love their children more than they hate us."
Golda Meir

My freedom bird landed in Colorado Springs on February 17th, 2006 on the same frozen tarmac that I took off from 352 days ago. We were greeted by a 7-degree temperature and an entourage of the city's political and business leaders and handed a Quarter Pounder with cheese from the local McDonald's crew as we stepped off the ramp. The Colorado Springs Police Department escorted our busses and blocked off all of the intersections as we made our way back to Fort Carson. I'll always remember the chills running down my spine as I watched the people in their cars and the pedestrians along the route stand up to cheer and clap as we passed. By this time, our families and friends at the post's Special Events Center had been waiting for over three hours, but we had to stop at the motor pool for another anxiety-filled hour to turn in weapons, sensitive items, and classified materials before marching in to embrace them.

The thousand or so returning soldiers in my group quickly gathered into a formation outside of the center and marched in to the patriotic music of Toby Keith and a rousing ovation from the crowd. There was no way Jen and the kids could see me from my position in the back of the soldiers, but I quickly spotted them under the purple balloons that Jen told me she'd be holding. I was itching to run to them, but found myself very content taking in the moment and staring at my beautiful wife and children from afar. After a couple of short speeches, the command of "dismissed" was bellowed and soldiers and families scampered over each other in a sloppy and passionate attempt to meet in the middle. I made my way into the bleachers and once again felt Jen's warm tears flowing onto my face and soaked up the clean, fresh, smooth smell and feel of my children with McKenna's sweet embrace around my neck and Cade playfully rubbing my nose and ears to reacquaint himself with his dad's face. In the last 48 hours, I went from the most seemingly hopeless place in the world to the most wonderful, secure, and comforting place. I'll always look back on February 17th as one of the most peaceful days of my life.

A month after my return, I found myself getting a pedicure at the Broadmoor Resort overlooking the Cheyenne Mountains on a gorgeous sunny Colorado springtime day. It was strange to think that a war was going on and soldiers were dying only 15 hours in the air from the lounge chair where I found myself snoring and soaking my calloused feet in a Jacuzzi tub. In the short time since my return I rarely gave Iraq, or the past year of my life, a second thought. My biggest stress was getting the kids to stay somewhat quiet during mass every Saturday night at the post chapel—I didn't have the heart to tell Jen that my new Saturday night routine was harder than any single thing I've done over the past year. I still read the paper religiously, but I found that I had to go out of my way to research what was going on back in Iraq unless one of the suicide bombers blew himself up in a crowd of Shia in a continued attempt to entice them into retaliation and an all-out sectarian war. I had to download the *Stars & Stripes Mid-East* edition once in a while to remind myself that there were still bad men being caught, terror and death squad cells being destroyed, large caches being found with the help of courageous Iraqis who had little reason to assist us, and infrastructure and schools being built to help the previously-oppressed. In fact, without the *Stripes* I would never have known that my unit's old area was turned over to the Iraqis in May, bringing me a nice feeling of closure that we were successful in at least securing and giving a new life to the people in the northwestern part of Iraq.

Life in garrison upon our return was exceptionally laid back and allowed both soldiers and officers to reconnect with their families and evaluate their future before making any rash decisions on getting out or not. We had no vehicles to maintain and no real-world missions to plan for, so we were left biding our time and pondering the future while squatting in some buildings that were recently vacated by a brigade in the 4th Infantry Division after they deployed to Baghdad. Jen wasn't exactly ecstatic that I brought home strep throat for the kids after my final week in Iraq of living on top of each other in confined tents and planes, but family life quickly returned to incredible, and incredibly busy (I have to take the newspaper to work where I can relax and read it), once again. Now that the kids are big enough to get themselves up and out of bed in the morning, I have found that there is absolutely nothing better in this world than being pounced on and awakened by giggling children and I sometimes wonder if guys like Zarqawi or Bin Laden ever get to, or even feel the need to, enjoy those simple pleasures in life. I feel great physically, even after a year of processed chow and sleeping on a tight cot, and Jen tells me that the only visible part of me that is just not right is my hearing. I guess that my ears were always on around the clock for an entire year as the generators and helicopters ran non-stop. I relish the silence now and make it a point to take some time each day to listen to the wind, crickets, rain, and birds.

Cade and McKenna are as beautiful as when I left them and I can watch them make up songs and laugh together all day. Cade took on many of his mom's cute obsessions with order and always ensures things are in their correct place—he even intently studies his pacifier before inserting it into his mouth to ensure that the two holes are always exactly at the top, even in his sleep when his eyes are closed. McKenna is still the leader and rubs off on her brother (an envious Cade wore Mac's blue Princess dress on a visit to Sea World) and she is becoming more girly and chatty by the day, changing her future job desire from a football player to a cheerleader (even though we still have to pull her off of Cade after she wrestles him to the ground when she's mad at him). The two are turning out as different as Felix and Oscar in The Odd Couple, with Mac leaving a trail of crumbs and chaos behind her wherever she scurries off to and Cade ensuring everything is in its place and reciting the "do's and don'ts" to his disinterested sister. The potty training process emphasizes this divergence in personality—Mac is in such a hurry that she once shit on the stool, whereas Cade has a time-consuming ritual after going potty where he has to tuck his wiener back in at just the right angle and then hike his waistband up to the perfect spot or else he has to start over. Unfortunately, the two of them still think I'm heading to Iraq every day to work; whenever they see my photos of the desert they both say "Look, Eye-rak—Daddy's work".

We had a handful of ceremonies and parades on base during our first month back, both welcoming us home and memorializing all of the troopers from Fort Carson who lost their lives over the past three years. One of the services was for a Specialist who was struck and killed by a drunk driver in Colorado Springs after being home for less than a month. After losing only four soldiers in the Squadron to combat over the past year, we had to experience that insane loss. His memorial was attended by hundreds of his fellow "Freedom Riders", the group of mostly Harley riders who block off the whackos demonstrating at the funerals of American soldiers. Another unit on post, the 2nd Brigade, 2nd Infantry Division, lost two soldiers in a three-week span as they conducted their pre-deployment training in preparation for an end of year trip to Iraq, once again illustrating the dangers of being a soldier even when you're far away from the combat zone.

One of our most uplifting ceremonies was a mass reenlistment in which hundreds of 3rd ACR soldiers "re-upped" to continue their career. That answered my question about battle-hardened veterans staying in the Army. Some great officers and soldiers called it quits after the three-month stability period ended (to include a buddy of mine who moved to New Orleans but decided against joining the National Guard there lest he be deployed in his new downtown to stop the murders), but a mass exodus out of the Army certainly didn't materialize in our unit or any other units that I'm familiar with and our Army will be stronger for it. I was one of those soldiers who were seriously debating whether to leave the service because of the strains the year overseas put on my family. Like many of the other undecided soldiers and families, Jen and I decided to stay in and we were assigned to a military intelligence unit at Fort Sam Houston in San Antonio, where driving on Interstate 410 during rush hour is often more frightening than taking a convoy down Route Santa Fe in Iraq. The decision to take the assignment turned out to be a huge mental relief as it meant that I was going to stay in for the long haul (eight more years) and retire as a career soldier and officer. It certainly is a nomadic lifestyle—the kids are barely three and they have already lived in four different states.

News reporting on Iraq remained sparse in my first six months back, during the spring and well into the summer months of 2006. It wasn't until we were hit with a run of bad news, to include the Marine atrocities in Haditha, the savage deaths of the two U.S. soldiers who were taken from a checkpoint in the "Triangle of Death", and the alleged murders of Iraqi civilians in Balad and south of Baghdad, that our actions in Iraq actually made the front pages. The media coverage of the search for Natalie Holloway, a teenager missing after a night of partying in Aruba, was still ongoing after one year, but I never did read anything about our continued searches for Staff Sergeant Matt Maulpin, who remains the only American soldier missing in action in Iraq after he was captured over two years ago when he was a PFC. There was a nugget of hope during that run when Abu Musab al-Zarqawi was killed north of Baghdad, but several national headlines actually questioned whether the death of the Al Qaeda in Iraq leader was good or bad. The media remained a tough crowd—the only "feel good" stories I read featured soldiers returning to their lives after losing a limb or most of their skin rather than uplifting stories about one of our many soldiers who have received a Silver Star or a human-interest piece on the successes of the Iraqi Army or the rebirth of a village that was previously suffering under Sadaam. In place of anything "good", we received box-score accounts of our deaths without a corresponding enemy tally, in-depth reporting of the government's infringements on the rights of non-U.S. citizens and public debates of our tactics and strategy, and even the divulgence of sensitive and classified information that surely didn't make the ground pounder's or leatherneck's job any easier and allowed the enemy to conduct their own surges prior to whatever strategy was to be enacted.

For the most part, our overseas fight against terrorism remained back page news and you wouldn't really know what was going on in Iraq or Afghanistan unless you were over there fighting it or knew someone who is. Israel's short fight against the Hezbollah in Lebanon gained far more national attention and they initially went in fighting with fewer ground troops than we used to clear and hold Tal Afar—that was before the Israelis quickly realized that you can't fight this new kind of war, against an enemy who is wearing a jogging suit with the wife and kids in tow, with air power alone. Hezbollah claimed victory in their fight against Israel because they survived; by that rationale, I guess all of us Americans are victorious so far in the war on terror because we continue to not only survive, but also thrive.

All in all, I returned home and found things to be pretty rosy in America—unemployment is ridiculously low, the economy continues to be on a roll in spite of fighting on two fronts, the high price of oil, and the exorbitant cost of rebuilding New Orleans, home ownership is higher than it's ever been, we're living in a country where most of our poor people can even afford a washer, dryer, and cable TV, and our lifestyle continues unimpeded with the biggest complaints being the possible increase in our unconventionally funded home loans and the cost to fill up the SUV as we accelerate to 85 mph on the way out of town for the weekend, thinking that maybe a hybrid or carpool may be an option if gas hits five or six bucks a gallon. We may not be winning the Ryder Cup in golf or World Championship in basketball anymore, but we're still dominating in the Nobel prizes in the sciences and the people of the world overwhelmingly clamor to become a citizen or at least attend our universities. Despite our grumbling about the stock market's gyrations or a real estate bubble or the threat of inflation or our unethical politicians, we are still by far the most industrious, entrepreneurial, generous, wealthy, and patriotic country in the world and will likely stay that way as all of us continue to strive for an

American Dream that just isn't possible in other countries. If nothing else, I realized yet again what a blessed life we all lead and how grateful we should be for our livelihoods and quality of life relative to the rest of the world.

The control of illegal immigrants was at the forefront of hot topics when I returned and all of the banter rekindled fond and frustrating memories of the Pillsbury Doughboy phenomenon that we experienced while trying to secure the Syrian border (plug up one point and they just squeeze over to a less secure one). The government does have the right and the duty to secure our borders and it takes on even more importance than ever now that Iran is openly cozying up to Hugo Chavez in Venezuela, but the tough part about securing America is that she offers a lot more room to squeeze into, to include the land bordering two oceans and two border countries with weak security. Plus, most of our illegals don't enter by simply cruising across the open borders; most of them enter legally and then just overstay their visas forever. Immigration is necessary; after all, we are a nation of immigrants and the only industrialized country in the world that is not predicted to experience a work-force loss in the coming decades largely thanks to our generous immigration policies and the legal immigrants whose hunger for the dream helps to keep our economy sharp. It may seem intuitive to me, since our main mission once we left Baghdad was to seal the Syrian border, but you will never be able to effectively secure a border as long as the incentives (profiteering from gas, sheep, and cigarettes in Iraq and free schools, health care, citizenship for newborns, and employers willing to hire illegals to save some money in the U.S.) to commit a crime greatly outweigh the punishment (catch and release in both Iraq and the U.S.).

Once the rallies with all of the Mexican flags fizzled out, the illegal immigration issue died down and other less explosive issues, like same-sex benefits and marriage, global warming, flag burning, scandalous Congressional behavior, Jon Benet's possible murderer, and Terrell Owens's possible overdose filled the headlines while news from Iraq remained on page 17. Mel Gibson's drunken anti-Semitic remarks to a policeman even gained more print and national publicity than a Muslim man in Seattle who shot up unarmed women at a Jewish Center. All in all, the dull political and social landscape and lack of passion over state-side terrorism was exactly what I hoped for because it assured me that if times are good here then whatever it is we are doing to keep everyone safe and happy at home seemed to be working.

It wasn't until a few months before the Congressional elections in November that I noticed our own country becoming increasingly fragmented and starting to show great concern for a war that directly affected an insignificant number of Americans—a war whose burden was borne by a small segment of society who volunteered to serve while the rest of the nation lived peacefully with no shared sacrifices like a draft or compulsory service, higher taxes, or even a mandated decrease in the speed limit to 55 (like the government did during the 1973 oil crisis) to reduce the price of oil and send less revenue to our sworn enemies. All of a sudden, everything that happened in Iraq and about Iraq became front page news and, for the first time in my life, I really paid attention to and grew angry towards our bickering political leaders and influential media as they teamed up to become divisive forces in the war effort and seemed to do an exceptional job at undermining the fight, clouding the battlefield with legal rulings, aiding the enemy with publicized leaks of sensitive material, and indulging the enemy's strategy of civilian mass murders to sway public opinion.

By the time November and the elections came around, our own country seemed to become polarized to the point where I wouldn't have been surprised to see violence erupt between the Republicans and Democrats—much along the lines of the Sunni and Shia, the Hamas and Fatah, and even the Jolaqs and the Farhats of Tal Afar. I never thought I'd see the day where two former Presidents badmouthed a sitting President or a movie depicting the assassination of a sitting President was shown in our theaters. I certainly didn't think I'd ever watch an American network tag along with a group of insurgents and air footage showing our enemy sniping a U.S. soldier (meanwhile, the Department of Defense was chastised about buying media exposure in the Middle East press to spread the word of positive accomplishments taking place). Much ado was made about the war lasting longer than World War II and surpassing the mark of 3,000 dead American soldiers, but little said about the fact that WW II witnessed over 406,000 dead and 600,000 wounded Americans, tens of millions of dead Allies and civilians, and a continent left in rubble, let alone the fact that it took two atomic bombs to bring it to a close. It's like we all conveniently forgot that our current actions in Iraq and Afghanistan freed over 50 million people from harsh, tyrannical, and oppressive regimes that alienated and enslaved most of the populace and that outcome alone was something that we all agreed upon in the not-so-distant past (the overriding goal of the majority of our military's 180-plus international missions during the post-Cold War period of 1991-2002 was to promote democracy and freedom and safeguard liberties—in fact, the military was so overstretched back in the '90s, between the drawdown of 425,000 soldiers and the increased deployments to meet these goals, that George Bush used the promise of reducing the overseas military deployments to increase military morale, recruitment, and retention that was suffering under the Clinton foreign policy when he ran against Al Gore for the Presidency in 2000).

As we neared the Congressional elections, I felt the public's mood swinging towards a pullout or drawdown with the death of every soldier and with every suicide bomb going off in a Baghdad barbershop that was aimed to sway U.S. opinion far more than it was meant to kill their Muslim brothers. Our governmentally unsanctioned enemies realized that it's much easier and cheaper for them to demoralize a population and force submission by blowing up a car in a market and ensuring that the pictures of the dead children made the front page and evening news. Weakness photographs much better than strength—after all, the world even felt sympathy for us after watching the towers collapse on 9-11—and terrorists play the victim very well at the expense of serving up their own children and neighbors as the "collateral" for their public relation purposes. Where we had no courageous voices opposing the war four years ago (not even Colin Powell), those voices to oppose our actions flourished once the going got tough, once the evidence of WMD "barely" materialized (depending on one's definition of WMD), and once the opinion polls started to turn. Amazingly, one poll showed that over 30 percent of Democrats and 10 percent of Republicans don't even want the current plan to succeed and many of our political "leaders" have their career riding on our failure in a non-binding kind of way.

Collectively, as a nation, we seemed to have made up our mind to get out of there and leave the Iraqis to decide their own fate, hoping all will go well and we'll just face a more positive unknown future, sometime when the next big bang goes off in our homeland and we get upset again and ask the current President and administration the tough questions about how they failed to stop the imminent attack or perhaps when the region all goes to hell and we're forced to send in half a million soldiers to clean up the mess because nobody else in the world gives a shit. Unfortunately, it will take something much bigger than being forced to discard the Mary Kaye lip-gloss prior to boarding an airplane to get all of us to believe that this game is for real and many Americans will continue to believe that the Christian movement to keep "In God We Trust" on a coin is more of a threat than radical Islam. Maybe the radical Islamists are correct and God does favor them in this fight, like they claim. After all, He did put most of the world's most precious mineral on their land (leaving even Israel dry). Or maybe He just put it there to test humanity.

Reflecting back on Iraq, it's too bad that the Iraqi people didn't pull together after Sadaam's regime fell like Americans did after 9-11. If things worked out, we would have had a partner dead center in the hotbed of radical Islam and Iran and Syria's violent influence in the region and world would be drastically altered. We assumed that the Iraqis would embrace freedom and unity—80 percent of them did embrace their new freedom, but few of them seem to be embracing the unity and they will likely always prioritize their tribe and religion over nationalism. It's no coincidence that the Kurds up north, the only group who actively cooperated with our rebuilding and security efforts right off the bat, are flourishing and living peacefully while the Sunni and Shia are killing each other off.

Ironically, the anti-war movement in the U.S. only served to deepen the chaos and increase the danger for our soldiers as we totally lost the trust of the Iraqi populace when it became widespread knowledge that the U.S. was not going to be there for long and the Iraqis quickly realized that they better side with another power broker in this fight. The only way to find an IED or to stop a suicide bomber is to gain information from the locals who trust us, and that trust faded away as quickly as the anti-war drumbeat heated up back home. Despite the Herculean efforts of our own anti-war movement, the new Iraqi government (in its failure to unite), the terrorists, the sympathizers, and the criminals to widen the Shia-Sunni schism and maintain the chaos, it wasn't until Al Qaeda in Iraq blew up the Shia's most holy shrine in Samarra in February (some call it Iraq's 9-11) that the country seemed to fall into disarray, even though we still don't see a mass mobilization of sectarian communities under militarized structures that would indicate a full-fledged civil war for control of the land or government (if, indeed, the multiple factions, death squads, and thugs of Iraq are even capable of organizing themselves into fighting a "normal" civil war). Iraq will remain Al Qaeda's self-declared central front of their war as they attempt to gain a foothold in the Cradle of Civilization and enjoy the close support of the neighboring Syrian and Iranian governments. The for-profit criminal element will also continue to play a huge role in causing and taking advantage of the instability until the Iraqi security forces gain the confidence, respect, and cooperation they need to take the thugs off the streets. We've only been actively recruiting and training the new Army, police, and border patrol for about two years and it takes much more time than that to see results—on the positive side, we really only need the Army to be the respected security force, like in Mexico, and they really only have to be as strong as Ethiopia's ground forces to take out Al Qaeda or as strong as Sadaam's old battered Army to fight Iran to a draw.

Our soldiers take a frustratingly painstaking process to fight the war on terrorism and err on the side of caution in everything they do, even at the risk of putting their own lives on the line to avoid hurting innocent people or damaging property. I partly attribute the isolated events like Abu Ghraib and Haditha (events that caused far more damage to our cause than any IED or suicide bomber ever did) to the frustrations of fighting this complex battle against an enemy who not only hides and fights among the women and children but also makes the women and children do the fighting, an enemy who is protected by the U.S. Constitution and Geneva Conventions but doesn't have to abide to either. There's a reason that you never see the bodies of young, military-aged men being pulled out of bombed buildings on CNN—they run away after shooting off their rockets or IED's and leave their sleeping families to become the face of their fight.

Even though the world remains largely silent when the enemy tortures and maims our soldiers and civilians (as they did to the two U.S. soldiers who were captured in Yusufiyah, the dirty city south of Baghdad where I experienced my first taste of the war chills one year ago), our guys continue to persevere in the most humane, civilized, and lawful means possible. Historically, fighting against a barbaric enemy does have a tendency to bring the troops down to their level of savagery the longer the battle and the frustrations are drawn out, although I am skeptical about some of the alleged war crimes when the government's key witness is an Iraqi from the Sunni Triangle who lives next to the IED crater. It's even more frustrating to the troops when there's greater international furor over a Danish drawing depicting Mohammed (and no furor when Iran put on a display calling the Holocaust a Western lie—not even a word of condemnation from our most prominent Jewish leaders) than there is over the brutal and barbaric slaying and beheading of our two young soldiers. Some politicians came out and said the slayings are a grim reminder of how our soldiers are put into harms way. It's more like a grim reminder of our enemy's character and what they would gladly do to each of us if we don't constantly stay aggressive and vigilant in the worldwide fight against these sick men. You know that nobody is immune from this fight when an active Al Qaeda cell is even caught plotting to blow up the Parliament of peace-loving Canada and behead the Prime Minister on television. Unfortunately, the handful of despicable incidents like Abu Ghraib and the Marine atrocities in Haditha and the rape and murders south of Baghdad caught and kept the world's attention far easier than our soldiers' disciplined, restrained, and civil (to the point where soldiers are issued non-lethal ammo) fighting and they only furthered the perception of the U.S. forces as the occupier and painted our enemy as the victim.

Who knows where our military's next stop will be. You would think that it will be quite a while before we unilaterally exert our influence with military power, as our experience in Iraq will weigh on our leader's minds for a couple of decades and should make us somewhat gun shy and longing for the simple, Cold War days of mutually assured self-destruction. Unfortunately, that may be our best option to continue to affect regime change in the future and ensure rogue states and groups fail to gain power and leverage, especially with Russia and China sitting on the UN Security Council with their vetoes at the ready against any negative action towards the well-known madmen ruling Iran and North Korea. Just like we experienced negotiating with Iraq under Sadaam, Iran and North Korea's negotiating leverage and self-importance relies on the perceived threat of WMD. The actions and statements of their crazed heads-of-state only serve to make those threats believable (along with raising the price of oil and their state revenues (Iran) and gaining more food, money, and technical aid (North Korea) with every public boast). Again, just like with pre-war Iraq, we will be forced to deal with the unknown and best intelligence available as if they will make good on their threats to destroy our people, our allies, and our way of life. I don't know if we'll ever have four better cases that highlight the failures of appeasement and negotiation than Iraq, Iran, North Korea, and the "land for peace" deal in Israel (which turned out to be "land for a forward-based assembly area from where we can launch our attacks"—one thing I took away from my summer job on an Israeli kibbutz in 1990 was the memory of friendly Arabs telling me that they just wanted some land of their own so they can live peacefully and grow an Army that would one day be strong enough to destroy the Jews). If negotiation doesn't work with sovereign nations and heads of state, especially in the Middle East where a desire for peace shows a weakness that will be exploited, then they surely won't work with those who declared Jihad on us over a decade ago. Besides, the militant Islamic demands of our annihilation and the formation of an Islamic caliphate dominating the world wouldn't exactly be in our best interest.

We can always outsource our fights like we did in Somalia, employing the same warlords who were once our enemies to fight against the extremist Islamic Courts Union and then relying on the U.S. trained and equipped Ethiopians to rescue them. Or we can rely on the United Nations or NATO, but they come with their own agendas, problems, baggage, and forces that may not be powerful enough to do the job without our assistance. The UN observers sitting in Lebanon for six years didn't exactly warn anyone of Hezbollah's military build-up in the south and the poor guys served as Hezbollah's cannon fodder and human shield along with the women and children. And the President of Sudan makes it well-known that if the U.S. intervenes in Darfur (ironically, some anti-war activists in the U.S. would like for us to become militarily involved in that civil war to save the oppressed people—at least until the first American soldier's body is shipped home in a coffin) then it will face another Jihad. As much as the average Joe and Jane America is going to detest it and possibly not understand it, we'll likely have to continue acting unilaterally to defend our interests and continue going to bed with our more friendly enemies and opposition groups to defeat our most evil enemies instead of waiting on approval from a lame-duck UN and international community that has a less-than-stellar track record when it comes to morals, ethics, criminal behavior, and timely decisions on stopping problems before it's too late. As evidenced by the Israeli Crisis, the international community may detest us in front of the TV cameras and press (even though more people apply for citizenship to our country than the rest of the world combined), but they still demand our leadership and money to solve the world's problems in both times of peace and war.

As I found out firsthand over the past year, war is never a popular or desired option and it can steal the lives and destroy the families of both the innocent and the guilty, soldiers and civilians alike. Let's all hope that the world can get along and most of us will never feel the emotions of war or experience the taste of combat, but it's a naïve concept to accept that as reality while living in the most powerful nation in the world who is expected (some may say ordained) and has a responsibility and a duty to use its wealth and resources to protect our citizens, our freedoms, and our way of life and attempt to broker peace between other warring parties and help the world's oppressed in the process. There's a good reason that I felt like I was in heaven when I disembarked the plane on February 17th. It's because our forefathers made those unpopular decisions over the past 230 years to fight for freedom, for a world of civilized norms, and a world free from the tyrants who want to take these freedoms, norms, and our way of life away from us.

So that was war. And I hope neither my kids nor I will ever experience another one.

OFFICE OF THE MAYOR
CITY OF TALL 'AFAR

In the Name of God the Compassionate and Merciful

To the Courageous Men and Women of the 3[d] Armored Cavalry Regiment, who have changed the city of Tall' Afar from a ghost town, in which terrorists spread death and destruction, to a secure city flourishing with life.

To the lion-hearts who liberated our city from the grasp of terrorists who were beheading men, women and children in the streets for many months.

To those who spread smiles on the faces of our children, and gave us restored hope, through their personal sacrifice and brave fighting, and gave new life to the city after hopelessness darkened our days, and stole our confidence in our ability to reestablish our city.

Our city was the main base of operations for Abu Mousab Al Zarqawi. The city was completely held hostage in the hands of his henchmen. Our schools, governmental services, businesses and offices were closed. Our streets were silent, and no one dared to walk them. Our people were barricaded in their homes out of fear; death awaited them around every corner. Terrorists occupied and controlled the only hospital in the city. Their savagery reached such a level that they stuffed the corpses of children with explosives and tossed them into the streets in order to kill grieving parents attempting to retrieve the bodies of their young. This was the

193

situation of our city until God prepared and delivered unto them the courageous soldiers of the 3ᵈ Armored Cavalry Regiment, who liberated this city, ridding it of Zarqawi's followers after harsh fighting, killing many terrorists, and forcing the remaining butchers to flee the city like rats to the surrounding areas, where the bravery of other 3ᵈ ACR soldiers in Sinjar, Rabiah, Zumar and Avgani finally destroyed them.

I have met many soldiers of the 3ᵈ Armored Cavalry Regiment; they are not only courageous men and women, but avenging angels sent by The God Himself to fight the evil of terrorism.

The leaders of this Regiment; COL McMaster, COL Armstrong, LTC Hickey, LTC Gibson, and LTC Reilly embody courage, strength, vision and wisdom. Officers and soldiers alike bristle with the confidence and character of knights in a bygone era. The mission they have accomplished, by means of a unique military operation, stands among the finest military feats to date in Operation Iraqi Freedom, and truly deserves to be studied in military science. This military operation was clean, with little collateral damage, despite the ferocity of the enemy. With the skill and precision of surgeons they dealt with the terrorist cancers in the city without causing unnecessary damage.

God bless this brave Regiment; God bless the families who dedicated these brave men and women. From the bottom of our hearts we thank the families. They have given us something we will never forget. To the families of those who have given their holy blood for our land, we all bow to you in reverence and to the souls of your loved ones. Their sacrifice was not in vain. They are not dead, but alive, and their souls hovering around us every second of every minute. They will never be forgotten for giving their precious lives. They have sacrificed that which is most valuable. We see them in the smile of every child, and in every flower growing in this land. Let America, their families, and the world be proud of their sacrifice for humanity and life.

Finally, no matter how much I write or speak about this brave Regiment, I haven't the words to describe the courage of its officers and soldiers. I pray to God to grant happiness and health to these legendary heroes and their brave families.

NAJIM ABDULLAH ABID AL-JIBOURI
Mayor of Tall 'Afar, Ninewa, Iraq

HOW TO PREPARE FOR A TOUR IN IRAQ

(Taken from an Internet posting making its' rounds with a couple of additions thrown in to realize the full Sinjar effect)

Set your alarm clock to go off at random times during the night. When it goes off, jump out of bed and get to the shower as fast as you can. Simulate there is no hot water by running out into your yard and breaking out the garden hose.

Mount a garden hose at chest level for a shower. Ensure the shower floor is an uneven dirt mound and leave a minimum of four inches of cold water on it at all times.

Urinate everywhere except in the toilet. For a more realistic deployed-latrine experience, use the shitter of a neighbor who lives at least a quarter-mile away. Don't flush.

Get a haircut from the paperboy.

Leave wet, freshly laundered clothes in a ball in the corner where the cat pees. After a week, unroll them and proudly wear to work and family gatherings. Pretend you don't know what you look or smell like.

Shoot bullet holes in the walls for ambience and spread gravel and river rock throughout your house and yard to keep down the dust.

Sandbag the floor of your car to protect it from IED blasts and fragmentation.

Take out a chicken breast, freeze it for a year, boil it, refrigerate it for a week, reheat, sprinkle with dust, and then serve it every other night with a side serving of cold okra and a warm Strawberry Fanta.

Lay out crumbs in your garage to attract spiders or mice under the cot placed next to the water heater. Replace the garage door with a curtain and hire a neighbor to open it, crank up his lawn blower, and proceed to blast sand into your sleeping area every two hours throughout the night in an effort to recreate random helicopter landings.

Two hours after you go to sleep in the garage, have your significant other whip open the curtain, shine a flashlight in your eyes and mumble, "Sorry, wrong cot." Repeat in two hours.

Never use a mirror to shave or look at yourself for a year.

Every time there is a thunderstorm, go sit in a wobbly rocking chair and dump dirt on your head.

Use 18 scoops of coffee per pot and, after brewing, allow it to sit in the off position for five or six hours before drinking.

Invite at least 185 people you do not really like to visit you for a year. Exchange clothes with them.

Keep a roll of toilet paper on your nightstand and bring it to the bathroom with you. And bring your gun and a flashlight.

Go to the worst crime-infested place you can find, go heavily armed, wearing a flak jacket and a Kevlar helmet. Set up shop in a tent in a vacant lot. Announce to the residents that you are there to help them.

Eat a single M&M every Sunday and convince yourself it's for Malaria.

Sandbag the floor of your car to protect from mine blasts and fragmentation.

Announce to your family that the dog is a vector for disease and shoot it. Throw the dog in a burn pit you dug in your neighbor's backyard.

Wait for the hottest day of the year and announce to your family that there will be no air conditioning that day so you can perform much needed maintenance on the air conditioner. Tell them you are doing this so they won't get hot.

ABOUT THE AUTHOR

Craig Olson is originally from Phoenix, but has lived around the world and is currently serving in San Antonio, TX. Craig is a graduate of West Point and holds two Masters Degrees from Arizona State University. He is an Army Ranger and Bronze Star recipient for his service in Iraq. "So This is War" is Craig's first published work; however, the joy of writing takes a backseat to being a husband to Jennifer and a father to his twins, Cade and McKenna.

Printed in the United States
78776LV00003B/144